The Drummond Affair

Murder and Mystery in Provence

Stephanie Matthews and Daniel Smith

ICON

DEDICATIONS

Stephanie – *For Tony, my partner in crime.*
Dan – *For Mum.*

Published in the UK and USA in 2024 by
Icon Books Ltd, Omnibus Business Centre,
39–41 North Road, London N7 9DP
email: info@iconbooks.com
www.iconbooks.com

ISBN: 978-183773-058-2
ebook: 978-183773-060-5

Typesetting by SJmagic DESIGN SERVICES, India

Printed and bound in the UK

CONTENTS

PREFACE: TRAGEDY IN THE DURANCE VALLEY

On the morning of Friday 25 July 1952, Jack Drummond was packing up the family car – a new, dark green Hillman estate – parked up outside his Nottingham home. As he heaved the suitcases into the boot, his taste buds were already tingling at the thought of the cheese and wine he would soon be feasting upon. This was a trip for indulging his culinary passions. Elizabeth, his ten-year-old daughter, was bouncing with excitement at the prospect of the exotic adventure that lay ahead. Jack was a well-travelled man but even so, there was something special about a family holiday.

Until recently, a driving holiday to France would have been entirely unthinkable for most people. It was just seven years since the war had ended and only eight since France was liberated from Nazi occupation. The scars were still fresh, the rebuilding a work in progress. The spectre of fascism may have been vanquished from Europe but new battle lines had been drawn up, the inferno of the Second World War now replaced by the frost of the Cold War. But for those who could afford it, a bit of continental travel was now a possibility.

This was the dawn of the package holiday age. Horizon had been the first company down this route, a couple of years previously in 1950 – an all-in-one trip to Corsica including flights. By 1952 the same company was offering all-inclusives to Palma. But the Drummonds had other plans. They were going to travel under their own steam. A ferry across the Channel and then the long drive down to the French Riviera.

French sun and glamour were just what Jack and his wife Anne needed. She was younger than him by some sixteen years. She was smart too, a civil servant by profession but these days, to the world at large, a housewife. The couple had met through work and all in all they rubbed along well, but there had been a big argument the previous night. Hopefully things would calm down once they were on the road.

They were keen to give Elizabeth a real treat too. There weren't many kids in Nottingham going on a fancy holiday like this, but then again Jack Drummond wasn't an average sort of dad. He had made something of himself. People knew who he was. As a scientist who had provided crucial advice to the government in arguably the nation's greatest moment of crisis, his work had impacted the lives of pretty much every-one in the country. He might have been 'Daddy' to Elizabeth, but to the wider public he was *Sir* Jack Drummond. So, the South of France it was.

As she watched the luggage piling up in the Hillman, Elizabeth mulled over the plans she had for the trip. There would be the sun-kissed beaches to play upon, new foods to try, not to mention hours on the road to kill. Their ultimate destination was Villefranche, an attractive port town between Nice and Monaco. The intention was to meet up with an old friend and colleague of Jack's, Guy Marrian, along with his wife and two daughters.

The adventure began at a leisurely pace. Their car, although modern by 1952 standards, had a top speed of only 40 miles per hour or so. The Drummonds did not arrive in Dunkirk until Monday 28 July. Then the odyssey began in earnest. Not that it would be high living all the way. British tourists could take no more than £25 out of the country – a little over £600 in today's money – so they would need to make it last. Wandering through the countryside of eastern France en route to the Riviera, they were on the road for five days in all, passing through a mixture of grand old cities, like Reims, and smaller towns. The roads themselves frequently showed the evidence of their wartime bombardment, ensuring that passenger comfort was in short supply.

But that is not to say that the sense of adventure was in any way diminished. Elizabeth persuaded her parents to make a detour to Domrémy, the birthplace of Joan of Arc. There she wrote a postcard and mailed it to her teacher back in Nottingham. They stopped in Digne too, a small town close to the Alps. During the war, it had been a focal point of the Resistance movement and suffered both Italian and German occupation. The Drummonds parked up for the night and stayed at the Grand Hôtel. While having lunch there, Elizabeth spotted a poster for a bullfight and asked that they return to see it later in the week. Or so the Marrians, their hosts at Villefranche, would later claim.

Finally, on 2 August, the family arrived at Villefranche, where they dined with the Marrians and wallowed in the midsummer heat. But they were back on the road again on the 4th, taking the N85 – the Route Napoleon – back to Digne to watch the matadors in action. This road had formed part of the route taken by troops after the Allied landings on the beaches of the Côte d'Azur in 1944 and was still badly damaged. They set out early, at around six in the morning, although the bullfighting was not until four. Still, more time to take in the sights along the way.

That evening was hot and sultry in Provence. For reasons unknown, the Drummonds did not take the Route Napoleon on the return journey. Instead, they opted for the route nationale N96, which follows the valley of the River Durance. As the night drew in, they parked the Hillman on a stretch of dusty roadside near a mulberry tree. A signpost pointed in the direction of Lurs, a little village that nestled on the plateau above.

The banks of the Durance were no more than a hundred metres away. Just up the road stood an old farmhouse. Its name was La Grand Terre, but if it was ever grand, those days were long past. The peasant farming family who lived there, the Dominicis, had allowed it to become rather ramshackle. The head of the household, Gaston, was no spring chicken. He'd turned 75 on his last birthday. He shared the house with his wife Marie, his son Gustave, Gustave's wife Yvette, and their baby son Alain.

As night drew in, Elizabeth stretched out across the Hillman's back seats, while her parents slept under the stars on camp beds by the side of the car. When the sun came up, they would pile back in and get on the road again. A new day for new adventures and more memories to make. But at around 1 a.m. the silence around La Grand Terre was shattered. Several of the Dominicis were awoken by the noise. There was a succession of sharp cracks and what sounded like screaming. The inhabitants seemingly convinced themselves it was likely just a poacher. They did not bother to investigate.

A few hours later, according to witness testimony, Gaston was first to rise in the household, going out at four to take his goats to pasture, up a path that led in the opposite direction from the Drummonds' car. Gustave was next up, about an hour later, going to inspect some land damage that needed attention. Some overenthusiastic watering of the family's crops had caused a mini-landslide that threatened to halt the local trains. If that happened, the Dominicis would face a fine.

As he made his way to inspect the problem, so it would be reported, he stumbled upon a scene that chilled his blood. He spotted Jack Drummond first, lying prone at the roadside across from the parked car, one of the camp beds covering him. Then he saw Anne, lying next to the car. Both, he realised with rising dread, were dead. They had been shot. But there was worse to come. Some seventy or eighty metres away, on a track that led to a railway bridge in the direction of the river, was the body of poor Elizabeth. Had she tried to outrun whomever had attacked her parents? She had not been shot like her mum and dad. Her attacker (or attackers) had seemingly run out of bullets. So instead, her assailant had caught up with her and beaten her with the butt of a rifle until her skull fractured.

So, a tragedy began to unfold under the dawn sun of a beautiful Provence morning. A holiday adventure turned to horror. Innocents abroad slaughtered in paradise. Within the hour, the local police had been summoned and the area around La Grand Terre marked out as a crime scene. It was the beginning of a saga that would sear itself into the French psyche, the first bumbling steps in an affair that would become among the most notorious in French judicial history: *l'affaire Dominici*.

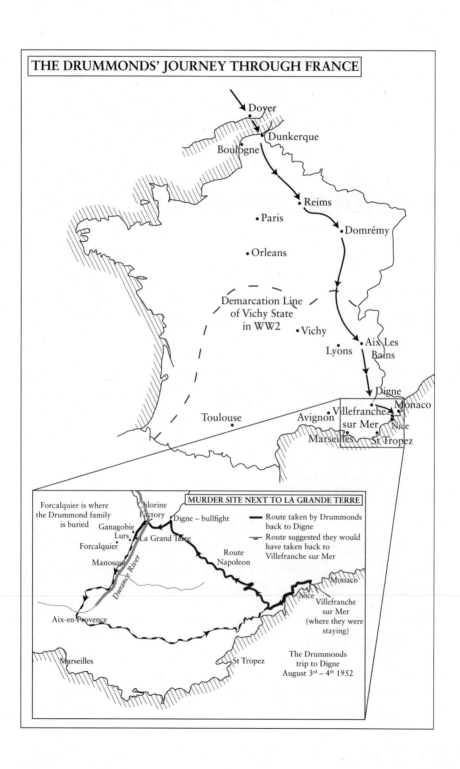

THE DRUMMONDS' JOURNEY THROUGH FRANCE

Dover

Dunkerque

Boulogne

Reims

Paris

Domrémy

Orleans

Demarcation Line
of Vichy State
in WW2

Vichy

Aix Les
Bains

Lyons

Digne

Monaco

Villefranche
sur Mer

Nice

Toulouse

Avignon

Marseilles

St Tropez

MURDER SITE NEXT TO LA GRANDE TERRE

Forcalquier is where
the Drummond family
is buried

Chlorine
Factory

Digne – bullfight

Ganagobie
Lurs

La Grand Terre

Forcalquier

Route
Napoleon

Manosque

Durance River

Monaco

Nice

Aix-en-Provence

Villefranche
sur Mer
(where they were
staying)

Marseilles

St Tropez

━━ Route taken by Drummonds
back to Digne

╌╌ Route suggested they would
have taken back to
Villefranche sur Mer

The Drummonds
trip to Digne
August 3rd – 4th 1952

RECOVERING THE DRUMMONDS 1

The journey down to the south of France that took the Drummonds several days in that summer of 1952 can be done today in closer to ten hours. Modern autoroutes and more efficient cars have vastly reduced the time – or, at least, that is the case for most of the year. Not, though, at the beginning of August when the roads are jam-packed with Parisians, Dutch and Germans all heading in that direction for the traditional month-long break. The traffic jams then – aptly called *bouchons* (corks) by the French – can stretch for miles, providing plenty of time for those so inclined to contemplate the Drummonds' terrible end and wonder at what secrets lie in the beautiful and rugged countryside of Provence even now, yet come to light almost three-quarters of a century later?

There are still a few pilgrims who go to visit the graves of the victims. The funerals for all three were conducted two days after their bodies were discovered. They had been taken some 10 km away to the local hospital in Forcalquier, a small town of less than 3,000 people that had been Provence's capital in medieval times. After the post-mortems were complete, the bodies rested in the hospital chapel until a Protestant priest was located to conduct the service. The chapel was tiny, only just big enough for a few mourners. Jack's godson and a couple of his colleagues from Nottingham were able to make the trip. The Marrians, the friends the Drummonds had met in Villefranche, were also there, as was the Consul General from Marseilles.

Jack, Anne and Elizabeth made their final journey together by horse-drawn hearse to Forcalquier's beautiful yew-lined cemetery with spectacular hillside views of the Provençal landscape. It was another stiflingly hot day. The locals followed the cortege in their Sunday best, accompanied by holiday-makers in bright summer attire. The outrage at the crime was still raw and many locals were in tears. Flowers were piled outside the chapel and strewn along the route by local children. Then the three simple plain oak coffins, each adorned with a wreath ('To Elizabeth from Grannie' read the one for the little girl, touching in its simplicity), were lowered into the ground. Elizabeth lay in between her parents. Some peace for the child, it is to be hoped, after the appalling tumult. But there is something not quite right about the scene. A detail out of place that points to the chaotic circumstances that have seen them laid to rest here. The family name on each of the headstones has been misspelt. Just the one 'm' where there should be two: 'Drumond'.

There are remnants of the tragedy on the road where it occurred too. The mulberry tree near the site of the killings is still there and you can see the pockmarks on a stone wall where some of the bullets ricocheted. At the spot where Elizabeth fell is a homemade wooden shrine, well tended to this day, adorned with ribbons and surrounded by teddy bears. Totems of the violence and innocence that collided here. But in France, those who still remember the crimes do not speak of the Drummond murders. To them, they are routinely *l'affaire Dominici*. To those of us looking back on the events from a historical distance, this is troubling. It is too often that the names of victims are treated as secondary to those of the perpetrators of monstrous crimes. It is why almost everyone has heard of Jack the Ripper but only a few of us could name any of his victims. But in the case of *l'affaire Dominici*, the erasure of the victims is even stranger. Jack the Ripper's victims were not public figures, unlike Jack Drummond. Sir Jack Drummond, let us not forget. His was a name that was known up and down the land. Yet at the moment of his slaughter and that of his family, his famous name was superseded by that of another. If Jack's relegation is puzzling, even more outrageous is the sexist manner in which Anne has been shoved into the shadows of history. Why is it that so few people in Britain have any inkling of who this family were? It is rare to find even senior academics in Jack's own discipline of biochemistry who have come across him.

L'affaire Dominici was a painful episode for France, and one of the most contested cases in the nation's history. Yet in Britain, it has all but faded from memory. The seemingly inexplicable and savage massacre of the family of one of the country's most esteemed scientific figures ought to have been a touchstone event. The Drummond murders should be one of those shared cultural reference points that everyone knows about, at least vaguely.

In France, there have been numerous books about the events,[1] along with major films[2] and hit TV shows.[3] But there has been nothing comparable in the homeland of the victims. Even at the time, there were far fewer serious obituaries of Drummond than might have been expected. Today, his groundbreaking work – for which Anne deserves vastly more credit – is hardly known by those who don't have a specific academic interest in it.[4] So, what has prompted this collective case of amnesia?

Is it possible that the death of Jack and his family was nothing so much as a great big inconvenience for certain parties? A source of potential embarrassment or discomfort? Was Jack perhaps not all that he appeared – or perhaps he was all he appeared, and more besides? Well known for his public health work, was he also involved in other work that was rather less well known about?

In part, this book aims to rebalance history. Jack Drummond is a forgotten hero. The story of him and his family has been hijacked. The mystery of their murders holds a compulsive fascination, but it is only one aspect of their tale. And even when it comes to their deaths, they have been rendered as little more than extras, incidental victims in a French melodrama. Ever since that hot summer night in 1952, the truth of what happened along the route nationale N96 has remained elusive and fiercely debated. It seems that our best chance of uncovering the answers lies as much in understanding the victims as in studying the apparent perpetrators.

The mystery of the Drummonds' deaths quickly turned into a French saga of bumbling gendarmes, class conflict and a judicial system under scrutiny. In short order, interest in the Drummonds was replaced by a focus on the perceived botched police inquiry and the possibility of a gross perversion of justice. These are, it is true, all elements of the story but they came to dominate and ultimately obfuscate the truth.

An unhelpful legend grew up around the bizarre theatre of the killings. Where sober minds were required to look outwards for the truth, instead they turned inwards. The case became a conduit for French introspection. With each new newspaper editorial, book, documentary and film (the vast majority originating in France), the truth receded. The evidence suggests that while a beautiful corner of France was the setting for the drama, its nature was much more international in scope.

When the news of the murders hit the British press late on 5 August 1952,[5] Jack Drummond was a well-known name, someone who had saved the lives of innumerable individuals. As such, there was an immediate outcry both loud and sincere. The horror of the crime was compounded because of the fate of young, innocent Elizabeth. It was headline news for two days. But soon the clamour subsided. The process of forgetting began. The story was supplanted on the front pages by the arrest of two Royal Navy sailors accused of stealing a taxi in Tokyo, and so causing a deterioration of relations with Japan. The Drummond case, commonly illustrated with affecting photographs of little Elizabeth, was consigned to the inside pages for a few more days, and then … a curious quiet. There was sporadic coverage when the case took on its many unexpected twists, but not the intense focus one might have expected.

With all this in mind, we hope this book will go some way to transforming *l'affaire Dominici* into 'The Drummond Affair'. Not just a titular change but a fundamental re-slanting of the entire narrative. This story is part murder-mystery but it is biography too. It is high time that Jack Drummond is resurrected from the fate he has suffered as a footnote in others' histories. His life, remarkable in so many respects long before it was cruelly cut short, is worthy of a biography regardless of the manner of his death. His wife, Anne, was a woman of note too, and the extent of her contribution to her husband's groundbreaking work is ripe for reappraisal. The more their story is studied, the more vividly they emerge – not as poor victims of a seemingly random act of brutality but as living, breathing individuals leading authentic lives of adventure and achievement. People who left a positive mark on the world in an era marked out by conflict and destruction.

Piecing together the evidence from contemporary accounts, personal memoirs and official documents, we have come to realise that the solution to the question of what befell the Drummonds in Provence almost certainly lies in better understanding who they were as people. It is a quest for truth that has taken us down some unexpected paths and thrown up more than a few surprises along the way. At times, it has been spine-tingling – like when a handwritten note jumps out from the margins of a letter stamped 'Top Secret'. A few scrawled words here and there that point in the right direction far more effectively than reams of carefully crafted official documents.

By returning the focus to Jack and Anne (and, of course, to Elizabeth, who was not granted the time to make her mark on the world but who surely would have done so, as her parents had before her), we hope this book will go some way to restoring the Drummond name. Jack's achievements, many in partnership with Anne, are deserving of a recognition that has been denied them for too long. But nor is this a work of hagiography. The Drummonds were not saints. They were fully rounded human beings. They did much good for the world, but there are areas of their lives that are shrouded in shade. While it is not possible to drown that shade with light, we have sufficient clues to at least illuminate some of its recesses. In this process of recovering the victims as real human beings, we may even find ourselves several steps further towards discerning the truth behind their deaths that has lain hidden for so many years.

WHO WAS JACK DRUMMOND? 2

On 27 December 1952, a letter appeared in the esteemed scientific journal *Nature*.[1] It was signed by five senior Canadian academics. Their reason for writing to arguably the world's most prestigious multidisciplinary scientific publication was to remember Jack Drummond.

'The news of the tragic death of Sir Jack Drummond came as a severe shock to his many friends in America,' it began:

> Only after the initial paralysing numbness associated with the sporadic news flashes of his murder had worn off could the enormity of this crime be appreciated. Although the loss to the scientific world has been great, a deep feeling of the personal loss of a friend has been experienced by many of us in Canada. Over the years Jack Drummond has made numerous Canadians his associates. His interest and hospitality was extended to many junior men of science, and all of us will remember the impact of his personality as he blended the science of nutrition and the art of entertainment into a formula as palatable as his Englishman's Food. Perhaps no one has done so much to help so many Canadian medical

research students attain a balanced perspective of scientific life in England. To many of us the pleasure of informal evenings, and the charm of Drummond as a host, will remain as our most vivid memory of a man who was truly more than a great man of science.

It is quite the eulogy. Proof, if it were needed, that the victim who died such a violent death on a French roadside was by no means run of the mill. Not only 'a great man of science', but a decent and engaging fellow whose influence straddled oceans and continents. It was as a biochemist and nutritionist that Jack found fame, especially as one of the chief architects of the British rationing system during the Second World War. But such were his abilities that many other countries would benefit from his expertise. In a world where epidemics of hunger and malnutrition threatened under the particular circumstances of war, it is impossible to say just how many lives Jack helped save, and how many more he rescued from the deformities of malnutrition, but it must be counted in at least thousands and it is almost certainly not an exaggeration to talk in the realms of millions. A claim very few have ever been able to make.

Jack was born on 12 January 1891. Queen Victoria was in the 57th year of her reign. A new magazine called the *Strand* was about to publish the first short story featuring a detective called Sherlock Holmes. Meanwhile, Oscar Wilde was applying his final edits to *The Picture of Dorian Gray* and Thomas Hardy was readying himself to publish *Tess of the d'Urbervilles*. Notable people doing great things. Yet there were not many obvious signs that Jack was destined for such greatness. As we will see, the exact details of his birth and early years are uncertain and even his birth certificate bears a different name. Some obituaries say he was born in Leicester, others in south London. What is certain is that he was not raised by his mother, but by an aunt and her husband, and the man identified as his father was, in fact, not.

If Jack wasn't particularly blessed by advantageous circumstances in his earliest years, it was not long before it was apparent that he boasted a first-rate scientific mind. This would be the key to his success. In 1912, he took a first-class degree in chemistry from East London College (which would evolve into Queen Mary University of London). He then held a series of research posts, first at King's College London and then, from 1914, at the Cancer Hospital Research Institute. He assisted Casimir Funk, who was then emerging as a pioneer in the nascent field of vitamins.[2] It was Funk, in fact, who minted the word 'vitamine', as a shortened form of 'vital amine' (an amine being a particular type of organic compound), and Jack who would subsequently remove the 'e' to call them vitamins. Jack was entranced by his mentor's work, which set him on the path of a specialism in nutrition.

While his contemporaries were making their way to the battlefields of the First World War, many never to return, Jack stayed in London. He was seemingly prevented from signing up by a medical condition, although – as with so much in his life – the precise details are elusive. But he was certainly gainfully employed at this time, a key member of the skeleton staff who kept the research work of the Cancer Hospital going during those years. In July 1915, he became a husband too, marrying Mabel Straw, a fellow undergraduate at East London College.

In 1917, Jack went to work with one of his old bosses from King's, William Dobinson Halliburton, and a year later published a paper on infant nutrition in the *Lancet*,[3] the leading journal of general medical practice. Still only in his mid-twenties, it was clear Jack's star was in the ascendancy. The following year, he received his doctorate and was appointed Funk's successor as physiological chemist at the Cancer Hospital. Then University College London (UCL) poached him and in 1922, aged just 31, he was named as its first chair of biochemistry, an appointment funded by the Rockefeller Foundation.

From there it was onwards and upwards, carrying out world-leading work into vitamins and their nutritional value. Not least, he was the first to isolate almost pure vitamin A and vitamin E,[4] but did not get the kudos for this. It all ensured that he was a well-established name in the scientific firmament before the onset of the Second World War provided him with the opportunity for his most high-profile work.

In 1939, as war loomed, Jack published *The Englishman's Food*,[5] an academic but nonetheless accessible historical survey of the eating habits of the English people over some half a millennium. In preparing the book, he worked closely with Anne Wilbraham, who in their subsequent obituaries was described as his secretary but who in fact held an important position in the civil service and whose contribution, it is safe to say, amounted to more than typing up his notes. The two were lovers, and when Jack and Mabel divorced after 24 years together, Anne Wilbraham became the second Mrs Drummond in 1940. Two years later they would toast the arrival of a baby girl, Elizabeth.

The Englishman's Food was in part an attempt by Jack to get to grips with the nation's nutrition in a highly practical way. It was timely, too. With Britain about to fling itself into a headlong conflict in Europe and beyond, there were undoubtedly going to be stresses on the food supply chain. The First World War had shown very clearly how conflict impacted domestic food production and international trade concurrently. If he wasn't already, Drummond soon found himself on the government's radar.

At the outbreak of hostilities in September 1939, the Ministry of Food called on his expertise with regard to the risks of gas contamination of food.[6] This, together with his submission of a memorandum explaining the needs and risks facing Britain as it strived to feed itself,[7] made such an impression that in February 1940 he became the Ministry's scientific advisor.

If the early months of the conflict were 'the Phoney War', it all soon took on a grim immediacy, not least for Jack. In May 1940, Winston Churchill's accession to 10 Downing Street in place of Neville Chamberlain saw the arrival of the dynamic Lord Woolton at the Ministry of Food. He promptly set Jack to work on a food acquisition plan that was practical and rooted in sound nutritional principles. In other words, Jack was about to design the rationing system that would ensure Britain did not starve over the coming years. It was, perhaps, the crowning triumph of his career. Where others may have been cowed by the size of the task, Jack embraced it. Instead of seeing an insurmountable hurdle, he sensed an opportunity. A chance to address the serial inadequacies of the British diet.

Plundering the knowledge gained from his decades of lab research and his grasp of the eating habits that he had so recently written about, he built a system that saw the population emerge from the war nutritionally better off than when it had started. He made sure that the most vulnerable were at the centre of consideration – the young and the old, the weak and the sick, the working classes, and expectant and nursing mothers. The poorest parts of the population found themselves consuming more protein and vitamins than ever before, while the better off were guided away from those culinary excesses that were slowly killing them.

The magnitude of Jack's achievement did not go unnoticed, and there were accolades aplenty, including a knighthood in 1944. Arguably an even greater honour came in 1947 when a 'Lasker Group Award' was bestowed by the American Public Health Association on the British Ministries of Food and Health. Established in 1945 and administered by the Lasker Foundation, the Lasker Prize is awarded annually to those deemed to have made major contributions to medical science or carried out extraordinary public service in the medical field. It stands perhaps second only to the Nobel Prize. The prize was given to the two ministries for what was described as 'the unprecedented program of food distribution in Great Britain, with resulting improvement in the health of the people'. The citation continued:

> ... Although almost all other environmental factors which might influence the public health deteriorated under the stress of war, the public health in Great Britain was maintained and in many respects improved. The rates of infantile, neo-natal and maternal mortality and stillbirths all reached the lowest levels in the history of the country. The incidence of anaemia and dental caries declined, the rate of growth of schoolchildren improved, progress was made in the control of tuberculosis, and the general state of nutrition of the population as a whole was up to or an improvement upon pre-war standards.

... In the opinion of the Lasker Awards Committee, this has been one of the greatest demonstrations in public health administration that the world has ever seen. The Lasker Awards Committee of the American Public Health Association therefore takes great satisfaction in recommending awards for scientific and administrative achievement to the British Ministries of Food and Health and to the four great leaders in this historic enterprise, Lord Woolton, Sir Jack Drummond, Sir Wilson Jameson and Sir John Boyd Orr.

Jack's efforts had come to the attention of the international community some years earlier, and his expertise was called upon across hot spots in Europe throughout the war. He was also a regular commuter to the US, advising on the intricacies of the food transports undertaken as part of the Lend-Lease deal with Washington, and in 1943 was a delegate at the creation of the United Nations Food and Agricultural Organisation, charged with improving the world's nutrition levels. As the end of the war came into sight from 1944, he assumed various new consulting positions to prepare Europe for the food challenges ahead, both immediate and longer-term. In May 1945, he undertook particularly arduous work in the recently occupied and famine-stricken Netherlands, as well as making a mercy dash to the just-liberated Belsen concentration camp.

In the immediate post-war period, Jack took a career change of direction that wrong-footed many of his colleagues. In 1945, he resigned his position as Professor of Biochemistry at UCL to become Director of Research at Boots Pure Drug Company. Once his posting with the Ministry of Food ran its course the following year, he transplanted his family to Nottingham, home of Boots, and threw himself into his new role with typical gusto. Leveraging his unrivalled reputation, he set about bridging the gap between the often dislocated worlds of academic and commercial research.

It was a task he was still diligently involved in right up until his final moments. He died a man of multiple and formidable achievements. A skilled and wise scientific researcher. The first Professor of Biochemistry at one of the world's great academic institutions. The saviour of the health of the British people in wartime. A courageous and compassionate helper of those in direst need behind enemy lines. A knight of the realm.

Which makes the mystery of why we have forgotten Jack Drummond and the slaughter of his family all the more perplexing.

THE INVESTIGATION BEGINS 3

It was a little after six in the morning on 5 August 1952 that Gustave Dominici, the grown-up son who lived with his family at La Grand Terre, reared up from the side of the road close to where the body of Jack Drummond lay. He flagged down a passing motorcycle ridden by a stranger, Jean-Marie Olivier, who was on his way home from a night shift at the local chemical factory in nearby St Auban. The motorbike was in fact not the first vehicle Gustave had spotted on the road. A moment or two earlier he had let a car with Swiss plates go past. Perhaps he had assumed its inhabitants would lack the local knowledge necessary in the circumstances.

Regardless, M. Olivier braked heavily to a stop and Gustave breathlessly raced over to him. He told the motorcyclist that he had found a body on the slope by the edge of the road and asked him to go and inform the gendarmes at Oraison, some five miles away. Olivier, his heart racing, revved up his engine and rode directly to the station, where an officer immediately passed on the intelligence to Captain Henri Albert at the larger Forcalquier station.

By the time the police contingent from Forcalquier arrived at 7.15 a.m., a small crowd had already passed through or near to the crime scene. Among them was a railway worker, Faustin Roure, who had come to inspect the damage caused by the landslide that Gustave had reported the night before and was known to the Dominicis. Gustave's brother, Clovis, and Clovis's brother-in-law, Marcel Boyer, also arrived on push bikes on their way to work at the train station at Lurs. It was apparent that word had quickly spread about the spectacle at the roadside by La Grand Terre.

But when Sgt Louis Romanet and Gendarme Raymond Bouchier turned up in their motorcycle and sidecar, all was temporarily quiet. Only as they neared the Drummonds' Hillman did Gustave approach them from behind and lead them to the victims. The police did not, as one might have expected, fence off any of the crime scene, nor did they have the necessary equipment – that is to say, a roll or two of tape – to do so. That they needed to protect the physical evidence at the earliest opportunity does not even seem to have occurred to them.

The grisly nature of the scene threw them. Expecting to find a run-of-the-mill local road accident and instead stumbling upon a British-registered car, three dead people and a notebook containing the name and address of one Sir Jack Drummond persuaded them that this was a serious crime involving foreign dignitaries and was far beyond their remit. It was time to pass this up the line of command. While Bouchier shot some photos of the scene, Romanet rushed to the village of Lurs, some four kilometres away up a very steep road, where he found a telephone and informed Captain Albert that they were dealing with a massacre. Albert escalated matters further up the chain of command, notifying his superior,

Commandant Bernier, in Digne and also the judicial police in Nice. Before long, the British Consulate at Marseilles was put in the picture too.

Albert now jumped in his standard-issue Peugeot and headed for La Grand Terre, with Bernier arriving sometime around eight o'clock. Yet still neither man, in spite of their wealth of experience, addressed the issue of cordoning off the area. The focus was less on preservation of evidence and more on informal interviews with potential witnesses in the hopes of honing in on a suspect and establishing motive. All the while, the scene grew increasingly chaotic, trampled by any number of passers-by and whoever fancied playing amateur detective. A colony of journalists was already starting to amass. Fifty by the end of the day, expanding to over eighty in the days to come. Proof, if it were needed, that this was not just any old crime.

Captain Albert was keen to get eyes on the ground with relatively free rein. He knew he had limited time to flex his detective muscles before bigger guns than him arrived. Soon the Drummond killings would serve as the backdrop for the latest bout in the perennial battle between the gendarmes (essentially local police affiliated with the armed forces) and the judicial police, a civilian body with responsibility for policing major urban areas and taking over other serious and complex investigations too.

But even as the clock was ticking, Albert had the luxury of a little more time than usual. Being the middle of summer, the judicial police were particularly busy, what with the influx of tourists creating extra work on the Riviera on top of the usual levels of localised criminality, not to mention officers taking time off for vacations of their own. The Nice police were utterly overwhelmed so opted to pass the case over to their counterparts in Marseilles. Albert knew it would likely take several hours for the crime to be registered, a suitably senior officer assigned, and for that officer to make the not insignificant journey to La Grand Terre. In the event, it was not until after 9 a.m. that news of the slaughter even made it to the station in Marseille.

Nonetheless, Albert would soon have other interested company at the murder site in the shape of three officers from the court in Digne, who turned up together at about 9.30. This trio represented yet another layer of technocratic complication. The law in France required that where there is a murder, the investigation be initiated by a public prosecutor (an employee of the state), who then hands it to a prosecuting magistrate (in theory, an independent, non-political appointment), who then oversees the conduct of the case. In practice, this meant the magistrate had the authority to guide the investigation of the judicial police, deciding which witnesses may be interrogated and when, as well as providing oversight of medical and other experts. In the end, it was also the prosecuting magistrate's duty to decide whether there was sufficient evidence to indict a defendant and enter a case into the court system. The prosecuting magistrate was thus a hybrid of police officer and judge. As might be expected, the relationship between the prosecuting magistrate, the public prosecutor and the police (both gendarmes and judicial police) did not always run smoothly.

Albert must have valued the golden hour-and-a-half he had before any of his potential professional rivals appeared. But how his heart must have sunk a little with the arrival of Deputy Public Prosecutor Louis Sabatier, Examining Magistrate Roger Périès, and Clerk of the Court Émile Barras – all officials of the court in Digne – in their regulation Peugeot.

By then, some other significant new arrivals were already in situ. The Mayor of Lurs had turned up with a local country doctor by the name of Henri Dragon.

There is nothing to suggest that Dr Dragon was anything other than highly competent in the day-to-day business of looking after the poorly and ailing. But he was utterly inexperienced when it came to making a forensic study of the scattered victims of a murder. Despite giving what might most charitably be described as a superficial examination of the victims, he nonetheless managed to sully the crime scene yet further. Most crucially, he turned the Drummonds' bodies over in the course of making his rudimentary assessment, as well as moving other items of evidence. Exactly how he manipulated the bodies was not properly documented, so those that followed could not be sure that the scene before them truly resembled the state in which the bodies were discovered.

While so compromising the integrity of the scene, Dr Dragon failed to make anything in the way of an incisive evaluation. On the contrary, he brought only further confusion and doubt. There was, for example, no precise description of the wounds each victim had suffered, which surely must have been the least expected of him. In the case of Elizabeth, he noticed that her bare feet showed no signs of abrasion. A later police report would contradict this, suggesting that there were multiple signs of minor injury. This question was important, because if Dr Dragon was to be believed, Elizabeth was likely killed and then moved across the rough track that ran to the water's edge. But if the later report was correct, then Elizabeth may well have been fleeing when she was caught and beaten to death. Uncertainty was already overwhelming the crime scene as a result of avoidable failings in procedure.

In only one direction did the doctor seem to shed any real light. Having made his examination of the Drummonds, he went to the farmhouse of the Dominicis to ask for some water to wash his hands. He was greeted, if that is the word, by Gaston Dominici, who seemed in a state of shock. The two were old friends, yet Dominici was adamant that the doctor should not come indoors but instead use the outdoor pump to wash his hands. When the doctor made to fill a basin, the old farmer prevented him, saying the smell of the blood would put his horses off ever drinking from it again. Dominici seemed determined to prevent the doctor from coming into his home at any cost. It was hardly the kind of compassionate cooperation one might have expected given the circumstances. But the incident did add to the fast-growing sense that the inhabitants of the farmhouse were not your typical helpful neighbours. Moreover, in time it would prompt some to ask what was in the house that morning that Dominici didn't want the doctor to see.

Later, at about ten o'clock, a sniffer dog arrived, a champion German shepherd from Digne. Accompanied by her handler, the hound proved almost as ineffectual as Dr Dragon, sniffing about the place without turning up any clues of note. She did not seem especially interested in the Dominicis, nor did she pursue any noticeable trails. Albert must have had the gnawing suspicion that his part of the investigation was getting nowhere at a canter.

Over in Marseille, where the chief inspector was on holiday and a skeleton staff was unprepared for such an involved crime as this, the case was assigned to Commissioner Edmond Sébeille. He was at the time finishing up another murder case and was looking forward to a well-earned holiday with his wife and daughter in the coming days. An early assessment by the gendarmerie in Forcalquier suggested that the killings might be the result of a robbery gone wrong. Sébeille voiced to a colleague his gut feeling that this one would be a tough nut to crack. But as the son of a celebrated detective and himself a member of the Marseille police's elite mobile 'Tiger Brigade', *Les Brigades du Tigre*, he could not pass up the chance to prove his mettle in what was already shaping up to be a sensational case. Known by some as the 'Maigret of Marseilles', Sébeille readied himself.

He was in one of two ancient black Citroën cars that eventually left Marseilles at 2.30 p.m., arriving at the scene some 130 km away at about 5.30 p.m. It was not an auspicious start. The bodies had already been removed. Sébeille failed to greet Albert and assumed something of a superior air, underscoring the natural rivalry between the two branches of the police. Albert was particularly unimpressed, as government directives meant that the gendarmerie had been severely hampered in what they could do in the absence of supervision from the judicial police. While he had been pleased to have a head start, for most of the day he had been hamstrung. In effect, eight or more daylight hours had been lost, during which time crucial clues went undiscovered or were severely jeopardised. Already the odds of identifying and convicting the perpetrator were greatly diminishing.

It was not all bad news, though. Before long, various ammunition was recovered and then the apparent murder weapon was found where it had been thrown into the river. It was an old American-issue Rock Ola M1 carbine rifle and bore a metal plate inscribed 'RMC'. For a while, it was speculated that these might be the initials of the murderer himself. But in due course, it was established that the firearm originated at the Royal Military College in Kingston, Ontario in Canada.

Such weapons were in plentiful supply in the area. It was almost certainly a leftover from the arming of the Maquis (the wartime French Resistance), whose network had been centred on the nearby Ganagobie plateau, where Allied troops had passed through in 1944 on their way to liberating Paris. Such weapons were illegal to own after the war but in an area where hunting wild boar was both necessary for food and beloved as a sport, this law was largely ignored. And now one of these rifles had been used for the most gruesome ends. But Sébeille was heartened by its discovery. Certain that the murderer was a local, he confidently told a contingent of the press that the 'weapon will talk' and implied it would not be long before it yielded the killer. That, however, proved to be an ambitious prognosis.

Rather, the investigation became bogged down in confusion and malaise. Even such basics as when vital pieces of evidence were retrieved and by whom saw frequent disagreement between officers. Perhaps most markedly, there were wildly at-odds stories concerning the discovery of a large splinter of wood that had become dislocated from the butt of the murder weapon during the attack. Moreover, after Dr Dragon's contribution, two other inexperienced doctors were given the job of conducting the autopsies. Neither consulted with Dr Dragon before they did so, nor did they think to document their procedures with photographs. The result was a collection of reports containing numerous disparities and contradictions.

There were wild-goose chases as well. When the discarded uniform of a legionnaire was discovered in woods a few miles away from La Grand Terre, there was initial excitement that this might be the frantically hidden clothing of the perpetrator. Conveniently, it contained papers that confirmed who its owner had been. This man was duly picked up by the police and interrogated, only for him to offer up a cast-iron alibi. A dead end.

All the while, the pressure was growing on Sébeille for a quick result. On 5 August, before word of the killings had spread, the French press were proclaiming the good news that the tourists were coming back, Errol Flynn and Clark Gable had just arrived in Deauville in Normandy, Egypt's deposed King Farouk was holding court in Capri, and St Tropez was becoming the go-to place for the wealthy, powerful and beautiful. The journalistic tone was resolutely upbeat – even the grim news of the fighting in Indochina was relegated to the small print. But when reports of the Drummond slayings hit a day later, they were all across the front pages.

Back in Britain, where Jack Drummond was still remembered as a national hero, the news caused a shockwave. It was headline news for two days but, as always, another story comes along to steal the attention. Reporting of the Drummond case, usually supported by photos that captured Elizabeth's girlish sweetness, was quickly relegated to the inside pages. Then almost nothing. But the interest lingered longer in France.

The diplomatic service jumped into action and funeral arrangements were promptly made. In place of permanent headstones, some wooden crosses were hurriedly ordered, complete with the correctly spelt 'Drummond' name, only for them to be misspelt (as 'Drumond') on the later permanent crosses. The funerals were held on 7 August with their meagre roll call of mourners. A memorial service for those who hadn't been able to make it from the UK (including Anne's distraught mother) was held in St Mary's Church, Nottingham on the 20th. For Sébeille, the ceremony in France was another chance to mine for information about the victims, but he did not learn much.

He was meeting brick walls everywhere he looked. Undoubtedly a respected officer in Marseille, out here in the countryside he was an outsider to the small, close-knit community. Convinced that the Rock Ola M1 was key to unlocking the puzzle of the murders, his attempts to identify its owner proved particularly frustrating. When not confronted with barely concealed hostility, he was met with near silence.

Despite the lack of progress, he nonetheless happily cultivated the press, entertaining journalists in the local bars, dishing out snippets of information along with cigarettes. Since the media circus had set up camp, he seemed intent on establishing himself as its ringmaster. But he was not the only one getting in on the act. So too were assorted members of the Dominici clan, who also seemed to be enjoying their moment in the limelight despite the trying circumstances.

Their willingness to engage with journalists did little to improve their relationship with the police, which was already tetchy. From the outset, their various testimonies had been inconsistent as to who was where, doing what when. On several occasions, they didn't merely contradict each other but rebutted their own previous individual testimonies – a damaging habit which would only get worse. Their conduct left many other questions. When they claimed to have heard gunshots in the night, why had no one bothered to check on the English campers they knew were just up the road? Did they really assume it was nothing more than poachers? And why had it taken so long that morning to alert the authorities to the horror scene?

The suspicions that quickly started to float around the family were not allayed when it became apparent that a protective arm, which came to be known as the Red Wall, *Le Mur Rouge*, was springing up around them. The family were well known for their communist leanings, very common in Provence at that time. The local Communist Party headquarters was in the railway station at Lurs, just a few miles from La Grand Terre. The Dominicis had longstanding links to prominent figures in the powerful movement. Building on an already deeply ingrained apathy towards and distrust of the police locally, the family and their allies seemed intent on being as uncooperative as possible.

But the Dominicis were playing a dangerous game. Their collective surly manner, especially that of the patriarch Gaston, and their erratic accounts of the night of the murders could not but make them subjects of interest. Furthermore, all the evidence suggested they lacked the wit and cooperative strategy to put one over Sébeille and his team for very long. But at the same time, the investigation was soon mired in confusion, stuck in a loop of unprovable hypotheses and working with a local community intent on self-censoring in its dealings with the police.

Sébeille on the one hand and the Dominicis on the other emerged as captivating personalities playing a game of cat and mouse as the country watched on. Already, the role of the Drummonds as the central figures in this tragedy had been usurped.

WRONG PLACE, WRONG TIME? 4

The slayings at La Grand Terre had all the ingredients for the most shocking kind of murder. A family slaughtered. A young girl battered to death. That most innocent of undertakings, a family holiday, turned into violent tragedy. And to top it all, the bloody drama played out in a foreign land.

The first instinct for many readers of the newspapers on both sides of the Channel was to wonder what sort of monster could be responsible. What depths of depravity could they possibly inhabit to stoop to such an unforgivable crime? The very act of seeking to establish a motive – to assert any sort of rationale – seemed almost distasteful. But, naturally, that is exactly what those charged with investigating the killings had to do. In order to solve the crime, they first had to try to understand how it came about.

So, what were the viable scenarios that might have culminated in the deaths of the Drummond family, a seemingly happy band posing no apparent threat to anybody? One possibility that had to be considered was that they were in no way targeted as victims, but rather found themselves in the wrong place at the wrong time. The scene was so chaotic that it was difficult to imagine the killings were in any way premeditated. How could they be? Who would have known that a carful of British holidaymakers would choose just that spot to camp? And who would want to kill an entire family on a summer break anyway? None of it made sense.

To survey the crime scene, and particularly Elizabeth's lifeless body, it was easy to believe that this was the work of a deranged mind, the act of a psychopath who stumbled upon his unwitting prey and took the opportunity to snuff out their lives to sate his own disturbed passions. But such brutal crimes rarely emerge fully formed and without some prior indication. This explosion of violence must surely have been the culmination of a long journey of pent-up aggression which would have left some trail behind it.

It is true that this corner of France had witnessed its fair share of violence and murder in recent years, several cases coming to national prominence for their bloody nature in the immediate post-war years. But most were in some sense explainable in terms of easily graspable motives – revenge killings for wartime injustices, the violent conclusions to robberies, or doomed love affairs, or festering political disputes. But there was nothing that seemed to suggest itself as a precursor to the Drummond incident. No sign of the madman within their midst who might serve as a bogeyman and whose eventual capture might bring the sorry saga to a conclusion that the public would find at once both appalling and reassuring. This was no ordinary murder; it was violent, out of the blue and shocking.

In the absence of an immediate 'crazed monster', there was no choice but to consider more mundane motives. Could three people really have lost their lives, for instance, as the result of a botched robbery? To an opportunist thief, or

WRONG PLACE, WRONG TIME? 29

perhaps a gang of thieves, spotting the foreign visitors sitting in their expensive-looking new car, the Drummonds might have seemed easy pickings. Imagine the Hillman parked up on a quiet stretch of road, conveniently far away from prying eyes. A middle-aged couple sleeping alongside the vehicle, neither giving off anything approaching an air of menace. Maybe Elizabeth, asleep in the back of the car, goes entirely unnoticed. It's known that foreign tourists are restricted in how much money they can carry, but nonetheless the living expenses even for just a few days are not to be sniffed at. There might be a camera too, and some personal effects – a lady like her is sure to carry some jewellery, isn't she? And then there's the car itself. Altogether a nice little haul.

But what if one of the family wakes and discovers what is afoot before the robber or robbers can incapacitate them? What if they disturb Elizabeth, who lets out a scream? Or maybe Jack stumbles back through the dark from a call of nature to discover the crime in progress. Does he attempt to see the assailants off? Is that when a weapon is drawn and shots fired? But what to do about the little girl? They can't just leave her now. What if she can describe them to the gendarmes? What had seemed like a straightforward job descends into panicked chaos and in the confusion she tries to run away and then …

But it was soon apparent to Sébeille and his colleagues that the idea of an impromptu act of thievery gone wrong did not hold water. While the Hillman had the look of being ransacked, it still contained untouched cash. A high-denomination bank note of 5,000 francs (equivalent to approximately £50 today) was found by investigators. It might be credible that a robbery could descend into violence to such an extent that the thieves decide to give up on their mission and exit the scene without delay. Yet, it was known that the criminals at La Grand Terre had made off with some plunder. Specifically, a camera and, more bizarrely, a canvas water bucket too. A camera is one thing, but if you are looking for material enrichment, why take a cumbersome bucket and leave behind readily accessible cash? At the Drummonds' funeral, Sébeille cornered the Marrians, the family's friends from Villefranche, and persuaded Guy to inspect the car. He was adamant that nothing else of note was missing. The motive that seemed to have initially offered the most straightforward explanation for the crime was convincingly undermined.

What else might have driven the atrocity, then? Sticking with the idea that the assault was impromptu, and with theft ruled out, a sexual motive became another highly favoured theory. Was Anne the focal point of the attack? It was certainly a notion that would gain traction in the weeks and months to come, although the putative (and, at various points, self-confessed) sexual predator who was about to come into public view was so surprising a proposition that many observers came to discount the idea altogether. But it could not be completely ruled out. As before, we can imagine a scenario where Elizabeth is unseen inside the car, and Jack temporarily absent. Anne is ostensibly there on her own at the roadside, perhaps already asleep or maybe in the process of readying herself for bed. What might have started as the opportunistic picking-off of a lone woman is again interrupted (either through the intervention of Elizabeth or Jack, or perhaps both), with bloodshed the ensuing result.

But once again, there is no obvious build-up to such a crime. No escalation of attacks over previous months or years in the surrounding region to suggest a criminal progression towards this ultimate violation of domestic peace. Nor does the location – a stretch of remote road but one which nonetheless was sporadically illuminated by the lights of passing vehicles – suggest itself as an obvious choice for someone on the lookout for victims.

Indeed, the question of why the Drummonds set up camp there at all was another baffling aspect of the affair. In a region of considerable beauty, that stretch of road was far from the most picturesque. Moreover, the Hillman was parked on a slight bend so that when the occasional vehicle did pass, its lights would cast their beams directly over the Drummonds – hardly conducive to a good night's sleep. It would have been easy enough to park up at a more sheltered spot nearby. Over time, it would be suggested that not only was the Drummonds' choice of parking spot disastrously unfortunate but also rather perplexing.

While the robbery and sexual assault theories were largely predicated on the notion that the attack was unprepared and spontaneous, other hypotheses had to be explored. Could it have been a targeted assault after all? If it was, nobody could quite fathom why. There were a few murmurings that perhaps Drummond was a spy. It was only a year earlier that Guy Burgess and Donald Maclean had scandalously defected to the Soviet Union. Espionage was a hot topic, part of the cultural landscape. But the idea that Drummond, bastion of the British establishment and champion of public nutrition, might be involved with such things was considered outlandish.

Besides, whatever one thought of Stalin and his totalitarian regime in Moscow, the Soviets at least had a reputation for the efficiency of their operatives. Three clean shots to the victims' heads and the theory might have won a more sympathetic hearing. But this horror scene lacked any hallmarks of a Russian plot. And if not the Soviets, then who on earth might come under realistic suspicion? No, this bloodbath suggested less a hit job than a botched job. The police had already recovered the murder weapon which, though North American in origin, very much pointed towards a local perpetrator. Who in the South of France could possibly have had a bone to pick with Jack, and one big enough to leave three people dead? If someone for some unknown reason had set out to exact a dreadful revenge, surely they would have hit upon a weapon more efficient than an old Second World War relic that seemingly ran out of bullets or failed before it could dispatch the third victim without recourse to close-hand battery.

The discovery of the gun had left Sébeille rather too confident that the solution to the crime was in sight. Setting aside the dismaying nature of the crime, it felt like it ought to be eminently solvable, not least because he saw little to suggest that he was facing a sophisticated criminal adversary. But a satisfactory explanation for *why* the Drummonds were killed was proving elusive, and would continue to be so. None of the obvious answers neatly fitted the facts, and from there explanations soon spiralled off into supposition and, on occasion, utter flights of fancy.

The Drummonds were depicted in the press as a happy family, minding their own business on a dream trip until they found themselves in that fixture of domestic paranoia – the wrong place at the wrong time. Three good and valuable lives suddenly at the mercy of an unseen malevolent force. And maybe that was exactly as it was. In lieu of watertight proof for some alternative theory, the notion seemed as likely as any other. But the truth was that no one could know for sure. Sébeille and his colleagues were left to play a game of probabilities.

Moreover, they were doing so in a corner of France at a moment in time when secrets and lies were part of the everyday currency.

SECRETS AND SPIES 5

The River Durance, a tributary of the mighty Rhône, travels for over 300 km from its source high up in the southwestern Alps. The valley through which it wends in Provence provides a spectacular backdrop, epitomising a certain kind of rugged natural beauty synonymous with the South of France. Hillsides dense with forest nestle up against lavender fields, vineyards, fruit orchards and expanses of olive trees. For those who like to climb or hike, cycle or kayak, it is an inviting playground. A land moulded by nature herself over here, and by the hand of man over there. A place of tranquillity, fun, friendship, sun, food and wine.

The landscape is dotted with ancient towns, ramparts of once-upon-a-time citadels, monasteries and tumbledown farmsteads. To the passing traveller in 1952, it would have seemed like a hymn to days long gone. But for those whose lives were rooted there, the reality was rather more complex. Their existences were of course subject to the natural elements and the rhythm of the seasons, but the passions of the human heart and the trends of national and international politics were just as important. Far from a retreat from the outside world, the region had so recently been at the fulcrum of world events that the ripple effects continued to permeate everything.

Lurs is a pretty hilltop village in a rolling hinterland nestling up to lush Mediterranean greenery. Beneath the Ganagobie monastery, the houses are built of hard mountain stone and the route to the river basin is steep and windy. In the Middle Ages, its remoteness allowed the locals to protect themselves from marauders who swept up the river plains, and when terrifying cholera epidemics drove the land, they could isolate themselves.

But as Provence became less turbulent and lawless, houses like La Grand Terre sprang up in the valleys where farmers scratched a living from the unwelcoming, stony soil. The hill villages and the settlements of the plain-dwellers evolved as distinct communities, separate from each other. According to many in these parts, the Drummond murders should never really have been given the label of 'the Tragedy of Lurs'.[1] It was, they considered, a bit of journalistic shorthand that did a great disservice to the village. In 1952 the River Durance, here a fast-moving major waterway, flowed just 100 metres behind La Grand Terre; today the river has been pushed aside to make way for the A51 autoroute.[2]

After the fall of France to Germany's invading forces in 1940, Provence found itself in the so-called 'unoccupied' zone controlled by the Vichy regime. Led by Maréchal Pétain, the Vichy government adopted an obsequious subservience towards the occupying authorities, their collaborationist agenda turning the proud South of France into a vassal state. Already-poor farmers became yet more impoverished as the Nazi regime stripped the land of its produce and its young men.

Public morale collapsed as Pétain imposed one indignity upon another. Resistance to German interference was virtually non-existent and the Vichy government even promoted a scheme whereby for every three skilled French workers sent into the service of the Germans, one French prisoner of war would be freed. Intent on sending some 250,000 men across the border, Pétain declared that volunteers were doing their patriotic duty. Meanwhile, the Milice – the Vichy state's German-sponsored military police – ensured their brand of far-right order held firm, earning the revulsion of those they oppressed.

Provence was a very uncomfortable place to be. With trusts betrayed and suspicion endemic, families and local communities closed ranks for their own safety. The Communist Party began to fill a political void, gaining significant popularity in the region, particularly after the German invasion of the Soviet Union in June 1941. The party provided a voice and a political identity for a swathe of people who felt abandoned, little more than pawns in a game of geopolitics. On top of that, the Communists became the lightning rod for a more active Resistance movement. Resistance fighters became known as the Maquis, or *maquisards*, a word borrowed from the Corsican-Italian dialect for rough scrubland.

In November 1942, the sands shifted again when Hitler responded to the Allied landings in North Africa by ordering an advance on Vichy territory that resulted in Provence's full occupation. The Nazis decreed that all young Provençal men should be sent to Germany and beyond to work in industries to help the German war effort. Things had been bad under the Vichy regime, but now the locals faced being rounded up for slave labour. For the Jewish population, the threat was even more immediately existential and many went into hiding, seeking refuge in remote villages and amid the hillsides. The Dominicis, meanwhile, endured an additional pressure, since the family were of Piedmontese stock and these Italian origins made some of the locals nervous, in light of Italy's wartime alliance with Germany.

Hunger, suspicion and fear became features of everyday life. But such social fracturing has consequences. More and more people were ready and willing to rise up against the occupying forces. Over in London, Winston Churchill was thinking hard about how to mobilise the patriotic French, firstly to frustrate the German invaders and ultimately to overthrow them. Churchill was 'on fire with enthusiasm for irregular warfare'. His secret weapon was the covert Special Operations Executive (SOE), created in July 1940 with the remit to coordinate all actions of espionage, subversion, sabotage and reconnaissance against the enemy in occupied Europe. Encouraged by Churchill, they 'set Europe ablaze'.

In 1943, the SOE operations in France were scaled up ahead of the prospective Allied landings the following year, in what became known as Operation Jedburgh. Because they were dropped by parachute, the Jedburgh teams were known by the locals as *les parachutistes*. The SOE network local to Lurs, known by the codename Jockey, was led by a charismatic British Belgian called Francis Cammaerts (Codename: Roger). He was a survivor who relied on his wits, a man with an instinctively suspicious nature and a penchant for exceptionally careful preparations. As head of the Jockey circuit, he effectively controlled thousands of *maquisards* within southeast France and the Rhône Valley. The network was primed for its role in paving the way for the Allied advance from the south in July 1944 as envisaged in Operation Dragoon.

Cammaerts headed to the Vercors plateau, about 100 miles north of where the Drummonds would be murdered. There he took charge of more than 3,000 young French fighters who had gone underground to avoid being sent as slave labour to Germany. The Allies supported them every step, not only with training and moral support but with arms and gold. But it was not long before disaster struck. Acting on intelligence, the Germans launched an attack, blocking the escape routes from the plateau and slaughtering 600 young freedom fighters, followed by a programme of savage reprisals against the local community.

Many of those who escaped Vercors went to the remote and difficult-to-access Ganagobie plateau, just up the road from Lurs. There had been fighters stationed there since the previous summer, waiting for orders that never seemed to arrive. It had been a tough winter for them, contending with the bitter cold with neither sufficient supplies nor adequate shelter. But the locals, as Cammaerts would later acknowledge, had come to their rescue, supplying food and clothes. Among them was Gaston Dominici, the ageing local farmer well known for his support of the Maquis. Was it Gaston himself who traipsed up to the plateau with goodies for the fighters – or perhaps his wife, or one of his daughters?

One story popular with locals today is that Jack Drummond had been one of Cammaert's *parachutistes*, and another myth suggests he was there in 1952 to recover lost money given to the Maquis (presumably the substantial funds handed over to Cammaerts prior to Operation Dragoon). Such theories, however, can be confidently filed as evidenceless fantasy. Operation Dragoon, though, proved a marked success. Allied troops swept along the Route Napoleon – so called because this was the path taken by Napoleon Bonaparte in 1815

– liberating town after town. The Germans suffered significant casualties as they beat their retreat, although many of their best units were able to effect an escape. For French civilians on the ground, it was a terrifying time. News had spread of the atrocities committed by German troops retreating in the north of the country after the Normandy landings, including mass slaughters and the razing of entire towns. The Dominici farm lay in the Germans' path but somehow escaped untouched.

It was the turn of the Allies to file past La Grand Terre on 20 August 1944. Did the Dominicis line the route and cheer their saviours? Or did they watch the troops in silence, wondering what the future held? The Allied advance was rapid and it was no ticker-tape procession. There was sufficient time, though, for some of the soldiers to trade their guns for supplies. A good many American-issue rifles had already been abandoned back on the plateau in the Maquis stronghold amid the chaos of the advance – weapons that in the years to come would become a familiar sight in the Durance Valley, and one of which would take the life of Jack Drummond, his wife and daughter.

Back in the Durance Valley, the Resistance did not engender the unequivocal affection and appreciation that might have been expected. This was mostly because it was not a single, clearly defined entity. Over the course of the war, three main groups had emerged. One of these was itself a coalition of previously separate groups that had been brought together by Jean Moulin, and which recognised Charles de Gaulle as its figurehead. A second group was led by Claude Renoir, grandson of the famous Impressionist painter Pierre-Auguste and son of the actor Pierre. This group maintained strong links with the British government in London and was closely aligned with the Jedburgh teams. A number of its members found refuge when necessary at Ganagobie Abbey, under the care of its sole inhabitant, an enigmatic figure called Father Lorenzi.

Then there was the Francs-Tireurs et Partisans (Français), also known as the FTP or FTPF and affiliated with the French Communists. To many locals they were a lawless group of trigger-happy assassins, and thieves when it suited them. Gustave Dominici counted himself among their ranks.

Once the Germans had been driven out of France, there was no seamless reversion to life as it had been before. In the immediate post-war period, things were chaotic. The nation's economy and its infrastructure had suffered devastating harm. Roads, bridges and railways had been bombed and ports destroyed by the departing Nazis. Industry was on its knees, starved of oil, coal and equipment that had been syphoned off to Germany. In the Durance Valley, people had long memories. By the time the Drummonds came visiting, just seven years after the end of the war, there were plenty who remained neither keen nor capable of forgetting the events of less than a decade earlier. Recollections of the brutal fighting on the Ganagobie plain and of German atrocities were still raw, made all the worse for the knowledge that some of those horrors might have been avoided, or at least lessened, were it not for the collaboration of fellow French citizens. Post-war Provence was, then, a place of intermittent violence inflicted in the name of revenge and settling old scores. Reprisals for perceived past infractions were part of the fabric of everyday life. Having been brutalised by its German occupiers, a certain savagery had seeped into the soul of the place.

When Maquis veterans, either by chance or design, caught up with former Miliciens, the old Vichy enforcers could expect to be beaten, tortured and even killed. Blood-letting as a feature of France's struggle to come to terms with its own recent past. Virtually every village had its tales to tell of local people, and sometimes entire families, who had been murdered during the war and into its aftermath. Gordon Young, a journalist for the *Daily Mail* at the time of the Drummond killings, put together an inventory of local murders from the preceding few years. His list quickly grew as revelations gushed from locals only too happy to speak their truths over a glass or two of pastis.

There was, for example, the case of a photographer from Forcalquier who one day in 1944 was marched out of his parents' tobacco shop and never seen again, until his bullet-riddled body turned up two years later. No clear motive for his killing was ever established. Or how about Mademoiselle Colette, a young hairdresser from the village of Les Mees who was accused of sleeping with the enemy? For many women charged with what was known as *collaboration horizontale*, the punishment was public humiliation, which might include having their heads shaved and sometimes tarring and feathering. But Mademoiselle Colette paid with her life. A similar fate befell a tobacconist and his wife in Mallefougasse, while the old, staunchly anti-communist Mayor of Peyruis, François Muzy, was assassinated in his own home after he was wrongly accused of betraying local Maquis. Another local official, a judge by the name of Stain, was murdered during the liberation, and on another occasion a local Communist leader issued an apology to a family after their two young sons were executed in error.

The Dominicis would have been familiar with many of these stories, but one in particular likely stuck with them. Half a mile from La Grand Terre as the crow flies and on the other side of the river was the Château de Paillerol, the home of the Cartier family. During the war, they had been harassed by local *maquisades* for money and supplies and at some point M. Cartier seems to have protested at the demands placed upon him. One evening, there was a fracas overheard by a family member, and the next morning Cartier and his wife were both dead from gunshot wounds to the head. Chief Commissioner Jean Stigny from the Nice mobile guard was brought in to investigate. A hero of the French Resistance himself, he had undertaken dangerous undercover work against the Gestapo and aided the escape of many Allied airmen. Now it was his task to clear up the post-war mess of accusations against police collaborators from Provence. He was having lunch at Les Mees a few days into the Cartier case when he was forced by unknown assailants into a car and driven away. His body was later dumped on ground outside La Grand Terre. He had apparently been denounced as a collaborator to local Communist operatives by a fellow police officer.

Many of the most ferocious acts of 'payback' – whether justified or not – were perpetrated by members of the FTP. After the war, one of the local Communist leaders in the valley was Paul Maillet, a man well known to the Dominicis and a contemporary of Gustave. Maillet worked on the railway out of Lurs station, which was kept open to service freight trains on the Marseilles–Digne line. It was here that Gustave had gone on the night of 4 August 1952 to report the landfall caused by overwatering on the Dominici farm. Maillet and his fellow Communists exerted a tight grip on the Durance Valley. To such men, violence and bloodshed did not represent shocking intrusions into their daily lives but were instead constant threads running through their normal existence. Moreover, Maillet and the people of the Durance Valley had learned to play their cards close to their chests. Institutions of authority, like the police, were to be kept at a safe distance. The less that prying was encouraged, the smaller the chance that a can of worms would be opened.

Such was the challenging climate of non-cooperation that confronted Inspector Sébeille, the 'outsider'. But for those who wondered what possible defence the Dominicis might have had for not investigating the gunshots they claimed to have heard in the middle of the night, there was perhaps at least one credible answer: in the valley, where dark secrets were fiercely guarded, you kept your nose out of other people's business or risked the consequences.

A SCIENTIFIC MIND

6

Amid the maelstrom of local politics, the turmoil of the murder investigation itself and the fact that here was a crime that had piqued international interest, it was easy to lose sight of just what a remarkable and noteworthy life Jack, in particular, had led. The most comprehensive of the obituaries dedicated to him was the 12,000-word eulogy published by the Royal Society and written by F. G. Young,[1] who had succeeded Jack as Professor of Biochemistry at University College London (UCL) in 1945. 'Artist, discoverer, reformer, historian, host,' Young had written of him. 'Whichever of his many facets caught the light shone brilliantly.'

But how had Jack navigated such a notable path through his 59 years? Seemingly drawing on just one or two sources, each of the eight or so major obituaries[2] published about him agreed that his father was John Drummond, a military man who rose to be a major in the Royal Artillery regiment. However, as will be seen in a later chapter, new evidence makes it appear unlikely that John was in fact his biological father. John lived with Gertrude, Jack's mother, at Wisteria Villa, Howard Road, Leicester, but both parents died when

Jack was still very young. Exactly how young was uncertain, as was the question of where they had died: Leicester, London and even India were variously offered up. Regardless, Jack consequently went to live with his paternal aunt, Maria Spinks, and her husband, George, a retired veteran of the Crimean War.

From around 1902, Jack attended the John Roan School in Greenwich, south London, a few miles from the Spinks family home. Named after its benefactor, a Yeoman of Harriers to King Charles I, it was at that time a grammar school specialising in science and maths. Jack left when he was sixteen to go to the Strand School, which was housed in two crowded basement rooms at King's College on the Strand. This was an interesting choice of school because at the time it specialised in training boys for entry into the civil service. It did so very successfully and charged accordingly expensive termly fees – more than the Spinkses could seemingly afford, raising the question of whether Jack might have had another sponsor.

As things turned out, Jack was not destined to go into the civil service. In 1909, when he was eighteen, he passed the London Matriculation Exam and won his place at East London College (now Queen Mary University of London), which only two years earlier had been admitted on a trial basis to the University of London and was fully admitted in 1915. Jack travelled to its campus at Mile End in the east of the city, where he studied chemistry. It was also here that he met and fell in love with a fellow undergraduate called Mabel Straw.

If Jack was a bright spark, so too was Mabel, and her determination to graduate in chemistry at a time when it was a subject off-limits to most women says much for her character. The pair would get married at St James Church, Clapton on

17 July 1915, by which time Jack would be a man of means. His guardian, George, had died back in 1908 and Maria was to follow in 1914, leaving Jack over £2,500 (close to £200,000 in modern money). In due course, Mabel won a reputation for being an excellent host to Jack's colleagues and students at evening and weekend parties, even starting a tradition of hosting events for female scientists and wives like herself at gatherings where the other entertainments were for men only. But, of course, this all came at the expense of her own academic career. It was perhaps an inevitable outcome given the age in which she lived, but it is difficult not to feel regret for what surely must have been the wasting of her own talents in the interests of his.

So, Jack graduated in 1912 with a first-class degree and, according to friends and co-workers, largely left his youth behind him. Later known for his love of privacy, he rarely spoke of these early years. After a few months developing his research skills in organic chemistry at East London College, he moved to the department of physiology at King's College to begin a new chapter.

With his reputation growing, Jack was deputed to the research team of Dr Otto Rosenheim. Having gone to school in the college's basement a few years earlier, this was a step up the ladder in every sense. The head of the physiology department at this time was Professor William D. Halliburton. Celebrated for his work on, variously, proteins in muscle, cholesterol and vitamin D, Halliburton had published a seminal textbook the year Jack was born. Entitled *Textbook of Chemical Physiology and Pathology*,[3] it is arguably the first great textbook of biochemistry. There can be little doubt that he was a major influence on Jack's decision to soon turn his own career towards that discipline.

Not that the work was always very glamorous. Early on, Rosenheim put Jack at the disposal of a Dr Bain, a physician with a successful practice in Harrogate, but also a frustrated research physiologist. Under Rosenheim's direction, Bain was investigating the presence of substances in urine that affect blood pressure (a subject still under investigation today). Jack was charged with using his chemistry skills to extract a substance called isoamyl amine oxalate from urine. In the end, he harvested some 400 mg – or about a tenth of a teaspoonful – but to do so he had to process about 400 litres of urine – roughly about three baths full. It is only a pity that Dr Bain did not feel the need to credit Jack in his paper other than to briefly acknowledge his 'chemical assistance'.[4]

Rosenheim, however, was not so slow to recognise Jack's value and offered him a collaboration identifying and measuring other substances in urine. Jack's first publication was written jointly with Rosenheim in 1914,[5] with his first solo paper coming a year later, after he succeeded in developing the chemical methods to measure sulphates and total sulphur in urine. He also took the opportunity to attend lectures in physiology, biology and medicine along with the college's medical students. Becoming impressively well informed about anatomy and histology, he was now well set to embark on his quest to apply his first love, chemistry, to medical sciences. With biochemistry the emerging discipline *du jour*, it was a classic case of right man, right place, right time.

But of course, there was a bigger picture at play. Europe had descended into conflict, a war so brutal that it would virtually wipe out a generation, including one of Jack's great friends at King's, a brilliant medical student called Richard Bevan – a loss that affected Jack deeply. Jack himself received his call-up in 1914 and the official line is that a weak heart trumped his desire to take his place in the front line. Instead, he remained at home, working on the front line of science. One can only wonder at the grief this must have caused him.

After being recommended for a post by Halliburton, Jack spent the years 1914–18 at the Cancer Hospital Research Institute at the Royal Marsden in Chelsea. But there was a gap of a few months before he took up the role, which he spent working as a 'government chemist' on what was described, rather enigmatically, as a 'biochemical problem of a somewhat unorthodox type'.

At the Marsden, he was employed as a chemist in the department of physiology. The impact of Rosenheim and Halliburton on his approach to his work was striking and his transformation from chemist to biochemist was set fair. It was here that the Polish-American Casimir Funk became his supervisor. Funk was already something of a scientific superstar, having gone public six years earlier with his theory that it was the absence of a series of what he called 'vitamines' (a contraction of 'vital amines', amines being a type of chemical compound) that contributed to the 'deficiency diseases' beri-beri, antiscorbutic (scurvy), pellagra and rickets.

Under Funk, Jack developed new expertise, experimenting with animals to tease out what were then called the essential accessory factors and which we now know as vitamins. The pair would go on to publish together in this area,[6] and their work led on to another crucial question: is cancer affected by the proteins and amino acids we consume? Jack explored the mystery by looking at the growth rate of experimental tumours in animals – a process that contributed to his growing understanding of nutrition in general.

Back at King's, Halliburton had been brought on to the Royal Society's Food (War) Committee, which had direct access to the Minister of Food to advise on rationing in the First World War. Against the backdrop of conflict and an impending food crisis rooted in the nation's overreliance on imports, it was work of vital importance. Halliburton was aware of the expanding volume of research into vitamins but had many unanswered questions and turned to Jack to help him research them. Specifically, Halliburton asked him to investigate the vitamin content of butter, margarine and other butter substitutes to establish their potential health-giving properties.[7]

There's no doubt that this was an exciting time to be a biochemist. It must have felt like being a pioneer on a new frontier. The onset of the war had given the field an even greater urgency, highlighting problems that had been decades and even centuries in the making, and offering hope of a way through. Not least, the government was playing catch-up in the face of overwhelming evidence that much of the country was malnourished and that ill-health and poverty were inextricably linked.

At the beginning of the twentieth century, many old and unhelpful assumptions still held strong. For instance, it was widely believed that if you had enough food to fend off hunger, you were adequately fed. The idea of a nutritionally balanced diet, with sufficient vitamins and minerals, simply did not exist in any meaningful way. Moreover, it was a popular party line in Westminster that if you did not have sufficient income to secure the required food to feed yourself and your family, then the blame rested at your door. Poverty was still widely regarded as a symptom of personal failure.

Governments had hitherto shown little interest in getting to grips with the problem of poverty and attendant malnutrition, despite the evidence being there for all to see – not only in landmark social studies like those by Charles Booth and Seebohm Rowntree,[8] but also anecdotally from the nation's military recruiters. Between the Crimean War in the mid-nineteenth century and the First World War, they consistently reported increasing occurrence of willing recruits being rejected on the grounds of poor health and stunted growth. Jack's life, though, had been a period of great leaps forward in terms of understanding nutrition.

It is worth remembering that germ theory – the idea that pathogens cause illnesses – had gained widespread consensus only in the twenty years or so before Jack Drummond's birth, replacing the earlier idea that disease is spread through 'miasma', or noxious air. It explained so much that had previously seemed inexplicable. But it could not explain everything. However hard science tried, there were certain diseases that seemed to resist the idea of pathogenic origin. Among them were a group of five ailments that regularly proved fatal: the aforementioned rickets, scurvy, beri-beri and pellagra, along with xerophthalmia (night blindness). Now almost unheard of in the Western world, in 1900 these conditions affected up to half the population. The pressure was on to find their cause and thus a strategy to fight them. Governments and big businesses pressed for quick results, aware that the ravages of these illnesses were bad for, on the one hand, the recruitment of healthy soldiers and, on the other, an industrial workforce to address faltering productivity.

The race to find solutions was exciting, intense, competitive, international and, at times, cut-throat. With the finest medical and scientific minds of the era on the case, the solutions edged nearer and the mysteries of the 'terrible five' were gradually exposed. They were the result neither of hidden infections nor lack of calories, but of vitamin deficiencies.

Vitamin A was the first vitamin to be discovered. In 1912, one of the fathers of British biochemistry, Frederick Gowland Hopkins, showed that there were other elements in milk required for growth besides protein, fat and carbohydrates.[9] One of these substances was isolated and identified by two competing teams in the US the following year, and referred to initially as 'fat soluble' A, before the vitamin A designation superseded it. Hopkins would win a Nobel Prize for his work and in time it became understood that vitamin A deficiency caused night blindness.

Around the same time Hopkins was making his break-through, Jack Drummond's future supervisor Funk was isolating vitamin B1 (thiamine),[10] which would prove pivotal in the fight against beri-beri. A deficiency of vitamin B3 would eventually be identified as the cause of pellagra; likewise vitamin C in the case of scurvy and vitamin D for rickets, but these would go undiscovered until the 1920s and 1930s. This was a fast-moving academic arena, where assumptions needed to be revised almost by the day. For all that Jack found his capacity for work and learning tested, it was incredibly exciting too.

At the hospital, Drummond and his colleague Dr Alexander Paine kept the work of the research and pathological departments going virtually on their own during the war. At the same time, he published papers with Halliburton on his work for the Royal Society, increasing his expertise in the field of vitamin research. Belatedly, Britain's decision-makers had realised the need for sound policy around nutrition; but nonetheless, much of the advice of the Food (War) Committee was frustratingly ignored or rejected – despite the public being told that policy was rooted in 'carefully considered advice by scientific and food experts'. Some scientists were appeased by being co-opted on to the Compulsory Rationing Committee, but again their advice was totally ignored when rationing of bread was introduced against their recommendations. Even as they felt hamstrung, the scientific community carried on, collecting data on the composition of food and exploring the nutritional requirements of men, women and children in different occupations. Research opportunities were sadly many and forthcoming, as when there were outbreaks of beri-beri among the troops in Gallipoli in 1916 and of scurvy in Mesopotamia in 1917.

The national diet was already changing rapidly before the First World War. Butter, for instance, had for a long time been relatively expensive, especially after a widespread cattle disease in the 1860s affected supply, and much that was sold was rancid and laden with water (especially that coming from Holland). Margarine (also known as 'butterine'), invented in the late 1860s by a French scientist at the request of the French navy seeking a cheap substitute for butter, became common in Britain and its popularity increased when the process of hardening the margarine with hydrogen was invented in 1910. This despite the fact that in truth it was not very pleasant. What people didn't realise was that it was also full of trans fats that increased the risk of heart disease, but empty of vitamins (unlike vitamin A- and D-rich butter). Partly in light of Jack's First World War work, come the 1920s, vitamins were eventually added to margarine.

Jack's desire to find practical applications for his research was exemplified by a paper he published towards the war's end on infant feeding,[11] in which he expounded the need for vitamins in early years and during periods of rapid growth. Orange juice was recommended for artificially fed babies, and since skimmed and condensed milk were seriously deficient in all vitamins, he suggested supplements of cream or cod-liver oil. 'It now remains,' he wrote, 'for the practical worker on infant nutrition to apply the results of these experimental studies as soon as he is convinced of their accuracy.' By the war's end, and thanks to his partnership with Halliburton, Jack was a nutritional expert with a broad platform.

In 1918, he was awarded his doctorate by the University of London and briefly succeeded Funk at the Cancer Hospital but the following year moved to UCL as a research assistant in physiological chemistry. The promotions came thick and fast, and in 1920 he was made a reader at the university. It was around this time that he published a paper entitled 'The Nomenclature of the so-called Accessory Food Factors (Vitamins)'. For well-argued reasons of academic protocol, Jack suggested renaming 'vitamines' as 'vitamins', at the same time freeing us from the far more cumbersome synonymous expression 'accessory food factor'.[12]

In 1922, UCL appointed him Professor of Biochemistry in the department of physiology. He thus became the college's first ever Professor of Biochemistry, and only the fourth in the entire United Kingdom.[13] He published over 50 scientific papers and pamphlets in the 1920s and 30s and remained at the forefront of nutritional science as he continued his work on vitamins. In the early 1920s, for example, he spent considerable energy trying to purify and quantify vitamin A. On several occasions, he came very close to making important discoveries but was repeatedly pipped to the post by others. In the mid-1930s, he was a hair's breadth from isolating vitamin E (alpha tocopherol) from wheat germ oil but faltered when it came to proving its purity. A year afterwards, Herbert Evans *et al.* published the definitive isolation as a crystalline allophanate, winning the kudos that had so nearly been Jack's.

Jack was nothing if not broad in his research interests and there were those who considered that he cast his net too widely, a sort of human quicksilver who jumped from problem to problem. There was the suspicion that he was sometimes too concerned with 'big picture' ideas and, once convinced of a result, lacked the patience to painstakingly gather more supporting evidence. But no one could doubt his energy. The department he grew might have been small, but it routinely punched above its weight. He proved highly adept at establishing his own team of young research biochemists to help with his work, and he was nothing less than an inspiration to many of them.

Now and then, he could be blunt and brusque, his humour often mischievous and tinged with cynicism. Only a few, perhaps, could get really close to the soul of the man. But for all that, he was fun, loyal, approachable, kind and mostly sunny. If he could lend one of his students or colleagues a helping hand or a listening ear, he was happy to do so. His lectures were not just a hit with his students either, but won avid audiences among the public. He was a pioneering figure in what we would today describe as the public engagement of science.

But Jack was not all work and no play. The social side of life was vital to him – he was a regular on the capital's theatre and concerts scene, especially if it was opening night – and his wit and culture ensured a wide band of loyal friends. An enthusiastic and tireless cricketer, he loved his food and drink too, co-founding a dining club at which students and staff gathered informally. A member of the advisory council of the Wine and Food Society – set up by his friend, the wine merchant and gourmand André Simon – his interest in nutrition extended to a desire to reshape the UK's then generally poor reputation for cuisine. According to Simon, Jack was a man of great taste and absolute sincerity, with 'a keen sense of humour and a sense of fun far greater than that of many younger men'.[14] This no doubt helped him succeed as a canny networker, skills honed in the London gentlemen's clubs to which he belonged, the Savage and the Savile.

By the 1930s, more of Jack's time than ever was taken up with travel and he was active with the League of Nations Health Organisation (which would morph into the World Health Organisation in 1948). In 1933, for example, he visited politically volatile Spain on the organisation's behalf, the same year he was invited to deliver the prestigious Lane Medical Lectures at Stanford University on the American West Coast. Even with such demands on his time, he still managed to lecture and publish regularly, although from 1934 all his basic research publications were co-authored, suggesting he may have struggled to find the hours for practical work at the bench.

Most of his papers from this time centred on vitamin A but around 1937, vitamin E began to take more of his attention, along with matters of nutrition in general.[15] His sense of humour shines through in a paper he wrote about margarine, in which he exhibited an air of satire that would not be allowed today:

> It is unlike the French to be unmindful of a son of their country who has rendered notable service in so important a matter as food, yet I am not aware that the achievement of Mèges-Mouriès is commemorated in France by a public monument or inscription or even by a street name. Equally surprising is the scanty information supplied by biographical works of reference about that most ingenious inventor.

Perhaps we can attribute this to the lack of sympathy one would expect from a nation which appreciates above all other things good food and good cooks, towards one who hoped to pass off the greasy and rather unpalatable products of his laboratory as butter. Whatever the reason for such neglect, the fact remains that the French might well be proud to claim the inventor who made possible one of the greatest food industries of our time.[16]

In total, nine Nobel Prizes were awarded for vitamin discoveries between 1909 and 1952 and Jack must surely have counted himself unlucky not to get one of them. But his energy for work did not diminish as the years rolled by. He started researching a book, which would be published as *The Englishman's Food,* and was generous in supporting and reviewing research from others too. For instance, he took great interest in data collected at Christ's Hospital School, then a charitable trust boarding school, on its boys from pre-First World War until 1933. He assisted with the data analysis and found financial help from Distillers Company Limited and the Imperial Chemical Industries Limited to allow publication of the book *The Schoolboy: his nutrition and development* by G. E. Friend in 1935.[17] This book proved highly influential on prominent nutritionists like John Boyd Orr, who the following year published a landmark report on the relationship between health and income. The school's data revealed among other things that instances of fractures among its pupils increased nearly fivefold when butter was rationed between February 1918 and the summer of 1922 and substituted with margarine – evidence that seemed to confirm Jack's theories about vitamin D. As Jack had noted in a preface to the Christ's Hospital School book:

It is a fact at once surprising and humiliating that with thousands of years of human life and experience behind us we are actually engaged today in acquiring laboriously the knowledge necessary to enable us to feed and rear our children properly. Many a well to do father has given greater attention to the feeding of his own horses, dogs or farm stock than to the diet on which his son might be subsisting at a famous public school.

In the early months of 1936, he set out on an arduous European tour, surveying the nutritional picture (especially in relation to the poor) in Holland, Germany, Czechoslovakia, Austria, Hungary, Switzerland, Poland, Russia, Finland, Sweden, Norway and Denmark. Returning home with great enthusiasm for the canteen feeding he had witnessed in parts of eastern Europe, he was full of ideas for the future. He was increasingly occupied with the question of how to provide those whose health was impacted by bad diet not only with the necessary knowledge to correct it but with the very food itself. He would have a chance to put his theories into practice sooner than he might have imagined.

The clouds of war were gathering.

THE ENGLISHMAN'S FOOD   7

When Jack published *The Englishman's Food: Five Centuries of English Diet* with Anne Wilbraham in 1939,[1] he likely did not realise how quickly it would come to serve as his calling card. Released by the heavyweight publishing house Jonathan Cape Ltd, it soon established itself not only as a well-reviewed work of genuine scholarship and intellectual heft but as a bestseller too. Sir Alexander Walker II of the famous Johnnie Walker distilling dynasty had his part to play in this, giving financial help that allowed the book to be sold for twelve shillings and sixpence, a little over 60 pence in decimal currency – equivalent to about £30 in today's value, but much more reasonable than it would otherwise have been. Alexander Walker was some twenty years older than Jack but they inhabited shared social circles as members of the Savile and Savage clubs, as well as both being attendees at exclusive dinners hosted by Jack's close friend André Simon. It is distinctly possible that Walker regarded Jack as a protegé, and as such he was eager to support his book.

As its title suggests, the volume is a survey of how and what people ate over five centuries, and how it affected them.

Notably, the authors were interested not only in the food produced in the nation's grand houses but across all social strata. The emerging knowledge around dietary diseases and nutritional science is expertly described, from old wives' tales and folklore to the latest lab-based insights. A major reason behind the book's success was its readability. For an academic study drawing on historical sources in different languages (especially French), it skilfully avoided dryness in favour of an often wry, occasionally sarcastic, frequently funny and always engaging tone. Quite the authorial achievement – a fact attested to by the lesser quality of a great many subsequent books on dietary history that it inspired.

The question of authorship, however, is an interesting one. *The Englishman's Food* is a book by Jack Drummond and Anne Wilbraham. It says so, very clearly on the cover. Yet, the preface to the second edition[2] is a case study in how to erase a woman's contribution from the historical record. Norman C. Wright wrote the preface to that edition, published in 1957, five years after the murders in Provence. Sir Jack, he observes, had intended to publish an updated edition himself. Jack, notice – no mention of Anne at all. He goes on that 'his tragic death, together with that of his wife and daughter, came before he had found time to make the necessary revisions'. When there is at last a reference to Anne, it is not even by name and there is not so much as a nod to the fact that she co-authored the book. It is an extraordinary and depressing – if not wholly shocking – omission.

There was similar reluctance in the obituaries to Jack to acknowledge her role, with at best the impression given that professionally Anne was little more than his secretary. The fact that they would become husband and wife soon after publication seems to have done little to dim the idea that she was something akin to the Girl Friday who stole his heart. But there was a great deal more to Anne Wilbraham than that. She was no mere admin but helped elevate and add to Jack's work. They had published a paper together in the *Lancet* as far back as 1935[3] and Anne also received a nod hidden deep in the acknowledgements of the Christ's Hospital Schoolbook for 'data analysis'.[4] *The Englishman's Food* was not her first venture of this kind but she suffered the fate of so many women in what was then a masculine-dominated field in having her contribution shamelessly brushed under the carpet – something, one suspects, Jack would have found a grave affront too.

The book was dedicated to the subject of their *Lancet* paper, a young doctor, William Stark, an eighteenth-century pioneer of what we now recognise as nutritional science. His work had come at a heavy price. Bravely conducting dietary experiments upon himself, he contracted scurvy and died before his thirtieth birthday. As Jack and Anne Wilbraham sat down to write their book, Stark seemed a fitting cipher – a pioneering young man looking to improve public health through better understanding of nutrition but brought low through utter ignorance of vitamins.

The Englishman's Food was an outstanding and important work, but it was not alone in pleading for a new approach to nutrition. As previously mentioned, Jack's work at the Christ's School had been an influence on John Boyd Orr,[5] a doctor, biologist, teacher and politician and another of the age's great scientific communicators. When his *Food, Health and Income* was published by the Rowett Institute in 1936,[6] it was a slim volume that packed a big punch. The evidence it showed of the link between poverty and health was dumbfounding: the richest parts of society were able to pay for the better food that made them stronger and physically fitter. One-third of the British population, Boyd Orr said, were unable to afford the food needed to keep them healthy. The gap between the top third of income earners and the bottom in terms of diet was vast, with the top earners consuming the lion's share of the protective foods – meat, fish, butter, cheese and fruit – and the bottom third surviving on cheap, nutritionally bereft white bread, margarine, jam and sweet tea.

Unfortunately, the then Minister of Health, Kingsley Wood, simply wouldn't accept it. The welfare state, he insisted, had brought an end to malnourishment. No one was dying of starvation, after all. The government view was that dietary deficiencies were the consequence of ignorance, bad cooking and bad household economy. He went as far as to threaten Boyd Orr that his publication of data was not in keeping with the ethical standards of the medical profession and, as such, any doctors contributing to it risked being struck off the medical register. Despite voices like those of Boyd Orr and Jack, as war threatened again, the British public seemed scarcely better off in terms of food and nutrition than they had been in the First World War. The Great Depression had ensured some 15 million people in Britain lived in poverty and a third of the population suffered from malnutrition. Practical solutions were in short supply. Real-world change lagged far behind the growing list of impressive scientific breakthroughs. As the satirist Malcolm Muggeridge noted darkly in his 1940 work *The Thirties: 1930–1940 in Great Britain*:

The undernourished soon got forgotten in the excitement of deciding what was the measure of their under-nourishment. If it had been possible to make a meal of Nutrition, many who went hungry would have been fed; but, alas,

Nutrition allayed no hunger, except for self-importance and self-righteousness.[7]

As Europe cantered towards conflict and *The Englishman's Food* flew off the bookshelves, there were significant developments in Jack's personal life. In 1939, after some quarter of a century of marriage, he divorced Mabel. This was still a time when such a development was not only relatively unusual but distinctly socially unacceptable. Certainly not a decision to be taken lightly.

The couple had seemingly enjoyed an affluent lifestyle, despite Jack's fairly meagre academic income. Mabel had long ago surrendered any thoughts of a scientific career of her own and did not work, even though the absence of children from the relationship might have allowed her to do so relatively easily. To Jack's professional colleagues and their friends, they no doubt seemed to have a lot going for them. But somewhere along the way, Jack had fallen for the woman with whom he had done so much work over the years – his co-author, Anne Wilbraham. Within a year of the granting of the decree absolute dissolving his first marriage, Jack had embarked on his second. He was 49 and Anne was 33. It's worth noting, too, that he does not seem to have harboured ill-feeling towards Mabel, nor she to him. Mabel would be a significant beneficiary of Jack's will.

It must have stretched him to juggle these changes in personal circumstances with his work commitments in light of the fast-moving international scene. Yet he never really took his eye off the ball. As war seemed increasingly inevitable, he was conscious of the lessons to be carried from the previous World War. In that conflict, neither side had foreseen just how vitally important food, hunger and malnutrition would

be to the final outcome. Now Jack and his fellow professionals had a greater grasp of the need for those foods rich in the
'protective factors' (vitamins) necessary for life. Even though
it was a message still yet to be sufficiently communicated to
the nation's doctors, let alone the general public, it was an
area where Britain held a potential advantage. In Germany the
emphasis remained on a more old-fashioned view that total
calorie intake was what really mattered, with proteins, fats
and carbohydrates the focus at the expense of wider nutritional targets.

Britain's overreliance in the First World War on food
imports (accounting in 1914 for about half of food consumption in terms of monetary value) had almost proved disastrous
when Germany's relentless attacks on sea routes threatened
to starve the nation into submission. By 1917, the UK was
down to only three or four weeks' stocks. Eventually, an
effective and equitable system of rationing that took account
of nutritional necessity – including the need for protective
foods – was enacted, administered by the UK's first itera-
tion of a Ministry of Food, which operated between 1916 and
1921. In the end, it was the Allied blockade of Germany's supply routes that proved decisive in the war. Jack, however, was
determined that there should be no repeat of the short-lived
but damaging phase of voluntary food restrictions and bread
rationing that simply caused weight loss, illness and unhappiness among Britain's most patriotic and law-abiding
citizens. That the country should learn from the experiences
of the past was neatly encapsulated in the epigraph he chose
for *The Englishman's Food*, a quotation from Jean Anthelme
Brillat-Savarin's *La Physiologie du Gout*: 'La destinée des nations
dépend de la manière dont elles se nourrissent' ('The destiny
of nations depends on how they feed themselves').[8]

COMETH THE HOUR 8

It was in September 1939, with Britain having just declared war on Germany, that a new Ministry of Food was formed. It was created out of the small food department at the Board of Trade, itself set up in 1937 to ensure food security in case of war. The new ministry endured a faltering start. Ration books had already been printed and distributed to every person in the country ahead of the expected start of the rationing programme, but the programme would not come into force until the beginning of 1940. The government was struggling to isolate the swift, clear guidance it needed on the 'food position' amid a muddle of competing voices, some more expert than others.

Fortunately, the Ministry of Food possessed a powerful weapon to set things on the right path. Pulling its strings in the background was Sir Henry French, a Sir Humphrey Appleby-type career civil servant with a clear vision for the department and an unrivalled grasp of the Whitehall dark arts. He claimed humble beginnings as the third son of a leather seller and, like Jack, was an alumnus of King's College, although he had left several years before Jack went there. His first step into the civil service was as a second-division clerk at the Board of Agriculture but he worked his way up the ladder in open competition to become the board's general secretary for food production during the First World War. In 1936, he was seconded to the Board of Trade to develop 'food defence plans', where he cleverly used his network of secret contacts to stockpile supplies of what Lord Woolton – the wartime Minister of Food – would later describe as 'some of the more difficult commodities'. In the late 1930s, for example, the main source of animal oil in margarine production came from whales. With cunning and forethought, French sent agents into Norway who bought the season's supply of whale oil from right under the noses of the Germans.[1]

In 1937, he was pivotal to the establishment of the Food (Defence Plans) Department before transferring his team over to the Ministry of Food two years later. The first Minister of Food was W. S. Morrison, a soldier by training and formerly Minister for Agriculture and Fisheries. As it was for the Ministry of Food, and indeed for Morrison's former ministry, the food issue was also high on the agenda of the Ministry of Health, the Cabinet Food Policy Committee, the Scientific Food Committee, the Medical Research Committee and the British Medical Association – an instance of too many cooks jockeying for position around what threatened to be a quickly spoiled broth. French realised the massive job he faced in clarifying the jurisdictions of the various ministries and the national medical and scientific machinery. Moreover, he was conscious that his ministry was the new boy on the block. But he was up to the task.

Morrison lasted just a couple of months before he was moved on, quite possibly at French's behest, eventually to become governor-general of Australia. French now set about getting the right people into the right jobs. For the role of scientific advisor to the ministry, he had one particular man in mind: Jack Drummond. In fact, as long ago as September 1938, Jack had offered his services to any eventual Ministry of Food, although at the time he was told that should such a department come into existence, it was not intended that it should have its own scientific staff. But French knew a good option when he saw one.

At the outbreak of war, Jack was released on full pay from his duties at UCL, although he managed to carry on some research at the Courtauld Institute of Biochemistry (Middlesex Hospital) with Professor Charles Dodds. UCL fully expected him to undertake work for the 'national good' and, now aged 48, he was at the peak of his scientific career. Arguably, no one knew better than him exactly what, and how much, people should be eating to obtain sufficient calories to stave off hunger while accessing the protective vitamins and minerals they needed as well.

In addition, he had a reputation for patience and for being able to forge consensus between experts – skills French realised would be invaluable in bringing together officialdom, politicians, doctors, agricultural leaders and an array of other parties, all while working to get the public on board with necessary but potentially unpalatable measures too. French's plan to draft Jack into the Ministry swung into action on 16 October 1939 when Jack was named its chief advisor on food contamination. He duly produced a pamphlet, 'Food and its Protection Against Poison Gas: The Conservation of Food is Second Only to the Preservation of Life' (an update on one he had written in 1937).[2] Then, in January 1940, he was invited to attend a meeting to discuss the issue of wartime bread, along with representatives of the farming industry as well as flour millers and bakers, most of whom Jack knew personally. He presented his strongly held views, firmly grounded in scientific research, and drove home his message in an accompanying document presented to the Minister of Food, 'On certain nutritional aspects of the food position'.[3] This reviewed the current position and potential effects of the war, particularly in relation to poorer members of society.

It was a timely intervention. In response to questions about where it was getting its advice, the Ministry had been forced to admit that there was no one officially in position. But on 1 February, the day after Jack presented his paper and on the recommendation of French, he was appointed its scientific advisor. He soon discovered the atmosphere inside the department was dire. This was at a time when Neville Chamberlain was still prime minister but poised to be replaced by Churchill in May 1940. Lord Woolton was quickly announced as Minister of Food in Churchill's coalition and he would write of the Ministry: 'One's predecessors have not been entirely successful. I found the Ministry of Food suffering a general depression, the Press was against them, and they were dejected, and frankly puzzled by their unpopularity.'

Woolton, born Frederick James Marquis in 1883, had made his fortune in retail but was another who had clawed his way up from fairly humble beginnings. He had seen real poverty, recalling the shock when, as a student at Manchester University, a near neighbour – a woman, according to Woolton, of 'refined speech and appearance' – had died from starvation.[4] Woolton and Jack hit it off from the outset. With French the final third of the triumvirate, the Ministry was soon on a much better footing, taking the fight to the enemy on what became known as 'the kitchen front'. 'The war will be lost or won in the homes of the people,' Woolton would say. 'The strength of the home front depends on the spiritual and physical stamina of the people.' Jack found himself not only with a crucial wartime role but with an extraordinary opportunity to up the levels of public health in general. It was an unprecedented chance to conduct nutritional experimentation on a national scale. From small beginnings, the Ministry would eventually employ 15,000 people.

While Jack could say with accuracy what the British people needed to survive (and indeed prosper), the challenge of securing the necessary food was rather more imposing. But Woolton, French and Jack did a remarkable job of managing the various political, civil service and business interests involved. There was also an art to knowing how much information to share with the world at large. For instance, a secret study was undertaken in Cambridge in December 1939 in which volunteers were given a calculated diet restricted in eggs, meat, fish, milk and fat but with unlimited potatoes, vegetables and bread.[5] The volunteers took strenuous exercise to simulate the physical work needed to grow the food and after three months were found to have remained healthy. This gave confidence to the government that Britain could cope even if no imports were available. The downside, however, was a massive increase in flatulence and a two-and-a-half-fold increase in excrement volume – facts kept out of the public record until after the war.

The Ministry's food-distribution network became an exemplar of logistical genius, regularly demanding lateral thinking and quick action. For instance, the nation's storage facilities, including cold storage, had sensibly been built up over the years near ports, close to where the food that needed storing was arriving. However, these ports were now highly vulnerable to air attack and the contents of their storage facilities at grave risk. Money was therefore made available to build new facilities, often in the middle of nowhere and, ideally, underground for extra safety.

It was now understood within government that certain groups had particular dietary needs, with special provision made for babies and young children, pregnant women, and heavy manual labourers. It was also recognised that the dietary requirements of a child over fourteen years of age were equivalent to those of an adult. Jack was determined to convince his political masters of the good sense in retaining a healthy, balanced diet for all. There would be no repeat of the bread rationing of the previous war. Jack's main recommendations were to provide bread of high vitamin value, increase the consumption of potatoes, oatmeal, cheese and green vegetables, supply not less than a pint a day of whole milk to pregnant and nursing mothers and to all children up to the age of fifteen years, and to fortify margarine with vitamins A and D.

He was instrumental in the introduction of the National Loaf, a coarse brown bread enriched with vitamins that won no prizes for culinary finesse but was far more wholesome than the nutritionally deficient white bread beloved of the British housewife. Jack was able to leverage his contacts within the farming community and his knowledge of pesticides to advise on how supplies of the right sort of grain could be maintained, and how supplies could be shared between competing needs for flour, animal feed and the brewing industry. With sufficient bread, potatoes and oatmeal, he knew there'd be no hunger, and with sufficient milk, vegetables and potatoes, no malnutrition.

The National Loaf was loaded with the B vitamins, while vitamin C was provided in sufficient quantities by potatoes and vegetables as long as it was not lost through overcooking.

The fat-soluble vitamins, especially important to children, were more of a problem but vitamins A and E were known to be plentiful in cod liver oil, of which the government had sourced much from Newfoundland before the war. Cod liver oil, along with concentrated orange juice, became readily accessible from the local chemist, with a cash-prize contest launched to encourage the creation of a more palatable version of the supplement (quite a challenge given its origins in rotting fish livers).

When necessity demanded swingeing cuts in fat and sugar consumption, the reduced intake offered significant public health benefits. But Jack recognised the value of treats too and was determined that the country should not go without beer or fish and chips. While their nutritional value may have been limited, their part in keeping up popular morale was much clearer.

Another of Jack's major contributions was the development and production of safe, healthy dried foods. Their great advantage was that they offered maximum calories for the least amount of shipping space, relieving pressures on imports. At the start of the war, Britain was importing two-thirds of its food, amounting to 20 million tons a year. Just as in the First World War, the merchant navy took a hammering from U-boat torpedoes and over 30,000 merchant seamen (out of about 185,000) lost their lives over the course of the war, mostly in North Atlantic convoys – a death rate higher than any of the armed forces. Anything to take the weight off them was to be welcomed.

Milk, eggs, fruit, veg and mince were all investigated for their suitability to be dried. It did, however, necessitate a campaign to teach British housewives how to use them, along with other new foods being introduced into the national menu, like tinned Spam. Another of Jack's responsibilities was to make sure that the nutritional claims on labelling were true and honest – a task that required him to make several trips across the Atlantic as the war progressed.

While the popular memory has it that everybody was happy to do their bit for the war effort, the introduction of rationing in January 1940 was painful. Resistance and resentment were widespread. But the triumvirate at the Ministry of Food displayed not only good sense but an uncommon popular touch that helped to bring the general public quickly on board. Key to this was a system that not only seemed fair, but was so in practice. To keep the nation so well fed and nourished and in relatively good spirits in such circumstances was an achievement to be reckoned with, and one that Jack and his Ministry colleagues deserved to be proud of.

By the war's later stages, Jack's fame had spread internationally. Across a continent ravaged by war and pockmarked by hunger, his hand in what the UK had achieved was not ignored. In 1944, he was appointed advisor on nutrition to the newly formed SHAEF, the Supreme Headquarters Allied Expeditionary Force led by Dwight Eisenhower. Uppermost was the question of how to feed the hungry in areas imminently to be liberated but which for now remained behind enemy lines. The Netherlands in particular was known to be enduring savage famine conditions. Tragically, there was recent experience in dealing with famine. In 1943, in India's Bengal Province (now straddling India and Bangladesh but then entirely within British India), about 2–3 million people from a population of 60 million died of starvation and other diseases aggravated by malnutrition.

Jack chaired a committee at SHAEF whose remit was to maximise the efficiency of the people tasked with delivering aid. The regular troops tasked with liberating Europe were at the forefront of this effort; they were well trained in combat but not in administering humanitarian aid. Within a few weeks, in January 1945, a clear, concise, lucid and readable manual of about 100 pages was published as a handy, pocket-sized hardback.[6] It included practical advice on what food to give (taking into account different eating habits across Europe); how to recognise and document undernutrition and vitamin deficiency; how to source food, utensils and fuel; and how to store, handle and cook the food without destroying its vitamin content. *Nutrition and Relief Work: A Handbook for the Guidance of Relief Workers* was soon a bible for personnel at the sharp end.

In the UK, the administration of famine relief was bolstered by the emergence of new local organisations like Oxfam in Oxford and the national Famine Relief Committee, fully supported by nutritional experts including Jack. Plans were put in place to evaluate the scale of Europe's starvation problem, with Jack already experienced in going behind enemy lines. He had earlier ventured to Malta during its prolonged siege (June 1940–November 1942), during which children had died of starvation. He had flown to the island during a lull in fighting, assessing the situation and arranging for the provision of emergency supplies, including chocolate fortified with vitamins.

But his trip to the continent over the course of late April and early May 1945 must surely have ranked among the most intense periods of his life. On 20 April he arrived in Eindhoven in the Netherlands for four days of talks towards organising special feeding teams and milk supplies, readying

Red Cross stocks in Ellecom (in the central-eastern zone of the country) for mobilisation, and preparing F-treatment (a process of giving nutrients via intravenous infusion or a tube straight into the stomach to patients whose stomachs have atrophied through lack of use; the 'F' stands for 'famine') for some 70,000 people. On the 26th he briefly flew back to London to action various decisions, then immediately returned to Brussels, from where he travelled to the newly liberated Belsen concentration camp over 500 km away in northern Germany.

The reality of what had been going on in the Nazi camps had come to light on 15 April when British Special Air Service officer Lieutenant John Randall and his jeep driver discovered the camp by chance while on reconnaissance deep in the German forest. Alongside some 13,000 corpses left where they had fallen were 60,000 others clinging on to life in an almighty struggle. People died at a rate of 500 a day in the first phase after liberation; despite the liberators' Herculean efforts, there were 14,000 additional deaths in the first month.

Belsen, or Bergen-Belsen, was set up as a prisoner-of-war camp but in 1943 became a concentration camp to which thousands were transported from other camps, either by foot or by rail, as the Allies closed in and the Nazis attempted to hide their crimes. This resulted in extreme overcrowding and conditions ripe for typhus, dysentery, typhoid and tuberculosis to take hold. Anne Frank and her sister Margot arrived here from Auschwitz and died from typhus just a month before liberation. In the last days before its discovery, no food or water was available, most of the prison guards had left and there was evidence of cannibalism. Although it was still in German-held territory, Heinrich Himmler, head of the SS, agreed to hand it over to the Allies without a fight and designate the surrounding area a neutral zone. Nonetheless, for the British and then Canadian troops arriving from the 15th, it was a dangerous place to be. Even more so when four German fighter planes attacked it – whether deliberately or in error – on the 20th, causing further damage to the water supply and killing more prisoners along with three British medical orderlies. The place teemed with infectious diseases and a number of prisoners died when their bodies proved incapable of digesting the army rations some troops had selflessly given them.

Brigadier Kennedy sent word from the camp to Jack in the Netherlands, requesting his advice. Jack arrived on the 29th and, in his usual lucid and concise manner, evaluated the situation and the nutritional needs of the liberated prisoners. Inmates were divided into five categories: babies up to four years, children between four and fourteen years, those with extreme starvation, those with serious starvation but not thought to be close to death; and those able to eat a normal diet. With his own daughter now aged three and at home in relative safety in London, the sight of 900 under-fourteens living amid such horror affected him greatly. He wrote in his subsequent report:

> ... the children still presented a pitiable sight. Pallid wizened faces, devoid of any expression; limbs nothing but skin and bone; a desolating apathy and the weakness of sheer exhaustion. Many of those I saw could not be expected to live, however good the attention they received. Many others will be wrecked in health for life. Everything possible is being done to feed these poor little wretches suitably.[7]

He was full of admiration for the work already being done by British troops on the ground. He paid tribute to 'the magnificent job Colonel Johnson and Lt. Col. Lipscombe of 32nd C.C.S [Casualty Clearing Station], and their officers and men have done, and are still doing at Belsen':

> To have got the feeding of this great mass of sick and suf-
> fering humanity to a sound basis within a week of the camp
> being uncovered is itself an achievement bringing distinction
> to all concerned. When it is borne in mind that the feeding
> of these people was only one of the many truly Herculean
> tasks that these British officers engaged, their achievement
> seems nothing short of a miracle.

A roll-out of F-treatment, however, was problematic. Camp inmates had heard so many accounts of Auschwitz and the use of lethal injections there that many refused to have any-thing to do with a needle or, indeed, any medical equipment. Of those that did accept the treatment, some fell foul of the unhygienic conditions in which it was administered, although for others it was successful.

After Belsen, Jack returned to Brussels, where he heard that the Reichskommissar for the occupied Netherlands had agreed to permit four members of the Red Cross advisory committee to pass through German lines to discuss special feeding measures. At 11 a.m. on 6 May, Jack and three col-leagues crossed enemy lines under a white flag. At Bilthoven, they met General von Meyer, the senior German army med-ical officer, who gave Jack and his team the necessary passes to travel freely in occupied territory. A visit to Amsterdam later that day was distressing and led Jack to immediately call forward four special feeding teams. When Jack and his team then returned to get an agreement from General von Meyer, they discovered the Germans had capitulated and surrendered earlier that day. Under his own steam, Jack decided to press on with his plans without further consultation.

The next few days were a frenzy of activity involving trips to The Hague, Rotterdam, Amsterdam, Utrecht and Leiden – journeys made along bombed roads filled with desperate refugees, through checkpoints marshalled by jumpy, retreating German soldiers. On 14 May, Jack reported back to Major General Clarke and Brigadier Cazenove at SHAEF before arriving back in London on 16 May.[8]

Jack was horrified by what he had witnessed and immediately informed the British government as to the scale of the challenge ahead. From the surviving evidence, it appears that Jack personally drove the agenda and spearheaded the action that resulted in a European famine relief programme. As such, he was responsible for saving many thousands of lives, and many more were spared deformity and ongoing physiological impairment.

VE (Victory in Europe) Day came on Tuesday 8 May while Jack was still in the Netherlands. Plans were well established for the post-war occupation of Germany by Allied forces, with Jack appointed advisor on nutrition to the Control Commission for Germany and Austria (British Element) – a post that gave him virtually unfettered access to all corners of post-war Europe. His status as an important public figure was now beyond doubt. He had already been knighted by King George VI and now a flurry of other accolades came his way. He was awarded a fellowship of the Royal Society (an honour it was rumoured he did not particularly care for) and the New York Academy of Sciences elected him an honorary member, while the University of Paris presented him with an honorary degree. The French government topped even that by giving him the Légion d'honneur (the nation's highest order of merit) and his services to the Netherlands were recognised when he was made a Commander (Civil Division) of the Order of Orange Nassau. In the US, meanwhile, he was presented with the US Medal of Freedom, an honour created by President Truman for civilians in recognition of 'a meritorious act or service which has aided the United States in the prosecution of a war against an enemy or enemies'. Jack was one of only a handful of British citizens to receive the medal, complete with 'silver palm' – the second highest of four possible rankings.

Back in May 1943, Jack had flown to the States as the British delegate at the Hot Springs Conference in Virginia, where plans for a world food policy to defeat hunger and improve nutrition and food security were set in motion. After much work in the interim, in October 1945 in Quebec City the members of what was then still the League of Nations (soon to be superseded by the United Nations) put in place the foundations of the Food and Agricultural Organisation (FAO) – another accomplishment for which Jack could claim some credit, and further evidence of a dynamism that was never more evident than during the period 1939–45. An acknowledged expert at the war's start, he finished it a hero.

CAUSE CÉLÈBRE

9

The esteem in which Jack's work was held was evident in the shocked responses to his murder from those who knew him. In the days following the breaking of the news, Lord Woolton was among the many to pay public tribute:

When I went to the Ministry of Food, among my first inquiries was: 'Where is the scientific advisor to this Ministry, and who is he?' Then, for the first time, I got to know Jack Drummond, and we worked closely together throughout the whole period I was at the Ministry.

We decided on the import programme in order that we might bring the country essential and sustaining foods. It was he who told me of the importance of vitamins in these foods and gave me the knowledge which enabled us, during that period, to stamp out rickets among the children of this country. Together we worked out the welfare foods for expectant mothers and children. I shall ever be grateful to him for the knowledgeable and enthusiastic co-operation that he gave me. The nation is in his debt.

Sir Henry French was another to voice his admiration, praising Jack's 'knowledge of the chemistry of food and dietetics' that he believed was 'unique', while his 'modesty and personal charm made business relations with him a pleasure as well as a privilege'. Then there was Boyd Orr, by then raised to the peerage and a recipient of the Nobel Peace Prize:

> The death of Sir Jack Drummond is a great loss to the science of nutrition and its application to the promotion of health and physique of the people of this country ... His co-workers in this and in other countries will mourn the loss of a great scientist, a great administrator, and a great friend.

The *Nottingham Evening Post* of 6 August broadened the sympathetic and appreciative coverage to include Jack's daughter, carrying a few paragraphs headed 'Elizabeth was an Exceptionally Clever Girl'. That was according to her headmistress at the Wyvill School in Nottingham, Miss Hancock, who also described her as 'as nice a child as you could wish for'. 'She was what one would expect with such clever parents,' Hancock said, painting a picture of the Drummonds as a 'very united' family. Just a few days before their holiday, she added admiringly, Jack had taken time out of his hectic schedule to attend the school's sports day.

For the *Daily Mirror* on the same day, the slayings were front-page news, with the perpetrators described as 'machine-gunning bandits' motivated by robbery. There was a picture of Jack ('a sandy-haired man of 61'), Anne ('a petite, pretty brunette, several years younger than Sir Jack') and Elizabeth, taken when she was three years old. The very image of a happy family, hammering home the horror of it all. If there was any doubt as to the idyllic life they enjoyed, the report went on to describe their 'fifteen-roomed stucco-covered, green and white painted house ... set back among lime and chestnut trees' and referenced Jack's salary of 'not less than £4,000 a year'. The holiday, it said, was to help Jack recuperate from 'a slight spinal infection' of three months earlier. 'The millions of fine, healthy children in Britain today will be the finest memorial of all to Sir Jack Drummond,' the *Mirror* trumpeted. From Lurs, described by the newspaper as 'so tiny that it is not in any of the French guide books', the local shopkeeper, Henri Silve, was quoted: 'Everything has stopped in our little village. The police are everywhere. The bodies have now been moved to our little railway station where the trains no longer stop. It is quiet and peaceful there.'

Such press ensured the eyes of the world were directed towards the Durance Valley in anticipation of a speedy resolution to the murders. For Sébeille and the police over in France, the weight of expectation was intense. But Jack's status as a public figure was by no means the only driver for a result. There were wider political and economic considerations at stake. France was still in the early days of post-war rebuilding, which extended not only to its finances and national infrastructure, but to its very sense of self. It was bad enough that France had fallen to the Germans so quickly in 1940, but the widespread willingness to collaborate (or, at least, acquiesce) to the imposition of a fascist government had left a great dent in the nation's self-image.

The Fourth Republic created in 1946 was overseen by a series of coalitions that each crumbled as they grappled with reconstructing France while simultaneously dealing with demands for decolonisation in Indochina and Algeria (the latter being home to a million or so French nationals, to complicate matters further). It had all been too much for the country's biggest political beast, Charles de Gaulle, who resigned amid what he regarded as an impossible mess of partisan politics. By the time of the Drummond killings, he was just a year away from declaring his retirement from politics altogether to write his wartime memoirs, after several years on the relative periphery.

The murders came at a moment when France was trying to steer a course away from generalised political instability. They had implications, in addition, for a very particular strand of France's intended renaissance. Growing the underpowered tourism industry was a pillar of the Washington-sponsored Marshall Plan, which had envisaged revenues from the sector in France equivalent to some half a billion dollars in 1952. The travel agents' brochures sold essentially three visions of the country – all part of the plan to conjure a tourist's paradise. Firstly, there was the suave, chic sophistication of Paris. Next, the Hollywood-tinged glamour of the Riviera, with its white beaches and sun-dappled boulevards lined with palm trees. Then there was the rustic France of sprawling vineyards and noble peasants. It was this latter image into which the Durance Valley fitted.

There were promising signs that things were moving in the right direction. Tourist-class air fares were widely available for the first time in 1952, which brought a surge in arrivals from the USA, up to 260,000 from 180,000 the previous year. But it was the UK that supplied by far the most visitors. People like the Drummonds, each helping to fill the French coffers a little at a time. To have a tourist killed was, of course, a calamity. To lose a whole family, a disaster. But to have the family of a significant public figure so brutally murdered was an utter catastrophe.

Moreover, Anglo–French relations had been tetchy during de Gaulle's tenure and beyond – not least over the reluctance of the UK to share intelligence from its atomic bomb programme. In light of this frostiness, the murders only heightened tensions. Someone needed to be held responsible for the killings in order that the French might carry on looking the British in the eye. The investigation, and any subsequent trial, was inevitably going to be a public test of the still-nascent republic, and one that it simply could not afford to fail. How well was the country functioning after its catalogue of recent traumas? Was it in a fit state to consider itself still among the international elite of nations?

Never mind the yet-to-be-discovered assailant – the police, the judiciary and the government were just as much on trial. Then throw into the mix the press's insatiable desire for the story to move along. There was constant demand on Sébeille to provide updates that would fuel the next day's headlines. A job, it must be admitted, that Sébeille initially took up with some relish. But his early briefings were marked out by what was soon apparent as strident overconfidence. With the discovery of the rifle used in the attacks, he had assumed it would be plain sailing from there on in. He made the fatal error of overpromising.

With the offender still at large and undetected, the air of general frustration quickly grew. On 17 August, the British *Sunday Dispatch* offered a reward of 500,000 francs (about £500, equivalent to about £17,000 today) for information leading to the capture of the murderer or murderers. The accompanying article is illuminating in several respects. For one, it gives a strong sense of the weightiness of the case upon the collective French consciousness. The reward, the paper suggested, would 'help to allay the deep sense of personal responsibility which the French people feel for the crime'.

But the condescension of the article's unnamed author towards the peasant population of the Durance Valley simmers in the background. Even more striking is that it is an attitude seemingly shared by Sébeille. 'This offer,' the paper stated, 'is made as a result of statements by the French police that money may loosen the traditionally tight lips of the peasants in the area.' Sébeille, it explained, believed that 'at least 20 people in the district could give important information – if they were willing'. The article continues:

> For nearly two weeks the arid slopes of the lower French Alps have been combed by hundreds of local gendarmerie and members of the Marseilles murder squad. More often than not, the investigation has come to a frustrating halt in face of the local peasants' declaration: 'We know nothing.'

Of the newspaper's offer of a reward, Sébeille is said to have described it as an 'excellent idea': 'The peasants in this region … are very, very commercially minded. They tend to be stingy. If one mentioned money to them it would open their mouths. We'll be successful in the end but at the moment everybody is mute, like a wall.'

Yet this is all rather tame compared with some of the journalism in the French papers, especially when it grew apparent that the police had their eye upon a solution from within the local population. The case quickly became a distinctly hot political potato. There were none-too-discrete whispers that Jack's wartime government work may have strayed from the strictly above-board into the nether world of secret missions and espionage. The British authorities, including the Consulate in Marseilles and the British minister in Paris, moved quickly to quash such rumours. But they soon discovered that, however tenuous the basis for the allegations, this particular genie was not easy to get back into the bottle. Especially given the power of the Communist Party in the Durance Valley.

Le Figaro, the country's oldest national newspaper and one of that handful of newspapers whose fame carries round the world, served as the voice of the conservative middle and upper classes. So, when it speculated that the Drummonds may have been victims of a summary execution by French communist resistance for some presumed wartime affront, people sat up and took notice. The gloves were off, and other mass-circulation titles with their own agendas waded in. On the left, for example, was the daily L'Humanité. Founded in 1902 by Jean Jaurès, a leading figure in the French Section of the Workers' International until his assassination in 1914, the paper emerged as the mouthpiece of the French Communist Party. Although banned during the Second World War, it continued to publish clandestinely, cementing its image as an organ of resistance against the occupiers. After the war, amid surging popularity for the Communists, it achieved impressive circulation figures and became a mainstay of the French journalistic landscape. Naturally, it countered claims like those made in Le Figaro, implying instead that the police had embarked on some sort of anti-communist witch-hunt. It made much of the fact that Jack had gone behind enemy lines during the war and raised the question of whether there was more to this than merely a concession to allow Jack to undertake his hunger-fighting work in occupied territories.

L'Humanité's nemesis periodical was *L'Aurore*, first printed in secret in 1943 and hitting the mass market shortly after the liberation of Paris in 1944. Its name harked back to a famous earlier journal of the same name, founded in the nineteenth century by the then-future prime minister Georges Clemenceau and known for its intellectualism and liberal, socialist positioning. It was here that Émile Zola published his famous article on the Dreyfus affair – in which hardwired antisemitism had resulted in a great miscarriage of justice – under the now legendary headline 'J'accuse'. But by 1952, *L'Aurore* was owned by the industrialist Marcel Boussac, selling not far off half a million copies a day from its centre-right position on the political spectrum. For *L'Aurore*, there was little doubt that the answer to the murders lay among the Durance Valley's tight-lipped, left-wing peasants – the sort the *Sunday Dispatch* hoped might soon open up.

The French government found this type of scrutiny intensely uncomfortable. On the one hand, it understood the need to find a culprit to appease the British and assuage national shame. On the other, it had no great appetite to antagonise the Soviets with wild accusations of international communism's involvement in such a grisly crime on French territory. Although the French Communist Party had been excluded from Paris's governing coalitions since 1947, it retained a significant electoral presence and the implications of blithely linking it to the murders were considerable. Much more desirable and politically palatable was a quick and simple resolution. The presence of a psychopath or a band of heartless thieves or perhaps a sexual deviant hardly showed off the country in its best light, but it was preferable to the messy geopolitical soup being stirred by the media.

And there, on the ground, charged with finding the answers, was poor old Sébeille, his early confidence fading with every passing hour and day of inconclusive investigation. No wonder that when a viable suspect came into view, he was determined not to let his prey wrigglc free.

THE DOMINICIS 10

The buildings of La Grand Terre were run-down and tired. Its stone walls had that sturdy look bestowed only by the passage of time but there was a frailty about the place too. The weather-beaten roofs needed serious attention and a wooden lean-to appeared to be defying gravity by staying up at all. But it was big. Imposing, even in its unkempt state, with just a few small windows breaking up the rugged expanse of its walls. It had the air of a rustic fortress, its boundaries containing a world where strangers were not much welcome.

The farm was home to three generations but there was no doubting who bossed the place. Gaston Dominici, the septuagenarian patriarch, ruled his family with a rod of iron. The family had a complex dynamic, beset with ill-feeling and fear but also deep bonds of loyalty. In the immediate aftermath of the murders, they put on a united face to the outside world. They were, they wanted the world to believe, innocents caught up in a dreadful maelstrom.

Much of the early press depicted them as peasant simpletons, relics of a backward social class tinged with savagery. It was a take predominantly fuelled by prejudice and old-fashioned snobbery. While it was true that the family had limited formal education, the assumption that they were somehow stupid was difficult to justify. Gaston, in particular, had enjoyed very little schooling but possessed an impressive work ethic and an entrepreneurial streak that had enabled him to carve out a life for himself and his family, working his way up the ladder to become a landowner in his own right from the humblest of beginnings.

Clémence Dominici had been 20 years old when she had given birth to Gaston in a workhouse in Digne in 1877. This was the France only a few decades after Victor Hugo's *Les Misérables*, six years after the Paris Commune and with the Third Republic in its infancy. Indeed, *Les Misérables* opens in Digne. The literacy rate among French peasants was 33 per cent. Clémence's parents had come from Calabria in Italy to work on the Marseilles–Grenoble railway and ended up putting down roots. Clémence was unmarried and working as a servant when she fell pregnant. The father was unknown. Her parents tried to force her to give the child away but Clémence's midwife persuaded her otherwise, much to the new grandparents' unhappiness. The baby's life prospects were not promising.

Clémence and Gaston stayed in Digne and by the time he was ten he had two younger siblings, again with fathers unknown. All three were made wards of charity as Clémence struggled to cope, and Gaston was sent to a Catholic school where he pretended, for reasons unknown, to be illiterate. He was then put to work, at first as a farm labourer around Digne, during which time he first set eyes on Marie Germain, a pretty local girl a couple of years his junior. He lusted after her, much to the disapproval of her father, a successful farmer. Then, aged 21, he began a three-year stint in the army, when he was drafted into the 7th Regiment of Cuirassiers at Lyons. On discharge he became a shepherd and gained the reputation as a hell-raiser due to his hard drinking and fighting.

In August 1903, he married Marie after her father at last relented in his opposition. On the wedding night, Gaston realised why: she was already three months pregnant. The following April she gave birth to a daughter that Gaston would never acknowledge as his own. He was unable ever to let go this early deceit, a symbol of his disregard for his wife being his habit of unflatteringly referring to her as 'the Sardine' (La Sardine). Nonetheless, the following June, a son arrived, whom they named Clovis. In the coming years there would be a further four daughters and three sons.

In 1910, Gaston leased a farm at Ganagobie in a bid to assert his independence. Five years later, he moved to another tenant farm at La Serre in the Durance Valley, which had better soil. He did not fight in the First World War, having been granted an exemption because of his responsibility to provide for such a large family. Instead he threw himself into his agricultural work, scrimping and saving towards his lifetime aim of owning his own smallholding. This he achieved when, in 1922, he bought La Grand Terre. It was not much to look at and he paid 10,000 francs (worth about £400 then and equivalent to about £40,000 today) for the old-fashioned farmhouse set amid dry, stony land. Fiercely proud and independent, he eked out a living, somehow raising his nine children; and after nine years, it was ready for the family to move in.

To his loved ones and friends, he could be an excellent host when in the mood, ready to fill your empty wine glass. He also had a reputation for bravery after he once single-handedly apprehended a dangerous escaped criminal. It was 1923 and Gaston was tending his flock with Clovis. Two armed bandits were on the run from the gendarmes, and one, called Gauthier, came upon the two shepherds. Gaston confronted the stranger, demanding to know: 'Are you the robber?' Gauthier responded by opening fire. By some extraordinary fluke, the bullet he fired went down the barrel of Gaston's shotgun without injuring him. Gaston was recognised as a hero for his part in apprehending the escapee and he received a certificate of bravery from the prefect of the *département*, which he had framed and which was counted among his most prized possessions.[1]

A communist by political inclination, Gaston even thought about running for Mayor of Lurs around the time he purchased La Grand Terre, before deciding against it. Although he didn't fight in the Second World War, given that he was already in his sixties when it started, he was nonetheless active in assisting the Maquis, of which several of his sons were members. As well as helping to feed the Resistance cell hiding on the Ganagobie plain in 1944, Gaston also contributed to keeping the road and rail link from Cannes to Grenoble open for the Allied advance. All of which is to say that at the moment the bodies of the Drummonds were found strewn across the road close by his farm, Gaston Dominici was a man in the autumn of his life, surrounded by a close-knit if not always entirely harmonious family and in many respects a pillar of his local community.

To begin with, there was no suggestion that the Dominicis were anything but potentially valuable witnesses. But that soon changed. There is no doubt that Gaston was a tough man who'd lived a tough life. He did not feel the world had done him many favours, and that which he had he had got by going out and grasping it. He did what he had to do to get by, and he made sure that his family shared these values too.

Look out for yourself, because no one else will. Such attitudes were, as we have already seen, not uncommon in the Durance Valley, where it was hard to grind out a living and where old feuds and mistrusts proliferated. It should have come as no surprise, then, that the Dominicis were defensive as the police came to sniff around their lives. But a reluctance – or perhaps nervousness – to engage collided with inconsistencies between their various recollections of the night of the deaths. The result was that they quickly drew suspicion upon themselves.

For example, it was said that Gaston and his adult son Gustave – who lived at the property with his wife Yvette and their babe-in-arms Alain – had been woken at around 1 a.m. by five or six gunshots. However, the family claimed not to have heard any accompanying screams, contrary to the evidence of another farmer, who said he had heard screaming despite living much further away. There was also some puzzlement as to why, regardless of whether or not there was screaming, no one from La Grand Terre had thought to check on the campers they knew to be up the road.

Then there was the question of how the discovery of the bodies played out. Gustave claimed to have found Elizabeth when he went to inspect the landslide that had endangered the railway. This would have required him to go on a rather circuitous route which was possible, if unlikely. More problematic was his claim not to have found the bodies of the girl's parents at this stage, having decided not to go in search of them for fear that they were, in fact, alive and responsible for the girl's death. It is difficult to say what 'normal behaviour' would be in such circumstances, but his narrative of the discovery raised eyebrows.

Particularly damning was the reaction of Gaston's oldest son, Clovis, when confronted by Sébeille with the suspected murder weapon early on in proceedings. Clovis, an employee of the SNCF, the national rail company, was at work at the time. It is quite understandable that the recent turn of events had been shocking and his nerves were frayed, but on seeing the rifle, Clovis became noticeably flustered and refused to answer questions before falling to his knees and claiming never to have seen the gun before. Hardly a straightforward reaction.

Although Sébeille had no firm grounds for pointing the finger at the Dominicis, he certainly had reason to keep a close eye on them. La Grand Terre was searched on 7 August but nothing of much note was discovered. Gustave, however, was in bed on doctor's orders, apparently suffering from nervous exhaustion brought on by persistent badgering by journalists. The next day, however, he was sufficiently recovered to be questioned by Sébeille for several hours. Sébeille, opting not to play his cards close to his chest but to flash them teasingly at the press, told journalists that there were 'several contradictions' in Gustave's statements, while allowing that these could possibly be put down to his 'emotional state'. 'In any case,' he continued, 'we have no new evidence that might cast suspicion on the farmer.' But suspicion was nonetheless cast. In Sébeille's view at this time, it was the old man's son, Gustave, who was the man most likely.

The next days and weeks were intensely frustrating as the police investigation crawled along without significant breakthrough. All the while, the case was becoming increasingly politicised. The local Communist Party threw their 'Red Wall' of protection around the family, spearheaded by Gustave's old schoolmate, Paul Maillet. The communist press – local and national – was making its argument that the Dominicis were victims of a campaign of police harassment. Left-wing lawyers sent strongly worded letters to the most widely read newspapers and there were organised protests too, with demonstrators bussed in. Meanwhile, the right-wing press pushed back, its disdain for the Dominicis and their purported protectors thinly veiled.

The media circus reached one of many crescendos on 15 August, a public holiday to mark Assumption Day. By coincidence, it was also Gustave's birthday. He and Yvette took the opportunity to celebrate in the local village of Peyruis, famed for its Assumption Day festivities. Seemingly, the couple had never before attended but this year they went in their glad rags and presented as a stylish young couple. Sébeille turned up too, keen to keep an eye on goings-on from the shadows. The newspapers tracked the newly famous couple, flashbulbs flaring, one photo becoming a full-page image in *Paris Match*, no less. Gustave was evidently ill at ease with all the attention but Yvette seemed much more relaxed. Attending at all was quite a statement, given that they must have known the commotion it would cause.

Sébeille was becoming more stressed by the day. Unable to sleep, his nicotine and caffeine consumption went through the roof. Then, on the 17th, it looked like a breakthrough had come. A witness came forward, a travelling cheese salesman who had stopped his car for a call of nature close to where the Drummonds were camped. He claimed to have seen the murders and that he could likely identify the culprit. Sébeille was again quick off the mark with the press, promising that the end was in sight. It was another false dawn. The witness was soon shown to be a fantasist.

Armed with little more than his suspicions, Sébeille continued to pursue Gustave, questioning him for hours at a time. Gustave himself claimed intimidation and that threats had been made regarding his young son being taken into care. A letter was sent in his name (although likely written by his lawyer) to the communist daily *Ce Soir*. 'I am neither a murderer nor a coward, indifferent to the fate of respectable people who were struck down in a mad fury ... My one misfortune is to have notified the local police.'

Sébeille had put off a planned holiday in the hope of quickly wrapping up the case but, faced with an impasse, he now decided to take a break. His replacement was one Chief Inspector Constant, a native Provencieux from Manosque who had a natural repartee with the locals that broke through the Red Wall of silence so impenetrable to Sébeille. Something remarkable now happened. Paul Maillet, Dominici ally and coordinator of their communist defensive ring, told Constant that Gustave had admitted to him that Elizabeth had still been alive when he had discovered her. Gustave, in other words, had left the child to die. He was taken in for questioning on 15 October, during which he admitted that he had indeed heard her groan and saw her left arm move. In the early hours of the 16th, Gustave was charged with 'failing to give assistance to a person in danger'. The case came to trial the following month and he received what to many seemed a very lenient two-month prison sentence. But the Dominicis were regarded with more suspicion than ever.

By now the crime scene was virtually useless from the point of view of further detective work. Up to 500 cars a day had been passing through, many full of rubberneckers determined to catch a glimpse of the now-notorious site. Thousands of feet had trampled the ground, which was thick with cigarette butts, empty bottles and assorted other detritus. In light of time already served, Gustave was freed on

16 December. By now, money was growing tight and a family conference on how to share the burden of lawyers' costs ended in acrimony. For the first time, the broadly united front the Dominicis had maintained was stretched to breaking point. But for now, it just about held.

Sébeille returned to head up the investigation in January 1953, intent on a new approach. He was less forthcoming with the media and refocused on trying to break down the barriers in the local community. For a while, he turned up at La Grand Terre almost daily. Relations with Gaston were initially quite affable. The old man perhaps believed that as time passed, the heat on the family was receding. But the detective's regular appearances soon started to rankle and he made a complaint of intimidation.

More time rolled by, with the investigation going nowhere fast until Maillet decided to drop another bombshell. Now he told Sébeille that sometime the previous late August or early September – he couldn't be sure precisely when – he had gone to La Grand Terre to buy potatoes. While Yvette went off to fulfil his order, Maillet explained, Gustave said out of the blue: 'If you had seen it – if you had heard those terrible screams – I don't know what to do.' He then indicated that he had been standing in one of the fields when he heard 'those terrible screams'. Sébeille, not unreasonably, took this all to mean that Gustave had, despite his denials, witnessed the murders. And if he was a witness and not the perpetrator, then Sébeille needed a new chief suspect. Meanwhile, an eye-witness report from someone who passed through La Grand Terre as the police were on their way to the murder scene on the morning of 5 August suggested Anne was lying on her back. She had been on her front when officers arrived, so it now seemed very likely that her body had been moved a short time before the police turned up. Why on earth would that have been?

After this flurry of activity, the investigation went quiet again. While still piquing interest, the Drummond murders had lost their hard-hitting impact in the news cycle. As the anniversary of the deaths approached, Dwight Eisenhower succeeded Harry Truman as America's president, while the Soviet Union lost Joseph Stalin to a stroke. The Mau Mau were rebelling against the British in Kenya, and France was granting Cambodia its provisional independence as things heated up in Indochina. At the summit of Mount Everest stood Edmund Hillary and Tenzing Norgay, the first men to make it to the top of the world, all in time for the pomp and ceremony of the Coronation of Elizabeth II in Westminster Abbey. The Drummonds were not forgotten but the world was moving on.

Sébeille himself decided to pause the investigation in the summer of 1953 until after Armistice Day, 11 November. It was a puzzling decision but one that he ostensibly made in the belief that it would help protect the tourist season in the region and because he didn't want to be a disruptive presence during the harvest. On 12 November, however, it was back to business, with a re-enactment of the events of 4/5 August 1952 as far as they were known, involving the Drummonds' Hillman and as many key witnesses as possible. A large crowd of journalists and casual onlookers gathered to watch the unfolding drama, with food vendors providing snacks. Gustave and Clovis, meanwhile, were taken to Digne's law courts for hours of questioning, to the consternation of the wider Dominici clan.

Under interrogation, Gustave changed aspects of his story time and again, including the details of when exactly he had got up that night and what he had done. He did admit for the first time that he had visited the site where Jack and Anne had lain before the police arrived, and that he had indeed turned over and moved Anne's body. He initially said it was simply to ascertain for certain whether or not she was dead, but later claimed he had been checking around the body for anything incriminating, such as spent gun cartridges, that could link the deaths to La Grand Terre. He was relieved, he said, to find nothing. As for why he hadn't helped Elizabeth, he had panicked and was paralysed by fear of getting caught up in what was clearly a seriously bad affair. Gustave, in common with a good many others who had lived through the traumas of occupation and post-war recrimination, was firm in that you didn't look for trouble for fear that it would come looking for you.

Gustave spent a restless night in an armchair at the courthouse and questioning resumed the following morning. Sébeille shared the duties with the Examining Magistrate Roger Périès. It was as if Gustave could feel the walls closing in. Sébeille felt pangs of compassion for the man before him, struggling like an animal in a trap. At last, Gustave broke down and stated that at four o'clock in the morning of 5 August 1952, his elderly father had confessed to killing the Drummonds – the result, Gaston had told him, of an encounter with Jack as Gaston returned from a night-hunt. Gustave confirmed that Clovis also knew of their father's guilt, but both had been sworn to secrecy by the old man.

An initially incredulous Clovis was now brought in for questioning and confirmed his brother's testimony, the pair falling into a tearful embrace. Clovis told of how he had been to a family meal at La Grand Terre while Gustave had been in prison. It was a tetchy evening, with Gaston and 'the Sardine' going at each other, when Gaston exclaimed: 'I've already killed three, and could kill another!' before adding, 'I killed the English.' According to Clovis, his father explained that he had got into a fight with the campers when he went out to inspect the landslide by the railway line. He did not exhibit much in the way of remorse, Clovis indicated, and threatened him if he did not keep his mouth shut. Clovis was suitably fearful, although there was perhaps an element of relief too as he had until now wondered whether it wasn't Gustave who had been responsible for the deaths.

The troubled relations and unspoken suspicions within the family were becoming obvious. That Gaston had a temper was no surprise to Sébeille, but it was clear that his viperish tongue and the simmering threat of violence – brought to the fore by heavy drinking – weighed heavily on the family. A closer look at his record revealed that while he had once been commended for taking on that escaped criminal, on another occasion in his younger days he went at a neighbour with whom he was squabbling with an axe. Gaston could be a frightening man.

Now, enveloped by old age, much of his energy was drained. He had long ago started stepping back from the hardest of the farm work. Clovis, as the oldest son, was meant to have taken over the farm but he had accepted a job on the railways instead, prompting a dislocation from the family that saw them not speak for several years. He was in many ways the son most like his father – tough, stubborn and quick to anger. Perhaps he had sensed that La Grand Terre was too small for two such fiery personalities. The next son, Marcel, had left in 1939 to marry a widow fifteen years his senior and settle on her farm, while the youngest son, Aimé, had also married and moved on. Gustave, 33 years old in 1952, was the last man standing at the farm, the responsibility for its day-to-day running falling squarely on him as his father took to tending a few sheep and then, latterly, exchanging even them for the easier labour of goats. While Gaston remained king of the castle, Gustave felt resentful that he did the lion's share of the work for very little reward.

In the year and more since the killings, one can only imagine the multitude of feelings, fears and suspicions that coursed through the various members of the Dominici family. Now it was time for Gaston to go to Digne to be confronted with these new revelations. He arrived in a characteristically irritable mood, supping down a bowl of soup he was provided with and smoking his pipe before his latest interrogation began. When told that his sons had denounced him, he came out swinging. Both children, he insisted, were liars.

By the following day, rumour of the sensational developments had spilled out to the press. Sébeille assured them, as undiplomatic as ever, that the identity of the killer would be revealed within 24 hours. In the meantime, Gustave and Clovis were returned to the farm to point out exactly where their father had kept the murder weapon, on a shelf in the shed. Their arrival was met by a crowd of the extended family, all expressing their fury at the police and journalists, several also calling the brothers 'traitors' and 'bastards'. Yvette, whose position was among the most unenviable, was particularly vociferous in proclaiming the innocence of both her husband and her father-in-law – a difficult line to take just then.

What would one have given for Gaston's thoughts, back at the law courts? How to deflect the finger of suspicion pointed by his own flesh and blood? That night, a junior officer reported that Gaston now seemingly acknowledged responsibility, explaining that it had all been a terrible accident after the Drummonds had attacked him. Jack, Gaston said, had taken him for a marauder. But then his story went through the first of several contortions. He was not a murderer, he now claimed, but was taking the blame in order to save others – specifically Gustave. Gustave, in due course, would say that Sébeille had told him he knew either he or his father was responsible, and that if it were Gustave found guilty then he would be guillotined, but if it were his father then Gaston would likely only be sent to an institution. If the account of the exchange is true, it would have served as food for thought for both father and son looking to see the least damage inflicted upon their family.

On 14 November, Gaston dictated a statement, in which he described himself as 'the author of the drama which took place during the night of 4/5 August 1952'. He told of meeting the Drummonds and exchanging pleasantries while going to inspect the landslide before embarking on a hunting trip with the rifle. Later, he said, he watched from behind a mulberry bush as Anne undressed, describing the short, transparent chemise and dark grey or blue dress she wore. Then things took a surprising turn, according to his account: 'We exchanged a few words in a low voice, after which I touched her on several places on her body. She did not object.' In later interviews, Gaston would repeat this assertion, though in much more graphic language.

Gaston's statement then had Jack appearing in an understandably irate state, followed by angry words and a physical altercation: they grappled and Gaston reached for the gun that he had left on the ground beside Anne's bed. Jack grabbed at its barrel just as Gaston, who declared himself as having 'lost my head', fired it. The bullet passed through Jack's hand, at which point he made to run across the road as Gaston hit him with two or three shots. Anne was by now screaming, and Gaston believed he then fired a single shot at her, causing her to fall on the spot. It was now that he noticed Elizabeth exiting the car by the rear doors and running towards the Durance. He fired off another round but it missed her so he ran after her as she hurtled down the slope on the other side of the bridge. When he caught up with her, she was on her knees and he hit her once, he insisted, with the butt of the rifle while in a crazed state and not knowing what he was doing but desperate to ensure she didn't talk. He then proceeded down to the river, flinging the murder weapon away, washing his hands and returning to the farmhouse, where he remained until he took his goats out early the next morning.

Sébeille could hardly believe what he was being told. And on closer inspection, there were a multitude of holes in the account. For example, Gaston must have taken a very circuitous route to the landslide to go past the Drummonds since they were in opposite directions from the farmhouse. Other witnesses, meanwhile, had spoken of Anne having already changed her clothes several hours earlier, and anyway she was not wearing anything like that described by Gaston. The carbine was an excessively powerful weapon to go hunting with, an activity Gaston had reportedly not done for several years. Nor was Jack shot through the hand, while Anne was hit by more than the single round alleged by Gaston. An examination of the car, moreover, proved that Elizabeth could not have opened the back doors from the inside. But in some ways this was all incidental to the main complaint that the entire scenario lacked credibility. Was anyone really to believe that Anne would engage in intercourse with this aged stranger within metres of her husband and daughter? Even if the idea were to be entertained for a moment, Anne was discovered clothed and there was no sign of recent sexual activity. This was a confession, yes, but one that did not hold much water.

Nonetheless, Gaston stood by it the following day, although with a number of inconsistencies in narration and the addition of a significant caveat. He told Périès that he had not murdered the family but would reconfirm his statement in order to save his grandchildren's honour. Gustave, he said, was the real killer but, as the Dominici patriarch, he would sacrifice himself. Périès was infuriated. What was to be done with this confession-cum-non-confession, augmented by the accusation of another's guilt? If the drama were not already ramped up enough, Gustave and Clovis were now brought in to confront their father. When Clovis confirmed that his father, in his cups, had said he had killed 'all three of them' and could kill again if required (the 'kill again' being directed at his son, undoubtably an empty threat). Gaston acknowledged that he might have said it but couldn't remember. When Gustave reiterated his own accusation, Gaston sarcastically thanked him and the pair then hurled insults at each other.

The police still did not have the conclusive evidence guaranteed to win the day in court. This rampage of confessions and accusations in certain respects posed more questions than answers. Sébeille and Périès were reluctant to push too hard on many of the inconsistencies and dubious details for fear that the whole case might unravel. While he remained uncharged, Gaston had not officially appointed a lawyer, so the authorities took their chance to stage one more reconstruction in the company of the accused. Watched once again by hordes of journalists and sightseers, it was unclear whether it was the police or Gaston dictating the direction of events.

Little more was firmly established and new questions arose. Gaston initially indicated the murder weapon was stored on a different shelf to that described by his sons; there was uncertainty over the number of shots fired, from what angle and even whether the rifle needed reloading or not. There was even time for Gaston to make a lunge for the railway line in an apparent suicide bid before Pèriès intervened. Both men briefly lost their hats and some hilarity ensued when each ended up wearing the other's.

Then it was time to return to Digne. In the van taking him there, Gaston was formally charged with the murders of the Drummonds. The presumption of guilt was upon him as France's libel laws allowed the press to label him as the assassin. It was triumph at last for Sébeille, who received thousands of congratulatory letters from well-wishers, was wined and dined by the great and the good, and for whom there was even talk of the Légion d'honneur, France's highest award. It had taken far longer than he'd ever expected, but he had his man at last. Didn't he?

TRIAL

11

Gaston was imprisoned in Digne to await the trial at which he would proclaim his innocence. The focal point of what many legal minds had already identified as a problematic case with political undertones, he now found himself surrounded by a crack legal team who would normally have been beyond his financial means. Such was the public interest that the offers of help came pouring in, inspired both by genuine desire to help and by the realisation that such opportunities to boost one's own profile are few and far between for the average lawyer.

Meanwhile, any semblance of unity within the wider Dominici clan had dissipated as factions emerged according to whose version of events each person believed and whom each thought had committed the worst betrayal of the family. This splintering did not, however, much help the authorities as they rushed to get their case in order before it went to trial, aware of the many details that needed resolving. There were myriad loose threads that any defence lawyer worth his salt could pull at. Paul Maillet, for instance, was still adamant that Gustave had told him he had been outside in an alfalfa field at the time of the killings. Gustave, on the other hand, maintained that he had been indoors all night. Such glaring contradictions among key witnesses were dangerous for a prosecution, especially when the defendant boasted a more than competent legal team. If there was doubt around these seemingly lesser details, how could a jury trust the prosecution on the really big questions?

Even apparent steps forward were to be treated with caution. Yvette, Gustave's wife, now gave a more detailed account of the night of the murders, admitting that she had heard screaming as well as gunshots in the early hours of 5 August. She furthermore confirmed that Gustave had told her that night of his father's confession, and signed a document saying as much. It was corroboration of everything that Gustave and Clovis had alleged about their father. But there was a hitch. She soon denied ever making or signing such a statement – a clearly untenable line given that the police possessed it – and then said she had only professed it as Périès had threatened her that Gustave would be arrested as Gaston's accomplice if she did not. There was no evidence to back this assertion and there was little in Périès's record to suggest that this was typical of his modus operandi. The fact of the matter was that Yvette knew very well the peril her husband lived under, that he had been a chief suspect and might be again if Gaston were to wriggle free, and she was torn from moment to moment between backing her husband's account and not incriminating her father-in-law either.

On 30 December 1953, Gaston was again confronted by his two accusatory sons at the law courts in Digne. Gaston at this stage was claiming his earlier confession had been coerced. He accused the police of having presented him with an unenviable dilemma – confess and face life in prison, or see Gustave take the rap and suffer likely execution. Gaston now said that, worn down by prolonged interrogation, he had opted to confess despite his innocence.

There then played out another episode in the incredible psychodrama into which the Dominicis had become locked. In the presence of his father, Gustave was made to listen to the testimony he had given concerning Gaston's confession to him. When asked to confirm its veracity, he was at first silent and then denied it. Instead, he claimed his father had only 'to tell the truth'. What truth, though? If not that Gaston were the guilty party, which Gustave was now suggesting he wasn't, then what was the revelation that might acquit him, and what was so terrible about it that Gaston still chose not to voice it?

When questioned by Gaston's lawyers as to why he was now retracting his original denunciation, Gustave claimed that it was because it had been made under police duress. But when Clovis entered the fray, he maintained that his father had confessed to him over the dinner table, although the precise details of his account of that evening now varied from his original statement. Gaston was incandescent, calling him every name under the sun. Clovis responded: 'You've made us suffer too long.' When Gaston was returned to his cell that night, he seemed in remarkably good cheer, predicting to one of the guards that he would be back at La Grand Terre before the spring was out.

Later in January, Gaston received a letter from Gustave in which his son promised to 'tell the truth' in the face of unspecified threats, concluding: 'The truth must come to light.' Gustave by now was insistent that his father was, after all, innocent, although further questioning saw him reaffirm his claim that his father had, in fact, confessed. His changing story, he confided to Périès, was because of the pressure he was feeling from his family. Whatever the reason, there was little chance of claiming Gustave to be in any way a reliable witness.

Clovis, meanwhile, had written a letter to Yvette's father, asking him to talk Gustave into sticking with the denunciation of their father. In the letter, Clovis referred to 'the wrongs' that 'the old scoundrel' had made them suffer. But other members of the family were completely unconvinced by the allegations against Gaston, or at least said as much to the police. With little sign of any new and decisive evidence to be revealed, the investigation drew to a close in late April of 1954. The evidential dossier was reviewed by the court and a date for the trial of Gaston Dominici was set for Wednesday, 17 November.

Gaston arrived at the Digne Court of Assizes at quarter past nine in the morning on the first day of his trial, which was expected to last four days but would go on for ten. He was dressed in a smart suit and tie, an overcoat and a striped scarf. His white hair had been neatly shorn and his bushy moustache teased into respectability. He certainly did not fit the image of the peasant-savage that some of the press had been keen to conjure up. As he prepared to face the fight of his life, he seemed like nothing so much as a grandfather out in his Sunday best. Not terrifying. Not base. Instead, old and perhaps even a little vulnerable. It would be for others to decide which version was truer. The answer would depend on how good an actor you considered him to be.

Everything about the trial had a sense of theatre. As the defendant arrived at the courthouse gates, he was greeted by a great throng. Just as there had been at La Grand Terre on so many occasions recently, there were journalists, perhaps a hundred of them, and casual spectators, along with those who had some personal interest or other in the case. Groups of law students had also made the journey, eager to be present at what promised to be the greatest trial of the age. Then there were the great and the good – authors and playwrights, local officials and minor celebrities, representatives of the French prime minister himself. All ages, sexes and classes were represented – although it didn't escape the attention of many that several of the best seats in the house had been reserved for striking young women. Notable by their absence was anyone from the British Foreign Office. Apparently, the Consul in Marseille was concerned that any presence might appear to cast shade on the workings of the French judicial system. But to some it felt like the Drummonds had been abandoned by their own team at the most vital moment. Not for the first time, they seemed little more than bit-part players in the story of their own murders.

The trial's sense of theatricality was accentuated by the presence of white-gloved guards who presented arms every time the court stood. When the presiding judge, Marcel Bousquet, entered and got proceedings under way, so many flashbulbs went off that it felt like an assault of strobe lighting. In the end, Bousquet had to step in to restore order. In due course, there would be audience participation too, with testimony delivered to a sporadic soundtrack of screaming and booing, occasional fainting and even shouts of, 'Death!'

From the time of the Revolution, it had been a mainstay of the judicial system that major crimes were tried before a jury of twelve of the defendant's peers. However, this principle had not survived the vagaries of the Vichy government, who instead introduced a set-up whereby guilt or innocence (and any punishment resulting from the verdict) was decided by a jury of six laymen in consultation with a panel of three judges (the presiding judge and two assistant judges). This significantly stacked the odds in a great many trials. The increased rate of convictions since the new system was introduced in 1941 suggested professional judges were more inclined to find against a defendant than lay jurors. Moreover, since a majority verdict was deemed sufficient, if the judges voted as a block then they required the agreement of only two out of six jurors.

In Gaston's case, the judges and jury faced seven questions in total: three related to his innocence or guilt in regard to the three murders, a fourth concerning whether Elizabeth's murder was premeditated, and a further three related to whether or not the killings were contemporaneous. It was soon apparent that Gaston should not expect an easy ride. In introductory comments, the court clerk painted a picture of him as authoritarian, secretive and excessively fond of his liquor. Judge Bousquet did little to disguise his contempt for the defendant either, addressing him aggressively and witheringly throughout the trial. His approach rather shocked the courtroom's contingent of British pressmen, who nevertheless concluded that this was the French way, fuelling suspicions already voiced back in Britain that the judicial system might not be up to the job. But if they had been able to listen in to the conversations of their French counterparts, they may have been surprised to learn that they too found the judge's explicit hostility unsettling. The presumption of innocence was by no means the preserve of the British, but it was little in evidence in Digne.

At least Gaston could count on some heavyweight representation to hit back. His main man was Émile Pollak, a distinctive figure with thick, flowing hair that had turned a distinguished grey even though he was only in his late thirties. A Jew, he had spent much of the war in hiding and came to prominence in its aftermath when he defended a number of alleged collaborators. Now one of France's most famous legal faces, a cigarette semi-permanently clamped between his lips, he was a natural fit for a case as high-profile as this. Nicknamed 'The Word', *'Le Mot'*, for his loquaciousness, even in those moments when he did not seem entirely across the evidence, he was always a formidable presence in Gaston's corner.

Pollak made an excellent job of critiquing not only the substance of the case but also the treatment of his client. He condemned the conduct of investigators, whose questioning of Gaston was frequently poorly documented and suggestive of a disregard for protocol. He questioned why, for instance, Gaston had been deprived of legal representation during the crime reconstructions regarded as so key to the case and which had stoked press and popular antagonism towards the defendant. There was no doubt that there had been a purposeful delay in charging him (the point at which he could formally appoint representation) in order to conduct the reconstructions without the interference of troublesome lawyers.

Pollak also skilfully highlighted the copious inconsistencies and contradictions between the medical reports and the accounts Gaston gave in his various confessions. He was critical that such vital evidence as the Drummonds' Hillman car was not available for inspection, nor the camp beds that had been so prominent at the murder scene. The car was already back in the UK and shipping it back for the trial proved impracticable, not least because it now formed part of a display in a waxworks in Blackpool.

Gaston was vocal in his own defence, making regular interjections from his position in the dock. Others might have crumbled beneath the weight of the character assassination. The Mayor of Lurs was quoted early on as describing Gaston as living 'on the margins of society'. But Gaston hit back, at least initially, with a series of calmly delivered rebuffs. In between chewing on sugar lumps, he pointed out, when the prosecution raised the matter of his attacking a man with a cudgel, that they referred to an incident no less than 56 years in the past. When they said that he was a mean and brutalising father, he argued that Gustave was in fact a bone-idle liar.

The extended Dominici family was, of course, out in force throughout and all but Clovis were now on the side of the defence. This led to some curious exchanges, given that Gustave was of course a pivotal driver in Gaston being charged in the first place. Nor did Gaston hold back in attacking the integrity of his son even though they were now seemingly on the same team. When Gaston was formally questioned, another problem became apparent. He spoke a distinctive local Provençal dialect that diverged significantly from standard French. Sometimes shared words and phrases carried different meanings and tones. At one point, a witness referred to Gaston as authoritarian and crafty but the old man seemed delighted, as if he had been given a compliment. On the other hand, there were aspects of local slang delivered in evidence that utterly perplexed the judge and others unfamiliar with the local parlance.

When Gaston was questioned about the events of the night of the murder, his testimony was littered with assertions incompatible with his previous statements. At times, he had no choice but to admit as much. There was a debate, for example, as to whether or not he had found a splintered piece of the rifle butt and handed it to the police. Interrogated about his claim that he had done so on the morning that the bodies were discovered, he was forced to admit that he might have been mistaken and really could not remember. As for the question of why Clovis had denounced him, he hit back that if Sébeille had done his job properly, it would have been Clovis he had gone after rather than himself. Then, when Gaston was asked why he had previously fingered Gustave as the killer, he explained that he had made the accusations under severe mental duress, wearied by hour after hour of police questioning and deprived of refreshment. Throughout the entire trial, Gaston professed his total innocence even in those moments when he seemed tired and overwrought and when the complexities of specific questions got away from him.

The roll call of witnesses was long. There were the psychologists who tried to get inside the mind of Gaston, a job easier said than done. Then came the doctors who had carried out forensic examinations of the bodies and whose evidence regularly and unhelpfully contradicted one another's. Next, a succession of eye-witnesses who had passed through the crime scene in those critical hours of 4 and 5 August, from whom it was difficult to get much in the way of a consistent picture.

When Jack's old friend from Villefranche, Guy Marrian entered the witness box, he was permitted to testify in English and staunchly dismissed any suggestion that Jack was, as papers on both sides of the Channel persistently hinted at, a spy. The murders, he was adamant, could not possibly have been linked to any sort of clandestine work.

For those seeking sensation, the trial kept on delivering. When Gaston's teenage grandson, Roger (son of Gaston's daughter Germaine, and known in the family as Zézé), nervously took the stand, he proved as slippery, capricious and

unreliable as his earlier performances under police questioning had suggested. His ever-changing recall of events made it
impossible to accurately track his movements and there was
the suggestion, which he flatly denied, that he had been present at La Grand Terre for the entirety of the night on which
the murders occurred. All that could be determined with any
real degree of certainty was that not too much stock should
be set by his word. Gaston made his feelings clear, accusing
the boy of being a layabout and a poacher. But then he went
further. He could be, Gaston told the court, the murderer. He
simply didn't know. Then he doubled down – either Zézé or
Gustave might be guilty. The power of such words was somewhat mitigated when Gaston was reminded that he himself
had made nine separate confessions to the murders, as well as
attributing blame variously to Gustave and Clovis, alongside
this further suggestion that his grandson may have been the
one responsible.

Paul Maillet, the ally-turned-accuser, was at least consistent in his evidence, repeating what he said Gustave had told
him on the occasion of his visiting the farm to buy potatoes. Sébeille, meanwhile, reiterated that Gaston had told
him the killings had come about because of a 'romantic mis-
deed'. Gaston for his part now claimed he had only confessed
because his coffee had been drugged. There was further testimony from Victor Guérino, one of the officers on duty when
Gaston had made his original confession. He described how
he and Gaston had been relaxing and chatting together in
his cell, discussing different aspects of the old farmer's life,
from the wedding-night revelation of his wife's pregnancy
to his hunting prowess, when, out of nowhere, Gaston had
said: 'Yes, they attacked me. They thought I was a prowler.'
He had then made the claim to another officer that he was, in

fact, sacrificing himself for his grandchildren. Prison, he had apparently concluded, didn't represent too awful a fate just as long as he could take his dog. When Gaston was asked about these conversations, he somewhat unconvincingly claimed to have no memory of any of it.

When it came the turn of his poor wife Marie to face the court's scrutiny, she insisted that she had no relevant knowledge at all. Looking drawn and crushed, she denied having heard any shots during the night in question and only learned of the discovery of Elizabeth's body at six the next morning. When she was asked whether she had at any point considered going to see if there was anything to be done, she could not have been more dismissive of the idea: 'Good heavens no! I didn't think of it.' If she was a study in beleaguered despair, then Gustave's wife Yvette, by contrast, presented as composed and assured. Wearing a smart suit and jumper, her hair newly styled, she brought the same confident style that she had previously displayed at the Ascension Day festivities in Peyruis. But the impression left by her evidence was less good. She too had made no effort, she confirmed, to check on the girl. Instead, she had apparently gone about her business like it was just another day. There had been a leisurely lunch with her parents before she came back to La Grand Terre and casually viewed the bodies. More importantly, all the evidence she had previously given to investigators now appeared null and void. According to Yvette, no one got up after gunshots were heard and she had not heard any report of Gaston's purported confession to Gustave. Indeed, she couldn't really remember anything, although she did now claim that two previously unmentioned and unknown cars were present in the area in the immediate aftermath of the shooting. She also suggested that Zézé was mistaken when he said (as he had) that Anne and Elizabeth had earlier come to the house to ask for water. He had, she suggested, got them mixed up with some Swiss tourists who had made such a call on another occasion. She did not deign to explain how Zézé had accurately described Elizabeth and Anne. But she was a resilient witness if nothing else, holding firm to her lines throughout.

Clovis, looking dapper in velvet trousers and a jacket, also exuded calm as he began his testimony. He now testified that Gustave had told him that Elizabeth had been groaning when he'd first encountered her but was dead by the time he properly approached her. But it was not long before Clovis's demeanour cracked under questioning. The strain he had been under for over two years now broke through as he admitted how terrible a task it had been to accuse his own father. Gustave similarly showed signs of stress when his turn came to testify, even if he cut a handsome figure in the stand. In a high, reedy voice, he claimed pitifully: 'I've been lying all the time. My father is innocent!' His condemnation of his father, he said, had been extracted under pressure from an investigative team hell-bent on wrapping up their case. They had, he said, not only accused him, Gustave, of being responsible for the deaths but had beaten him. He also asserted that it was Clovis who had the idea of laying the blame on Gaston, at which point his father rose to his feet to animatedly point out that it was Gustave who had been the first of his accusers. It was all rather surreal to see the defendant taking issue with a witness who now, if somewhat belatedly, was declaring him innocent. Judge Bousquet took a very dim view of Gustave: 'You are a coward ... You claim that you were forced into lying. Thus you were prepared to lie and accuse your father of murder and you continue to lie. You are a coward and your behaviour is unconscionable.'

Gustave came across as both desperate and sadly inane as he sought to argue the innocence of the entire family. At one point he claimed, to some hilarity, that he had never once told a lie, despite the crux of his testimony being that he had indeed previously lied in accusing his father. The more he tried to own and explain his deceptions, the more untrustworthy he appeared. Yet the effects of his evidence were complex. If his aim was to assist in the acquittal of his father, then his changing story and rejection of his earlier denunciation certainly fostered confusion and doubt. But it also showed them all up in a terrible light. During a subsequent cross-examination of Clovis, Gaston adopted a characteristically aggressive posture as he embarked on an unseemly slanging match with his oldest son. This particular sideshow concerned an incidental debate on whether or not Clovis was hungover at Christmas lunch at La Grand Terre months after the murders. Clovis claimed not to have eaten anything because of his frayed nerves over his father's guilt. Gaston said it was because his son was sick from drinking too much at a party the night before. 'I have a clear conscience,' Gaston said, 'but your brother and you—'. At which point, the judge adjourned the session for lunch, no doubt sensing everyone needed to cool off.

Day eight witnessed one of the most extraordinary exchanges of the entire trial – quite an accolade, given the competition. Under more questioning, Gustave reasserted: 'I've been lying all the time. My father is innocent! They made me lie!' Gaston now interjected, saying that he forgave Gustave for his accusations against him, which he described as a mortal sin, and pleading with him to now tell the truth for the good of the family. Gustave responded by suggesting he had never accused his father of anything, which was self-evidently preposterous and rendered the court silent. Gaston then suggested that Gustave had been in the alfalfa field with an unnamed other at the time of the killings and, furthermore, knew that the murder weapon did not come from La Grand Terre but from somewhere else not far away. Gustave denied having been in the field with anyone, and the exchange drew to a close when the judge called for an adjournment. What did it all mean? To many looking on, it seemed like a moment of revelation had been close but the judge's intervention had snuffed out the opportunity, never to be reignited.

There was still time for the courtroom to witness a confrontation between Gustave and Clovis, and then a notably strange exchange even by the standards of this most curious trial. Angelin Araman, the husband of Gaston's daughter Clotilde, asked for the court to be cleared because of the unwelcome presence of someone who had stolen a cart. The individual concerned turned out to be Paul Maillet. When Araman was pushed on the matter, he conceded it had absolutely no bearing on the case in hand.

Saturday 27th proved to be the last day of the trial, with the rather rodenty Advocate General, Calixte Rozan, giving a theatrical and aggressive closing statement that again poo-pooed any suggestion that Jack was involved in espionage and re-emphasised the State's case that blame lay squarely with Gaston for all three murders, 'committed by a violent man in a fit of rage'. Several witnesses were ruthlessly dismissed as essentially worthless, with one even described in terms of excrement. Due to a technical fault, Rozan's words were broadcast over loudspeaker to the crowd gathered outside the court.

Pollak then energetically closed the defence, arguing that the prosecution case, with Gaston's confession the only real evidence, was irredeemably flawed. Not one for understatement, he likened Gaston's suffering at the hands of his accusers to that of Christ on the Cross and pleaded with Gustave to take this final opportunity to come and tell the whole truth. An entreaty met with silence. 'It is not crimes that remain unpunished that wring the hearts of governments and the people,' Pollak noted, 'but the condemnation of the innocent.'

Alongside the criminal case, there had also been a civil case brought against Gaston by Anne's mother, whose health suffered terribly in the aftermath of the murders. Her attorney, Claude Delorme, did arguably the best job of all the many lawyers present in summarising the trial's significance: 'In order for the immense strain on our country to be removed, and to give back to the population the peace of mind to which they are entitled, justice must be done by punishing this terrible crime ...'

At 12.15 p.m. Judge Bousquet drew proceedings to a close. It was difficult to see the trial as anything other than confusing and conflicting. From the judge whose prejudice against the defendant was about as clear as it could be, to questionable procedural issues, utterly unreliable witnesses and a family tearing itself apart in public, few dared claim this was the best of French justice in action. Such were the conflicting testimonies that it would take a sort of blind arrogance to assume one could possibly say with any confidence what had befallen the Drummonds that terrible night. Nonetheless, a little over two hours later, the bell tolled to call the hearing back. The jury were asked their seven questions, to all of which they responded that, yes, the matter had been proven. Gaston Dominici was guilty on all counts.

As he listened to the verdicts in the dock, yet another sugar lump slowly dissolving in his mouth, he mumbled something about bastards and why was he paying for others. Exactly to whom this was all directed was uncertain. In the civil case, Anne's mother was paid a symbolic one franc for the unquantifiable damage she had suffered.

As for Gaston, the judges and jury set down his punishment: 'Gaston Dominici est condamné a mort et aura la tête tranchée.' He was to be condemned to death by that most French of methods – the guillotine.

DOUBTS

12

After the pronouncement of Gaston's death sentence, most of the Dominicis reconvened at La Grand Terre, a gathering marked by distress as they attempted to absorb that their nightmare ending to this horror saga had come to pass. Notable by his absence was Clovis, who was entertaining a small coterie of journalists at his own home and tearfully explaining that he really hadn't expected his father to face execution.

For a great many others, the result only confirmed what they felt they already knew about Gaston. He was, the judicial system had affirmed, the beast they'd long suspected. It was the culmination of a case played out, in the words of *The Times*, against 'the dark background of a France where life is still primitive and passions are unchecked'. *The Times* was repeating a narrative that had been constructed by many hands and voices over a prolonged period, but among the most significant was the celebrated author Jean Giono.[1] Giono was famed for a series of novels set in Provence that drew on themes of classical mythology and routinely used peasants as major protagonists. Born in 1895 in Manosque, just up the road from where the Drummonds were killed, Giono was still living there as Gaston came to trial. As a chronicler of southern French peasant life, he took a close interest in the proceedings, talking to the locals, the press and the police, and framing himself as a sort of amateur psychological profiler long before such a figure had entered the public consciousness.

He sat through each day of the trial, sucking on his pipe, his pen poised to write up his notes that he would publish once the affair was over. His opinion of most of the cast of suspects and witnesses was low to say the least, his condemnations acerbic. With his local roots, he claimed to 'know' the peasants of the region, describing them as 'savages', with 'a savage's cunning' who 'lie as they breathe'. No member of the Dominici clan evaded his withering character assassinations. Gaston he described as 'stupid perhaps, cruel' with a 'vulgar background' and 'a very restricted vocabulary of not more than thirty five words'. As for Marie – whose uncomplimentary nickname 'the Sardine' Giono enthusiastically adopted – she was 'Hecuba in person, a small black woman grilled and roasted to the bone'. In drawing the allusion to the wife of Priam, King of Troy, Giono highlighted the depth of his own classical education against Marie's lack of formal learning, reflected, he suggested, in a vocabulary even narrower than her that of her husband.

What of that claim of Gaston's virtual illiteracy, so casually made and widely accepted? To this day, Gaston's grandson Alain possesses a stash of letters that Gaston wrote to his family.[2] Of course, Gaston could not call upon the same long and rich formal education as his critic-in-chief, but the notes prove that he was certainly not illiterate and had powers of expression that ranged far beyond those credited to him by

Giono. Marie, meanwhile, had contended with much in her life, not least raising nine children and running a home that she could call her own. That she was afforded no credit for this surely says more about Giono than about her. Even when the author depicted Gaston looking on with passion as his wife delivered her troubled, monosyllabic evidence as her world crashed around her, he took the opportunity to patronise and belittle the moment. Gaston's evident emotions at this critical moment were put down as belonging 'to his peasant race'.

His description of another of the Dominici women, Gaston's daughter Germaine, is also telling: 'She is a little wanton, who's got an itch: she sleeps with the gendarmes. She powders herself, dolls herself up in every way, uses scent, paints her lips, walks on high heels, awkwardly but resolutely. She is a travesty of a peasant woman.' In just a few lines, Giono provides a case study in snobbery and misogyny. How else to explain the utter decimation of a person who was not even on trial. And to what end? Should we simply excuse him on account that he was working in a different age, his troubling underlying assumptions unquestioned? Or did he write such words in the knowledge that his casual cruelty would bring him the attention his ego demanded?

Curiously, Giono missed the last day of the trial. Having been a spectre at the feast throughout, he wasn't there for the drama of the closing remarks, the verdict and the sentencing to death by guillotine. A no-show for the grand finale. How that must have grated with this professional people-studier. 'I draw no conclusion. Perhaps the accused is guilty,' he noted in summary of the trial. But it was clear that he had Gaston marked as guilty from the beginning, even as he acknowledged that the evidence presented in court fell short of the bar for conviction.

However much the modern reader might be struck by Giono's egotism, prejudice and pomposity, his take nonetheless carried weight in 1950s France. What the learned author, pillar of the cultural establishment, said must be true, according to those whose ingrained sense of deference demanded he and his ilk be revered. The prevailing narrative was that there was something feral and untameable in the peasant soul of Gaston. It did not matter if the evidence failed to prove the case because they – like Giono – felt it to be true and that was enough.

Little notice was made of the fact that Giono was at some level monetising France's biggest trial in years. His was not a neutral voice, but that of an opinion-influencer who understood how to build a story he could sell. It is very likely that he knew Gaston and his family personally, too; he even admitted that he might previously have met Clovis. How might that have influenced his attitude towards them? We know, for instance, that Giono had been imprisoned in 1944, accused of collaboration in the war. He subsequently had his works blacklisted for several years. With the Dominicis allied to the Resistance and the Communists at the other end of the political spectrum, there was surely a natural antipathy there. Given their status as near neighbours, it's not beyond the realms of possibility that the Dominicis or those close to them were among those to have accused him. Yet in Giono's book about the trial, the only mention he made of the recent war and its all-pervading impact was to accuse Gaston of belonging to 'the murky underworld of communism' and to describe 'the occupation, patriotism and its exploitation for selfish ends' amid 'the anarchy of the liberation'. It almost sounded like Giono had a score to settle, and he found a large audience eager to join in his denigration of Gaston's character, and by extension that of a whole swathe of French society that did not fit with the aspirational post-war vision championed by the cultural establishment.

If the guilty verdict satisfied the likes of Giono, others felt the trial provided rather less closure to the case – not least those tracking its progress back in Britain, where there was the feeling that if this wasn't a miscarriage, it was at the very least an abuse of due process. Even before the trial had started, back on 13 November, the *Daily Herald* ran with the headline 'police are on trial'. 'Two trials begin at the same time, in the same small courtroom of Digne,' the article read. 'On trial is 78-year-old [sic] Gaston Dominici ... On trial too – with the world watching – are French methods of murder investigation.'

Now that the verdict was through and the piece could be viewed in the whole, the scepticism only increased. On Monday 29 November 1954, the *Daily Mirror* neatly encapsulated widely shared concerns: 'Feelings had been mixed right to the last moment. It was felt that no jury could convict on the conflicting evidence heard in the 11-day trial.' In due course, *The Times* gave its own scathing assessment of the trial's myriad failings:

> ... confessions under pressure, the toleration of police methods which the law reproves, the prolonged detention of suspects before trial, the admission of irrelevant evidence, and the licence allowed to the Press, to witnesses, and even to magistrates to besmirch reputations and constantly to ignore the essential presumption of innocence.

To impartial observers, the feeling that something had gone badly wrong was almost inescapable. On what grounds had

Gaston been found guilty? Certainly not on the basis of incontrovertible forensic evidence. There was no smoking gun. What gun there was – a battered old Second World War relic – only added to the confusion, given the disagreement over who owned it and who had access to it. All that had pinned Gaston down were the confessions he made, altered and withdrew at will, along with the accusations from two of his sons, one of whom now disclaimed them.

Why, it was natural to ask, would Gaston have made a confession, or his sons their accusations, if he was not guilty? One potential, troubling answer was that a family naturally averse to the institutions of authority and unsophisticated in their dealings with them had unwittingly dug themselves into a hole from which it became impossible to escape. Faced with murder on their doorstep, they fell into a collective panic. Perhaps their first instinct was not, as the court believed, to cover up three murders for which one of them was responsible but simply to shy away from what was someone else's drama. That 'don't go looking for trouble' reflex.

As well as the impulse to shut up shop and keep one's counsel, the family's difficult dynamics undoubtedly complicated matters further. With several of their relationships having a tinderbox nature, various members began to eye each other with suspicion. 'What if he had done it?' 'Or him?' 'He certainly has a temper, especially when he's drunk.' The Dominicis were perhaps not thinking merely of keeping a low profile but of actively diverting suspicion away from themselves – not because they knew one of their party to be guilty, but because they feared that it could be possible. Some coped by taking up a defensive position, essentially stonewalling whenever questions were asked of them. Others were more proactive, making assertions that they hoped would persuade the police to cast their gaze elsewhere. But they each lost track of what the others were saying and got lost within their own testimonies. Without the urbanity to pull off these attempts at distracting and, on occasion, misleading, they in fact cast themselves as unreliable witnesses. A family for whom deceit seemed the default. Rather than avert attention, they brought suspicion upon themselves. Increasingly fearful that one of their number would be unmasked as a monster, their attempts to obfuscate lacked any subtlety: a false confession to protect a family member; accusations driven by bonds of brother-hood or other unseen loyalties. Then the refutations as the seriousness of the situation clarified. But by then, it was too late. Too many lies had been told, too much said to take back. The hole so deep that there was no chance of scrabbling out of it. The bid to keep out of trouble turned on its head. It is only a hypothesis, but one that goes some way to explain the family's car-crash response to the killings.

Maybe Gaston was guilty. Maybe Gustave was. But where was the evidence that told the story for sure? What if someone, somewhere else – the real, unknown killer – watched on as the adrenalin of escape pumped round their body, still trying to work out how it was that the Dominicis had got themselves into such a mess and how *they* had got away with murder.

———

The condemned Gaston sat alone in his cell, contemplating a future as dark as it could possibly be, the executioner's blade awaiting him, and the family he had built – for better or worse – in disarray. On 28 November, within hours of the jury returning, he wrote to his daughter, Clotilde. The contents of his letter were widely reported and much of it – instructions, for instance, on how best to tend his goats – was striking in its mundanity. Only the peculiar circumstances of their author-ship loaded each word with something between macabre fascination and outright pathos. But there was more besides animal husbandry. In a single paragraph, Gaston – undermin-ing Giono's assertions of his illiteracy – conveyed not only his grim despair but his intention to soon usher in the next explosive episode of the drama. 'The current grief that I suf-fer is due to an evil individual, who has dragged me into the greatest and cruellest dishonour that any man could endure,' he wrote. Then he went on to describe the multitude of lies told against him and his unfulfilled belief that the unnamed 'evil individual' would give himself up and admit the truth to the court. Gaston explained that he planned to speak to one of his legal counsels, Maître Léon Charles-Alfred, the following day on account of his being unable to 'stand such dishonour'.

Exactly what the letter meant was hotly debated. On the one hand, his instructions to his daughter about what needed to be done on the farm were interpreted as evidence that he expected to spend a long time locked up. But on the other, he was clearly not going to go quietly. Who was it that he expected to share the blame with him? Most had little doubt that Gaston had Gustave in mind. And few were bothered about keeping their suspicions about the son under wraps. The citizens of the Durance Valley had endured enough of the Dominicis and the ignominy they had brought upon the area. Whenever the family name was mentioned, it was usually with disdain. Gustave's father-in-law, for instance, voiced his contempt for the lot of them to whomever would listen in the market square at Forcalquier.

But still Gaston found the stomach to fight on. On 29 November, he met as promised with M. Charles-Alfred and signed off on an appeal. It just so happened that a Belgian newspaper had offered him a hefty sum for his life story that would go a long way towards paying for the new legal action. When the lawyer stepped out of the consultation with his client, he once more defended Gaston to the press, at times seeming to well up. Without giving details, he suggested a turning point had been reached. But to most listening, it all seemed rather late in the day for that.

For an appeal to succeed, it would be necessary to introduce new and significant evidence or to argue that there were sufficient procedural failings at trial. Most would have agreed that there were some questionable aspects to the case but nothing likely to convince the courts that the conviction itself was unsafe. As Gaston's team worked on its strategy, he was moved to the jail in Marseilles, Les Baumettes, which was better suited to providing the extra surveillance demanded for death row inmates. When allowed out of his cell for exercise, Gaston was shackled, and the only visits he was allowed were from his legal representatives. Nonetheless, there was a faint suggestion that the local mood music around the case was changing. There were plenty who still felt he was exactly where he ought to be, but the brooding disquiet at perceived police incompetence and an unsatisfactory trial were growing.

Gaston's team pushed for a new inquiry into the murders, which if granted would have been unprecedented. Never before had a successfully prosecuted capital case been reinvestigated. But Gaston had made several new claims to lawyers. He told them that not only did Gustave take part in the murders but also involved were Zézé and Jean Galizzi, Zézé's mother's lover. He also claimed to have heard Gustave and Yvette discussing the murders and apparently the theft of some jewellery that Gaston understood to have belonged to the Drummonds. The Minister of Justice, Jean-Michel Guérin du Boscq de Beaumont, ordered that Gaston be officially requestioned, a job that fell to the local Deputy Attorney General, Joseph Oddou. Almost at once, there was a familiar row-back by Gaston. While he continued to vaguely implicate Gustave and Zézé, Galizzi now seemed off the hook as the old man conceded that he didn't know for sure who was responsible for the killings.

De Beaumont, an urbane man of the Establishment, was unimpressed by Gaston but nevertheless agreed to further investigation. The papers were sent to the Ministry of the Interior, where they went through the hands of the future French president, François Mitterrand, who was then the Interior Minister. It was decided that the next phase of investigation would be headed by Commissioner Charles Chenevier, the Deputy Director General of the Central Directorate of the Judicial Police. Chenevier was a man with a reputation, famous for taking out high-profile gangland figures with the types of names you might expect to find in mob B-movies: names like 'Big Foot' Paturon and 'Walking Stick' Rene.[3] Nothing seemed to faze him, as might have been expected of a man who had survived torture by the Gestapo and a stint in the Neuengamme concentration camp. A holder of the Legion d'honneur, on one celebrated occasion he had foiled a gold heist while using his fourteen-year-old son to provide surveillance. His career was not without its blots, though – most damagingly, he had been in charge of an investigation into a murder on a train and had alighted upon the wrong suspect, an entirely innocent ticket inspector. The case had so haunted him that he had evolved into a more considered and circumspect character by the time he took over the Drummond inquiry. He certainly wasn't going to be arm-twisted into doing anything without a solid base of evidence to justify it.

When Chenevier arrived in Provence in mid-December 1954 on a fact-finding mission, he found obstruction wherever he turned. The local authorities were resistant to what they deemed interference from Paris, while the press questioned both his right to be there and what he hoped to achieve. He and three colleagues – including a detective from the capital, Commissioner Charles Gillard – made their way to Les Baumettes, its imposing whitewashed facades rearing up to look out over both the ocean and the cityscape. They found Gaston in his cell, dressed in a prison-issue grey outfit, trying to be as bright as he could for his guests.

Chenevier began proceedings in philosophical mood, questioning the old man about his religious beliefs. It was the prelude to a more specific line of questioning: why, if he'd sacrificed himself to save his family as he'd claimed, was he now changing his mind? There was no definitive answer from the old man. Just the same inconclusive raking-over of old ground. Chenevier's team left at around six o'clock as Gaston's evening meal arrived. They were back again the following afternoon, when they had a conference with Gaston's team of lawyers. Gaston was summoned to join them at 7 p.m. and told in no uncertain terms that this was his last chance to tell them the truth of what had happened to the Drummonds outside La Grand Terre. Gaston began a tale of how Gustave had gone out from the farm that night with Zézé, a little after 1 a.m. He knew, he said, because he had heard shots, gone down to the courtyard and seen them. But then ... the familiar self-contradictions, beginning with the claim that he had not in fact got up until the morning. With his story as incoherent as ever, no one listening to it considered an appeal against his conviction as anything other than unworkable.

Further interviews with other members of the family were similarly unhelpful, although the general ill-feeling towards Clovis and his role in Gaston's downfall was clear. Chenevier completed his intelligence-gathering on 23 December and handed his report to the Minister of Justice four days later. Although lacking new leads, he was highly critical of the original investigation and trial, particularly the overreliance on Gaston's shaky confessions. On those grounds, de Beaumont acceded to a new investigation into allegations against a suspect described in the official paperwork as 'unknown', to be completed prior to the conclusion of Gaston's appeal. However, a change of personnel at the Ministry of Justice saw de Beaumont moving on, to be replaced by Emmanuel Tempe. Tempe ordered that Gaston's appeal should be heard prior to the investigation, and so it was. On 18 February 1955, the case went before the appeal judges who dismissed it after just two hours of deliberation. Gaston's only hope now rested with a presidential decree in the event of the discovery of major new evidence.

When the new investigation began, Clovis refused to withdraw his accusations against his father despite renewed and intense pressure from the family. In what proved to be the Dominicis' final extended family gathering, Gustave accused his brother of having accepted a bribe from the police in exchange for his allegations – an extraordinary claim given Gustave's own accusations against his father and Gaston's accusation against him. The contretemps between the brothers ended in a full-blown fight, during which Clovis flung a chair at his brother.

Meanwhile, Gaston's lawyers clung to whatever new evidence they could find. For example, what appeared to have been some banter among labourers on a farm got out of hand, such that two of their number were briefly suspected of involvement in the killings – a story lacking credibility but which Gaston's team briefly seized upon. Pierre Carrias was the new examining magistrate and he arranged for Gaston to be reinterviewed, this time by the jurist Jacques Batigne, who hadn't actually read the case dossier and was innately opposed to any suggestion of police malpractice or incompetence. He found Gaston in the prison hospital, suffering with severe food poisoning. There were those who suspected Gaston was the victim of a deliberate act but nothing could be proven. By early March he was sufficiently recovered to be questioned, as well as to be confronted by Gustave and Yvette – a head-to-head that passed off remarkably amicably.

Carrias had little time for the investigators from Paris and aggressively defended the original execution of the case. But Gaston's nephew, Léon Dominici, had secured the services of a hot-shot lawyer from the capital, René Floriot, who felt that the plethora of inconsistencies and improbabilities in Gaston's various confessions rendered his conviction unsafe. Moreover, the press had sensed the local antipathy in Provence towards Chenevier and Gillard. Why, some journalists began to ask, might that be? Were the Parisians on to something that might be damaging to the local authorities? In the end, the local magistrates who now had to set the limits of the investigations had no choice but to accept the Paris team or risk losing public trust. But their parameters were narrow, restricted to discovering the activities and movements of Gustave and Zézé on the night of murders. Gustave and Yvette then threw their own curve ball, suggesting that official records of their questioning had been falsified. Under pressure from the Ministry of Justice, the investigation's remit was widened.

All the while, the press interest added its own spice. Several trial jurors now gave interviews to the newspapers, making it clear that the trial had left them with unanswered questions. One, it emerged, knew Gaston personally and should have been excluded on those grounds. The interview made it clear that he disliked the old man, not least for the suffering he put Marie through, and seemed never to have been in any doubt about his guilt. Then, out of nowhere, the world's greatest film director tumbled into town. Orson Welles arrived to make a film about the case for his series, *Around the World with Orson Welles*.[4] His presence infuriated many powerful people within the region, fearful that his Hollywood eye would catch them in an unfavourable light. It turned out that he was lacking the correct paperwork too and found himself under threat of prosecution. The film he produced in these circumstances was predictably incomplete and unbalanced and, ultimately, was banned in France.

It was all rather more dramatic than the investigation itself, which meandered and fizzled. Gaston had little to say, retracting his various earlier allegations. Clovis stuck to his story of his father's guilt, even as his family accused him of being driven by hatred and greed. In a final showdown with his father, he stuck to his guns. 'You told me that it was you who killed the English,' he proclaimed. Then he challenged Gaston to tell the investigators that he had not killed anyone if that was true, but not to deny that he had made a confession of guilt to his son. They were the last words he would ever utter to his father.

Chenevier finally submitted a 900-page report to the examining magistrate on 25 February 1956, arguing that the investigation should be continued. Carrias took nine months to respond. He noted, intriguingly, how 'the shadow of the resistance and the liberation hangs over the inquiry', and acknowledged that the case was beset by doubts but that he was unconvinced further investigation would yield positive results. On 13 November, the investigation into the role of 'unknown' in the murder of the Drummonds was closed down.

However, discomfort around Gaston's conviction persisted. In 1957, President René Coty commuted his death sentence to one of life imprisonment. Then, on 14 July 1960, Coty's successor, Charles de Gaulle, ordered Gaston's release. Now an octogenarian, Gaston moved in with his daughter, Clotilde, in Montfort back in Provence – in contravention of the law preventing convicted murderers from returning to the *département* in which they committed their crime. His return was greeted by some muted support but an awful lot more ill-feeling. He died on 4 April 1965, still officially recognised as the murderer of the Drummond family, a divisive figure until the end. The people of the Durance Valley, meanwhile, struggled to move on from the trauma for which the law had concluded Gaston Dominici was solely responsible.

A WEB OF INTRIGUES 13

Doubt has a habit of burrowing itself into the imagination, creating a space into which speculation and innuendo follow. In the case of the Drummond murders, doubt began its tunnelling early in the investigation and gained momentum as the authorities fumbled to lay their hands on the truth. Nor was it focused solely on Gaston and his family. The victims themselves were subjects of intense scrutiny and rumour, most significantly Jack. There were whispers – and sometimes more – in both the French and British press that he, and by extension the entire family, had been targeted because of the nature of his work. Several newspapers asserted that he had been involved with 'top secret' projects. Amid the paranoiac transition from World War to Cold War, such claims gave rise to all manner of theories, some informed and many not, ranging from the distinctly feasible to the frankly risible.

One theory expounded at the time in the *Daily Express* suggested that the Dominicis were cogs in a vast smuggling ring providing arms to leftist insurgents in Algeria.[1] In this story, the Drummonds were reduced to innocents abroad, caught up in the wrong place at the wrong time. But other speculation placed Jack right at the centre of the action. A persistent rumour was that he had been an operative for the Churchill-backed Special Operations Executive. The SOE, as we have seen, played a significant role in supporting the local *maquisards* during the war. Although the organisation was formally wound up in early 1946, much of the sort of work it had been involved in didn't cease entirely but was absorbed by MI6.

If one were to accept that Jack did indeed once have ties with the SOE, it is quite logical to think that he might have had unfinished business to tidy up in 1952. But it is at this point that many of the resulting theories diverge from the path of logic. One such hypothesis revolved around the assumption that British gold had been dropped via parachute into the Durance Valley during wartime, its purpose being to support the activities of the local SOE-backed Resistance network. As the story was told, by the early 1950s a good proportion of that gold remained hoarded in the French countryside and Jack was now charged with repatriating it. It undeniably makes for a good yarn but the proof is scant in all directions. While the SOE certainly provided supplies into the area, the suggestion that there were unclaimed troves of gold was but a local myth. Even if there had been more to it than that, there was nothing to suggest that Jack would be the obvious choice to return it to the UK. Of his many attributes, buccaneering was not an obvious one.

Another even more preposterous narrative was that Jack had been in the Durance Valley on a mission to secure secret papers for Winston Churchill, who had been returned to 10 Downing Street in October of 1951. The basis for this theory was elucidated in a controversial Italian television documentary in 2004.[2] The long-accepted version of how Benito

Mussolini – Italy's Fascist leader and Hitler's Axis partner – met his end begins with his arrest, along with that of his mistress Clara Petacci, by communist partisans on 27 April 1945. The couple were stopped near Lake Como while in the process of fleeing to Switzerland, aware that Italy was about to fall to the Allies. According to international agreement, Mussolini should have been handed into the custody of United Nations forces but instead he and his lover were summarily shot the next day, and their bodies strung upside down from a petrol-station roof in Milan. However, the makers of the Italian documentary offered an alternative take.

Extraordinarily, they asserted that Mussolini was executed not by Italian partisans but by SOE agents working on direct orders from Churchill. Churchill, it was claimed, had been intent on preventing the release of embarrassing clandestine correspondence between himself and the Italian leader, in which he was said to have cosied up to Mussolini in an attempt to induce him to abandon his alliance with Germany and make peace. One line of argument holds that by the time he made the break for Switzerland, Mussolini was using the letters to barter for protection from partisan vengeance, but that he had pushed Churchill's patience too far. Churchill's frequent post-war visits to the Italian Lakes, it has also been suggested, were tied into this quest to recover these compromising letters. Jack, it has been speculated, may have been in Provence in 1952 to pick up another batch of the missives and smuggle them to the safety of the UK.

Again, it is a neat story, but crumbles beneath even the most cursory of examinations. Although potentially incriminating letters between the two wartime leaders have emerged over the years, few serious historians take them to be anything other than crude forgeries. In a speech he gave in

1933,[3] Churchill described Mussolini as 'the greatest law giver among living men', a phrase often quoted to imply his admiration for the Italian. In fact, the general tenor of that speech was to reject fascism as a model for the British people. Churchill was doubtless aware of delicate negotiations at the time to ensure Italy paid its outstanding war debts to Britain. The future prime minister was simply being cautious in his words to describe a man with whom there was still much business to do. There is precious little evidence to suggest that he was ever a genuine admirer of *Il Duce* and his fascist policies. The only two known genuine letters from Churchill to Mussolini date to just prior to the war, when Churchill pleaded with his counterpart to reconsider his close alliance with Hitler. That Churchill would then sue for a back-door peace during the war seems unlikely in the extreme. The story can be fairly dismissed as fantasy even before we arrive at the question of why the job of retrieving any suspect letters might have fallen to Jack.

It is worth noting, too, that Francis Cammaerts, leader of the SOE's 'Jockey' network in southern France, claimed to have known of Jack as a civil servant of rare importance to the war effort but denied he ever had an association with the SOE. There are those who might point out that he would, of course, say that. Covert operatives do not, on the whole, go around shouting about themselves and their colleagues. It is certainly possible to track some indirect connections between Jack and the organisation. For instance, in the 1930s he had worked with M. B. Donald on the isolation of vitamins A and B. Like Jack, Donald forged a highly successful career for himself, eventually becoming honorary secretary of the Institution of Chemical Engineers. More pertinently, he is also known to have been a member of the Special Operations

Executive Inter Services Research Bureau. Jack's personal and professional networks and those of the SOE certainly ran close. Nonetheless, any evidence linking him directly to the organisation is yet to come to light.

Arguably the story that has stuck most over the years involves allegations of an international criminal enterprise emanating from the Kremlin. Its origins can be traced to Stuttgart, Germany and an arrest on 9 August 1952, four days after the Drummonds were killed. A Polish-born German by the name of Wilhelm Bartkowski was picked up by police on suspicion of committing a series of robberies, some involving weapons. Then, in October, some two months after his arrest, he came up with the most astonishing confession: he said he had been present on the road outside La Grand Terre during the killings. He was, he said, the getaway driver for a gang of hitmen comprising a Greek, a Spaniard and a Swiss national. It sounded like the beginning of a particularly unfunny and unsavoury joke.

This apparent admission of guilt was communicated to the French authorities, who promptly sent Commissioner Gillard to question the suspect. The British were duly informed, and they too were permitted to interrogate Bartkowski. But for some reason the British authorities were wary of wading into an investigation that, though the victims were British nationals, many on the UK side thought best left to the French and Germans. Great efforts were made to keep the Bartkowski revelations out of the press, and internally there was a good deal of scepticism expressed as to the suspect's credibility.

Bartkowski's story was certainly wild, not to mention prone to revision with each retelling, of which there were many in the late part of 1952. In his favour, he did provide some convincing details about the crime scene and its locale, although there was much discussion about how much of this knowledge he could have gleaned from international news reports. He also gave in-depth descriptions of items said to have been stolen from the Drummonds, including a wallet, a distinctive necklace and an unusual men's signet ring, none of which were included in press reporting. Members of the extended Drummond family and Guy Marrian were questioned as to whether such items had indeed been in the family's possessions, although there is no record of the outcome of that particular strand of inquiry. Along with the Drummond case, Bartkowski also held his hands up to dozens of other crimes, all of which were verified.

He provided his interrogators with an extraordinary account of his life, which he said included an aborted stint with the French Foreign Legion. However, his recollections were soon shown to be as leaky as a colander. The emerging truth seemed to be that here was a petty criminal who had made his way in the world by robbing, thieving and then moving on to the next target. He claimed to have been hooked up with his alleged band of hired assassins by Russian contacts he had met while serving a prison sentence. At least, that's what he told the French. To the Germans, he said he'd already been introduced to them prior to his stint in jail. Their crime spree, he said, became gradually more serious and included a kidnapping undertaken on behalf of the Czechoslovakian government.

Regarding the attack on the Drummonds, Bartkowski told how the gang had left from an upmarket hotel in the German town of Lindau on the morning of 4 August, driving a purple Buick with US number plates. Hardly an inconspicuous look, although no one at the hotel remembered them. Then on through Austria, Switzerland and down into France, eventually into the Durance Valley, to the site of the murders, where Bartkowski was ordered to stop the vehicle. He parked up by La Grand Terre, doors open and engine idling as his colleagues attended to business. A few minutes later, he told police, he heard the sound of shots. Within fifteen minutes, he and the gang were back on the road, arriving back in Lindau by seven the next evening.

Over the coming months, a consensus grew among the various international authorities that Bartkowski was not a credible witness. The flaws in his story were myriad. He spoke of the Drummonds having a tent, which they did not. His description of their camping site included some factual detail but in general bore little resemblance to reality. Nor could he give an accurate description of the weapons the gang were supposedly carrying. Then came the inevitable retraction by Bartkowski, followed by renewed confessions. It was like Gaston Dominici all over again. Bartkowski was increasingly characterised as a fantasist, and many years later Dominici's trial judge Marcel Bousquet gave an interview in which he dismissed Bartkowski as a crank intent on securing his extradition to France, from where he hoped it would be easier to escape. Perhaps indicative of some mental instability, Bartkowski's own grasp on where fact diverged from fiction seems to have clouded in his own mind.

Nevertheless, his story lingered through the decades. What if the suspect's outrageous claims masked a kernel of truth? Was it possible that the French, Germans and British were so keen to preserve the narrative of Gaston Dominici as the madman slayer that they failed to give Bartkowski's meandering account the due diligence it warranted? This was certainly the belief of Alain Dominici, Gaston's grandson and defender of the family name, who in 1997 partnered with

William Reymond, an investigative journalist, with a view to getting Gaston's conviction quashed. The pair set out their case in a book, *Dominici non coupable: Les assassins retrouvés* (Dominici Not Guilty: The Assassins Found),[4] and then in an open letter to the French government.[5] Their thesis was that Jack worked for the British intelligence services and was killed by Bartkowski's Kremlin-controlled hit squad. They further claimed that the French government knew this to be the case but opted to throw Dominici to the wolves so as not to disturb relations with the Soviet Union at a delicate moment in the Cold War. The authors claimed that the government additionally wanted to avoid exposing the weak underbelly of their own security services and of the French judicial system. The book was developed into a TV series in 2003 for the French channel TF1,[6] which won audiences of 12 million and more. Despite a good deal of public doubt as to its central argument, it put the case firmly back into the public consciousness, even if it failed to convince the government that a judicial review was necessary.

However, six years later, Alain's and Reymond's case received a crushing blow when Bartkowski submitted to an interview with another French journalist, Jean-Charles Deniau. Bartkowski now claimed to have been an eye-witness to the 1997 car crash in a Parisian underpass that resulted in Princess Diana's death – and that her death had been ordered by Buckingham Palace. To paraphrase Oscar Wilde, to have been present at one internationally masterminded political assassination may be regarded as a misfortune, but to be at two ... For many of those not already convinced that he was a weaver of tall tales, this proved the final straw.

Almost from the outset, the Drummond case drew an army of cranks and fantasists. A trip to the National Archives at

Kew, just outside of London, provides ample evidence. There, you can find police files bulging with all manner of crackpot letters, the authors ranging from those making unfounded accusations of guilt to others offering their psychic abilities to catch the killer. Their frequently flowery language and a penchant for hand-coloured notes tell a story all of their own.[7]

Whatever grains of truth may have existed amid the mire of conspiracy theory and speculation became all but impossible to fathom. Given Jack's status as a public figure, the wall of silence met by the case's original investigators, and the peculiar conditions of post-war southern France, it was perhaps always going to be like this. Most of the theories should undoubtedly be taken with a large dose of salt. Many are evidently stories manufactured by troubled, if sometimes well-intentioned minds and, even more commonly, concocted for their shock value. Facts were routinely moulded to fit a good yarn to be shared over a glass of wine and, of course, to support the next juicy headline by journalists determined to wring all that they could from the Drummonds' tragedy.

But there is a disconcerting fact that stands in the way of all those keen to dismiss every allegation and innuendo as pure fantasy. The antidote to conspiracy theory is truth, but in the Drummonds' case, that was always in short supply. The official explanation for what happened to the family – culminating in a death sentence for the old farmer who lived down the road – left too many gaps through which intrigue could emerge and flourish.

And then there was Jack himself. What did anyone really know about him?

MORE THAN MEETS THE EYE 14

While Gaston's character, justifiably or not, was subject to intense critique, Jack Drummond looked for all the world about as straight-batting and down-the-line as you could hope for. But a closer delve into his private affairs revealed a life that had been shrouded in mystery and secrecy virtually from the moment of his birth. Exploring his life is like opening a box of chocolates with many layers, each abounding with unusual and interesting tastes that become stronger, more exotic and more enigmatic the deeper through the layers you go.

From 1875, British law required that every birth was registered with the appropriate local authority. Yet in the case of Jack – born some sixteen years after this became a legal requirement – even finding a certificate proved a challenge. When the document was tracked down, the name Drummond appeared nowhere on it. Instead, he was registered as Jack Cecil McQuie, father unknown, born in Kennington, south London, and not Leicester as some would believe in years to come. His next appearance in the official records came a few months after his arrival into the world, in the 1891 census. There he is, a babe in arms, living with his parents in a leafy suburb of Leicester in a substantial Victorian house, complete with a servant. Jack, though, is now listed as Cecil Drummond, as he is on several other official documents from his early childhood.

Nor is everything straightforward with his parentage. They appear to have lied about their ages and marital status. According to the census data, Jack's father was then 45 years old and his mother 29. But the retired Major John Drummond was in fact 60 at the time, and Jack's mother Nora Gertrude (usually Gertrude) only 21. Tragedy struck in June that year when the Major died, not in India as some of Jack's obituaries would later state, but in Leicester, where he succumbed to bronchitis. Maybe had he survived he would have sorted out his affairs more comprehensively but as it was, his will stated that he was a bachelor with no dependents. His estate, worth £527 12s 6d (about £60,000 today; the figure was calculated twice at the time, suggesting some possible dissension), was left to his sister Maria Spinks, his only legal next of kin. He and Gertrude, evidently, were unmarried. For Jack, more tragedy lay just ahead. In 1893, he was orphaned when Gertrude died in Market Bosworth, Leicestershire aged just 24, from causes unknown. By then, she had given birth to another baby, a girl. Again, the identity of the father of this child is uncertain.

So, what is to be made of the information provided about Jack in the 1891 census? In an age when parlours up and down the country were epicentres of unforgiving judgement, the 39-year age gap between unwed parents would have been an utter scandal. It is also puzzling that Jack was born in London, not his mother's native Leicester. It is quite possible that John Drummond was not his father at all, as he didn't appear on the birth certificate. Did he instead step in to give a veneer of respectability – to provide a bastard child with a father – but without making it official? If this was the case – and it is speculative – why might he have felt the call to smooth Jack's beginnings in the world, and why go to the effort and risk of distorting his and Gertrude's real ages?

Whatever responsibility he felt to the woman and her son, the Major's death seriously complicated the picture. It is known that John Drummond's house was sold in 1891, the proceeds going to his sister, Maria, as per his will. In due course, Jack went to live with Maria and her husband, George Spinks, in London. What is unclear is whether he stayed in Leicestershire (making the short move to Market Bosworth) with his mother until her own untimely demise or whether he was already living with the Spinkses, who were otherwise childless. Whichever scenario, it must have been hard to bear for the seemingly now penniless Gertrude, not least because it had not always been like this for her. Nora Gertrude McQuie was the seventh of eight children from a well-to-do Lancashire family, her father described as a 'Gentleman' and employee of the East India Company in official documents. Their household had at times employed up to six servants.

Was she forced to leave this comfortable life when she fell pregnant? By 1893, she had been expecting for the second time, this time a daughter, whose birth certificate records her name as Mabel Muriel but who became known as Ena Constance. Some sources later described her as the daughter of Nora Gertrude's elder sister, Constance Gertrude, who had married Arthur Culbard in 1881 but had not conceived in twelve years. Other records further muddy the waters, suggesting Nora Gertrude was in fact married to Culbard and Ena was their child. Could Nora Gertrude have acted as a surrogate for her childless sister, or did Constance take responsibility for the child after Nora's death? Did Nora Gertrude, perhaps, die in childbirth? And was the infant Jack even aware of the existence of his half-sister, or was he already with Maria and George Spinks in an address down at the Woolwich dockyards, not yet in the handsome redbrick three-storey semi in leafy Greenwich that John Drummond's bequest would eventually make possible?

George Spinks was a retired army captain and quartermaster who fought in the Crimea. He was 57 when Jack was born, and Maria just a year younger. Having no children of their own, Jack's arrival into the household sometime between 1891 and 1893 must have brought enormous upheaval. Nonetheless, by all accounts they treated Jack as their own. In the 1901 census, he appears as 'Jack Cecil Spinks', with 67-year-old George and 66-year-old Maria listed as his parents. They provided him with a decent home and prospects, for which he must have been appreciative in light of the difficult circumstances of his early years. But how much fun life in the Spinks family was is another question. His elderly guardians were strict, insisting the boy accompany them to their Nonconformist church services. It is perhaps telling that at the first opportunity, before he was eighteen, Jack reverted to his previous surname. His admission form to the Strand School in 1908 clearly has him as 'Jack Cecil Drummond, previously C. J. Spinks'.

Fast forward to 1914 and the onset of war, when another puzzling mystery wraps itself around Jack – his lack of front-line service. While millions of his contemporaries left to fight in the trenches of western Europe, he stayed behind in London, engaged in scientific work. His efforts to join up were stymied, the obituaries would later say, by an unspecified

In Memoriam

Jack Cecil Drummond, Kt.
D.Sc., F.R.I.C., F.R.S.

Died
August 5th, 1952

Interred at
Forcalquier,
Southern France

ANNE
(his wife)

ELIZABETH ANNE
(their daughter)

Images of Jack, Anne and Elizabeth Drummond used in a tribute produced by the Boots Pure Drug Company, Jack's employer in the post-war period. He worked on various products, including agrochemicals.

The Boots Archive

The prestigious American Medal of Freedom with Silver Palms, awarded by the United States government to Jack in 1948 for 'exceptionally meritorious achievement which aided the US in the prosecution of the war against the enemy in Europe'.

Stephanie Matthews

This badly burned book was one of the few volumes of employment records that survived when University College London took a direct hit from a bomb during the Blitz in 1941. It provides crucial insights into Drummond's time at the institution.

Stephanie Matthews

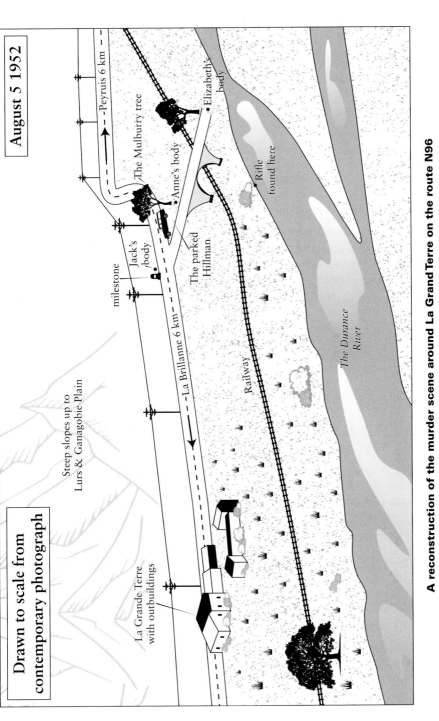

August 5 1952

Drawn to scale from contemporary photograph

Steep slopes up to
Lurs & Ganagobie Plain

La Grande Terre
with outbuildings

Railway

The Durance River

milestone

Jack's body

The parked Hillman

Anne's body

The Mulburry tree

Elizabeth's body

Rifle found here

Peyruis 6 km

La Brillanne 6 km

A reconstruction of the murder scene around La Grand Terre on the route N96 that greeted investigators on the fateful morning of 5 August 1952.

**A snap of Jack (right) on holiday in Harlech in Wales during the
1920s. He is pictured with his first wife, Mabel, and the other
figure is believed to be Guy Marrian, Jack's friend and colleague
who would become a key witness in the investigation.**

Courtesy of the Wellcome Collection

**Jack accepting his
honorary doctorate
from the University
of Paris in 1948 – one
of several prestigious
international accolades
he received in recognition
of his extraordinary
wartime work.**

Courtesy of the Wellcome Collection

**An adult's weekly ration
entitlement during the
Second World War. Jack
was instrumental in
ensuring the allowance was
scientifically calculated
and nutritionally balanced,
prompting an improvement
in public health.**

Alamy Stock Photo

Mourners gather for the joint funeral of Jack, Anne and Elizabeth at the cemetery in Forcalquier, a few miles from the crime scene. Many of those present were locals who had been traumatised by news of the killings.

Courtesy of the Wellcome Collection

Among the few mourners in attendance with direct links to the family were Jack's godson, Mike Austin-Smith; officials from Jack's employer, the Boots Pure Drug Company; and representatives of the British Consulate in Marseilles.

Courtesy of the Wellcome Collection

A shrine to Elizabeth Drummond – adorned with flowers, soft toys and messages of sympathy – is located at the end of the bridge near where her body was found. The memorial remains there today and is still tended by locals, seventy years after her murder.

Stephanie Matthews

Above left: A more youthful Gaston Dominici. Pictured here in 1922, around the time that he purchased La Grand Terre for 10,000 old francs.
Courtesy of Alain Dominici

Above right: Gaston, by now in his eighties, celebrating his release from prison in 1960 amid a climate of widespread unease around his trial and conviction.
Courtesy of Alain Dominici

Above left: Gaston in earlier times – a tough, uncompromising man who was well-known in his local community and had a reputation for hard work. He and his wife raised a family of nine children.
Courtesy of Alain Dominici

Above right: La Grand Terre was built on dry, stony land, but Gaston and the Dominicis eked out a living there for thirty years before the murders. Latterly, Gaston tended goats on the land.
Courtesy of Alain Dominici

Gustave Dominici, Gaston's son and eventual accuser. Pictured here with his mother, Marie – unflatteringly nicknamed 'The Sardine' by her husband – on the farm, c. 1950.

Courtesy of Alain Dominici

The farmhouse, La Grand Terre, in 1952, when for a while it was a focal point of national and international media interest. Was this really the home of a brutal mass murderer?

Courtesy of Alain Dominici

The family showing a united front at a reunion when Gaston was released in 1960. Front row, left to right: Christian, Bernard, Daniel, Marie, Gaston, Josiane, Claude, Alain.

Middle row, left to right: Marie, Georges, Gaston, Mauricette (Marie Christine being held), Aimé (Dominique being held), Clément, Marie Claude and Augusta Caillard, Ida Balmonnet, Gustave, Yvette, Clotilde Aramand.

Back row, left to right: Leon, Marcel, Angelin Aramand.

Courtesy of Alain Dominici

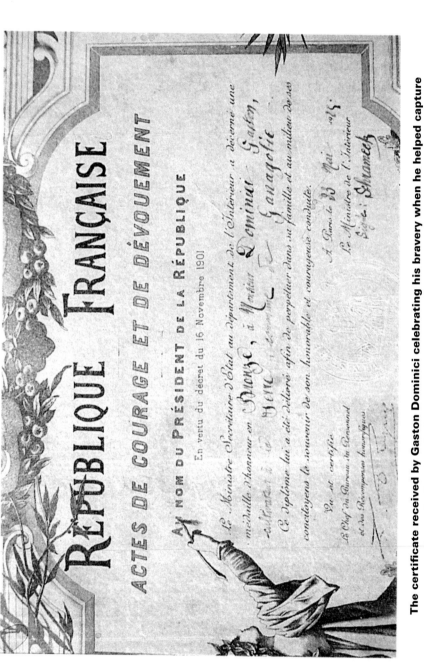

The certificate received by Gaston Dominici celebrating his bravery when he helped capture an armed convict in 1924. This was framed and hung on his wall with immense pride.

Courtesy of Alain Dominici

Investigators throng around the Drummonds' UK-plated green Hillman estate, which faces south in the direction it had been travelling. The farmhouse at La Grande Terre can be seen in the background.

Courtesy of the Wellcome Collection

Locals gather to spectate as the police stage a reconstruction of the murder scene in 1953, prior to Gaston being charged with the crimes.

Courtesy of the Wellcome Collection

The murder weapon is displayed in court – an American-
issue Rock Ola M1 carbine rifle that was found to have
originated from the Royal Military College in Kingston, Ontario
in Canada. It almost certainly once belonged to an Allied
soldier who passed through the area during the war.

Gaston Dominici, flanked by guards, arriving at the Digne Court of Assizes to face trial. Proceedings were originally expected to last for four days but actually went on for ten.

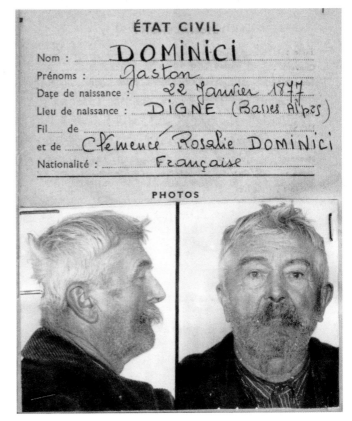

ÉTAT CIVIL

Nom : DOMINICI

Prénoms : Gaston

Date de naissance : 22 Janvier 1877

Lieu de naissance : DIGNE (Basses Alpes)

Fil de

et de Clémence Rosalie DOMINICI

Nationalité : Française

PHOTOS

Gaston's prison identity card, featuring two mugshots that give a glimpse of the toll events had taken upon him.

The view today from the village of Lurs on the plateau overlooking
the Durance valley. The river has been moved to make way for the
A51 motorway that now runs alongside the road where the murders
occurred (known as the N96 in 1952, subsequently renamed the D4096).

Stephanie Matthews

Above: A modern view of the bridge over the railway track that ran by the Dominicis' farmland, close to where Elizabeth was found. Her shrine can be seen to the right of the bridge.

Stephanie Matthews

Right: The modest grave of Jack Drummond, including his misspelt name. Jack and Anne lie either side of Elizabeth in the cemetery in Forcalquier.

Stephanie Matthews

Gaston and Marie Dominici, pictured after his release from prison in 1960. Although doubt surrounded his guilt, the couple were never able to escape the shadow of the events that took place on the road outside their property.

heart complaint. A heart complaint that none of the doctors who carried out post-mortem examinations on Jack in 1952 could detect. On the contrary, his heart was found to be in a healthy condition for his age.

If it wasn't his heart, the question remains as to what held him back. In Jack's obituary published by the Royal Society, there is one particularly haunting line that relates to the war. 'His biological outlook,' it reads, 'and his knowledge of physiology was widened by his friendship with one of the most brilliant of the medical students, who unfortunately was killed early in the 1914 war.' The student is unnamed but it is clear by his mere mention how much Jack valued the relationship. The doleful lists of the dead published by King's College between 1914 and 1918 throw up two leading candidates, both medical students killed in the first year of the war. The first to consider is Sydney Howard Hodges, at King's from 1912 until early 1914. He joined the 4th Battalion Royal Fusiliers and landed at Le Havre in August 1914 to serve on the Western Front. He was there at the Battle of Mons and the Battle of Le Cateau that same month, and at the First Battle of the Marne, the First Battle of the Aisne, the Battle of La Bassée, the Battle of Messines and the First Battle of Ypres in the torrid weeks that followed. And then his run of luck, if it may be called that, ran out. He was killed in action on 17 October, just three months after enlisting, and today lies in the British cemetery at Aubers Ridge in northern France, near the Belgian border. He was 23 years old, the same age as Jack. Sydney's older brother, Charles, who had also been at King's studying engineering, joined up at the same time. He lasted a few months more but was killed in June 1915, aged 30, and buried in the Zantvoorde Cemetery, just 20 miles away across the Belgian border. This was truly the lost generation.

The other likely candidate fitting the Royal Society's description was Richard Bevan, a young man with an impressive academic track record. When he was twelve, he won the junior foundation scholarship to attend the prestigious St Paul's public school in London (founded in 1509 and linked to the famous cathedral). He subsequently won a senior scholarship that allowed him to see out his schooling there. He took part in an array of competitions against rival public schools, emerging with many awards and accolades. Evidently, he was a boy who relied more on his brains than his family background for progression. To secure his place to study medicine at King's, he won the Huxley entrance scholarship, further evidence that he matched the Royal Society's descriptor 'brilliant'.

For many years part of the voluntary London Rifle Brigade, 5th City of London, he was remembered at King's as bright, enthusiastic and funny with unfailing good humour. Just the sort of character Jack would likely have been drawn to. Bevan was pivotal to the students' social life, serving as first junior and then senior club secretary in 1911 and 1912, responsible for organising college sporting activities and dances. As nineteen- and twenty-year-olds, Bevan and Jack might have taken the field together to play rugby or cricket or practised their volleying on the tennis court, working up a thirst before evenings of drinking and socialising, chewing over the great issues of the day, chasing girls and generally squeezing the joy from their youths. All, of course, while attending lectures and honing their extraordinary intellects.

It is, in the end, Bevan who emerges the more probable subject of the Royal Society reference, his path likelier to have crossed significantly with Jack's. After war was declared on 4 August 1914, maybe he and Jack discussed signing up, both conscious of the social pressure to do so. In London, they would have been bombarded by the famous image of Lord Kitchener with his proud walrus moustache, pointing his finger out from posters. The message for the nation's youth was simple: it is every young man's duty to fight for his country. Not that Jack or Bevan needed much persuading. The latter re-enlisted in his old regiment as soon as he could, as a private, his pleas to be allowed to make use of his medical expertise rejected. His regiment landed at Le Havre on 4 November, and from there it was on to Flanders. Full of vim and vigour, no doubt fuelled by certainty that all this trouble would soon be sorted out, Richard was among the first to die, shot by a sniper on 10 December in what the Tommies called Plug Street Wood in Wallonia. He had just stepped out of the trenches to fetch water. He succumbed to his wounds two days later, aged 21. A hitherto charmed life snuffed out.

The drip feed of news about lost friends was a succession of dagger blows even as lists of the fallen became a normalised part of daily life. But was Jack's grief bound up with a sense of guilt that he remained in the relative safety of his scientific lab back in England? In 1914, Jack was in the prime of life, not only a sparkling mind but a fine physical specimen. There would be no troubling the recruiting officer with a lack of height (the minimum height was no longer the 5ft 6ins demanded at the time of the Crimean War, but just 5ft) or poor conditioning as a result of malnutrition. With the clamour for recruits intense and popular disdain for those who ignored the call savage, he seemed well positioned to join his friends on the continent. Moreover, Jack had recently completed his degree but was not immersed in his career, nor did he have close family reliant upon him. His adoptive father, George, had died in 1908 and his adoptive mother, Maria, in early 1914. The timing of the call to serve seems to have been as good as it could be.

Jack had solid military heritage and showed interest in the army from a young age. George had been a veteran of the Crimea, while John Drummond, his purported natural father, was a major in the Royal Artillery. Jack had even lived by Charlton Park, with the Royal Artillery Barracks less than ten minutes' walk from his home. Sometime between 1905 and 1908, while a teenager, he joined the Special Cadet Force. By 1911, aged 20, he had reached the rank of corporal in the 1st Battalion, The Queen's Royal West Surrey Regiment, based at the Warley Barracks in Brentwood, Essex. A considerable achievement for a young man still in full-time education. How devastating, then – if the obituary writers are to be believed – to be told four years later that he was unfit to serve because of his heart condition.

Jack's post-mortem suggests that either his heart was subject of a preternatural recovery over the next 38 years or, more realistically, that this narrative was untruthful. So, why else might he have been diverted from frontline action? Many men were set to work in essential jobs but if this had been the case, it would surely have been recorded somewhere, for there was no shame in it. But a closer look at the available sources throws up something rather surprising.

The London Gazette is the most important journal of record for the British government. Looking through back copies from earlier in 1914, it reveals that on 14 February, Jack Drummond was seconded from the Royal Horse Artillery to the Territorial Force (i.e. the army's part-time volunteer section created in 1908 to augment its regular forces). In other words, Jack, far from being an invalid rejected for service, was serving in the military shortly before war broke out. Moreover, he was evidently promoted to the officer class, because on 4 November 1918 the *Gazette* reported that Lieutenant J. C. Drummond had resigned his commission. Come the Second World War, there are photographs of Jack in military uniform, as well as a report in August 1940 that he was a captain and had been transferred from the Royal Artillery to the supplementary reserve of officers. Jack was seemingly a lifelong military man after all.

Why, then, the obituaries' insistence that Jack's heart had been too weak for him to serve in the First World War? We know that shortly before the war, Jack had moved from King's to take up an appointment at the Cancer Hospital Research Institute. However, there was a gap in between, spanning roughly January to March 1914, during which time he was on the staff of the Government Chemist, an agency founded in 1842 and charged with looking out for consumer interests, particularly around the safety and quality of food and drink. Going back to Jack's Royal Society obituary, he was described as having been 'given a biochemical problem of a somewhat unorthodox type' while in this post. There are no known records to indicate precisely what this 'unorthodox' biochemical problem was. However, having recently graduated with a first in chemistry, it was likely a problem both complex and cutting-edge. At the time, the greatest questions of biochemistry occupying the collective mind of the British government were related to chemical weapons – a dreaded new wartime consideration. The nation's military and political leaders had been horrified at the potential carnage threatened by chemical weapons. Early proposals to make use of them in the Crimean War in the 1850s and the US Civil War the following decade had come to nothing, but they were employed in anger – if with limited success – during South America's War of the

Triple Alliance in 1868. Such were the levels of international concern that in 1899, delegates at the Hague Peace Conference adopted a convention prohibiting 'the use of projectiles with the sole object to spread asphyxiating poisonous gases'. Of the nations in attendance, only the United States demurred. But with war in Europe looming, the British did not want to leave anything to chance and upped their research in the field.

Both inorganic and organic chemistry were enjoying a golden age in terms of major fundamental discoveries in basic molecular forces and synthetic techniques. In 1913, just a year before the war, Marie Curie had been awarded the Nobel Prize in Chemistry for her discovery of radium and polonium. Other elements then coming to light included the inert gases and fluorine. Over in Germany, Fritz Haber was deep in the research that would ultimately win him a Nobel Prize, figuring out the means of producing ammonia from nitrogen. This would prove a crucial step towards the creation of chemical fertilisers that in due course revolutionised agriculture the world over. But it was more bleakly a vital building block in the development of new, more brutal chemical weapons. It remains a stain on the reputation of the Nobel Academy that one of its awards should have gone to a man who may justifiably be considered the architect of the gas warfare that marked out the First World War as among the most brutal, inhumane conflicts in world history. His veneration was all the more striking given that the creation of the Prizes was in some small part down to the desire of their founder, Alfred Nobel, to make amends for his own invention of dynamite, which he came to ruefully recognise had facilitated humanity's more destructive instincts.

Was Jack handpicked to serve as a supple-minded opponent to Haber on the British side? It is not too wild an idea to suggest that he might have been set to work on, say, looking at the potential impact on Britain's agriculture if Germany sought to disrupt production by use of chemical weapons. Or perhaps he was set to analysing what appalling new weapons the enemy might be in a position to deploy, and how the UK might seek to defend itself? Was there perhaps even work devoted to establishing what weapons of its own the country might hit back with? Chemists in the First World War were not considered among the protected professions, but such work would have been of the highest importance and necessarily highly secretive. It would certainly explain why the fit and healthy young Jack, already practised in military ways, was held back from the front line at the moment when the authorities were most eager to stock the army. A fighter after all – and certainly not a shirker or a white feather – but a soldier on another, secret front.

Whether Jack's obituary writers had a clue about the confusion surrounding his early biography is uncertain. Most were his colleagues in later phases of life and so may well have had no inkling of these mysterious gaps. With their information seemingly gathered from a limited number of family sources, they were likely merely trumpeting the lines as they received them in relation to those dim, distant days – a period he rarely spoke about latterly. The birth certificate in a different name, the untruths reported on census forms, the doubts surrounding his parentage, his repeatedly changing Christian name and surname, then the mystery of his wartime service represent a multitude of inconsistencies and intrigues that render Jack's early life enigmatic.

But the intrigues extended much further forward in time, on even past his death. Although the nature of his passing ensured an avalanche of headlines, Jack's name was soon pushed out of the public consciousness. Why, for example, was no obituary published by the esteemed Biochemical Society, of which Jack had served as both chairman and honorary secretary? There is a sense that he was quietly shuffled aside into obscurity, a man who had knocked on the door of greatness relegated to the recesses of the collective memory as quickly as possible. There is scant evidence that he caused sufficient personal offence in life to be so treated in death, which leaves another possibility: that deep scrutiny of Jack's life might throw up problems or embarrassments for those left behind. What is certain is that almost from the moment of his emergence into the world, secrecy wove itself around Jack and self-reinvention came naturally to him. Said without moral judgement, Jack Drummond was a chameleon.

BIG BOOTS TO FILL

15

After the war, Jack made a career move that astonished and perplexed many of those who knew him. In 1945, he resigned his professorship at UCL to take a job as Director of Research at the Boots Pure Drug Company. Not only was it a leap out of academia but it necessitated a move for the family to Nottingham in the English Midlands. At the time, the cross-over from the academic to the commercial world was taken far less regularly than today. They were, by and large, parallel worlds – one driven by the purity of intellectual enquiry, the other rendered murky by its underlying financial motivations. Jack's decision to jump ship was not only a surprise to many of his colleagues, but also a cause for sadness and even a betrayal. The academic's ultimate slap in the face.

Look at what he was leaving behind too – substituting the benefits of living in one of the world's great metropolises for life in a more subdued provincial city. It was goodbye to his beloved Food and Wine Society, to the exclusive London gentlemen's clubs and the West End opening nights. Post-war Nottingham was, by comparison, a bleak industrial heartland where unemployment was high, poverty rife and a good deal of the infrastructure in a state of dereliction. Jack did what he could to recreate his London life there but with inevitably limited success. He attempted to set up a branch of the Food and Wine Society, for example, which was described as 'a welcome oasis in a rather bare gastronomic desert' but it met only once before his death. He was also a director of the Playhouse Repertory Theatre, striving hard to keep the institution on its feet in hard times.

His commitments at the Ministry of Food and with the Control Commission in Germany ensured Jack did not begin his new role at Boots until 1946. And hard as it may have been for some to accept, the move made good sense in several ways. The war had been exhausting for him, working tirelessly for the Ministry and assorted other agencies at home and abroad, racking up thousands of miles in travel and repeatedly launching himself into difficult and dangerous situations. No longer a young man but deep into his mid-fifties, he had every right to consider his service to the public and to academia satisfied. There was his family to think about too. He had seen relatively little of his still quite new wife, a war bride, or Elizabeth, the apple of his eye, in her first few years. Corporate life offered at least the possibility of a moderately more stable working environment. Then there was the money. Jack was known to have complained in private about the relatively little he had earned as an academic and civil servant. He had been able to sustain a decent standard of life when there was just himself and Mabel to think about but now he had a family to support, an extra mouth to feed, school fees to pay. The Boots remuneration package would have turned most people's heads, and Jack doubtless welcomed the chance to make some serious financial progress.

Just as the cards stacked up well for Jack, they did so for his prospective employer as well. For their money, they were getting more than just a respected figurehead to bolster their public image – Jack was not intent on running down the clock until retirement. It was always the plan that he would undertake serious and challenging work. As his Royal Society obituary would in due course note: 'At Nottingham Drummond threw himself into the duties of his new post with the same energy and enthusiasm that had carried him through the difficult and strenuous years of the war.'

The Boots that emerged from the Second World War was very different to the high-street behemoth that we know today. The company can trace its roots back to 1849,[1] when John and Mary Boot opened a store in Nottingham selling herbal remedies – a lucrative market offering hope to those who could not afford to pay to see a doctor. When John died in 1860, his ten-year-old son Jesse stepped in to help his mother run the business, collecting, preparing and selling herbs. When he reached 21, he became a partner and his entrepreneurial skills shone as he built the firm into an industrial and retail empire. By 1913 he owned 560 shops across England, Wales and Scotland, with a turnover in excess of £2.5 million per year.

Boots played an important role in the war effort between 1914 and 1918, with Jesse anticipating many of the nation's supply challenges and duly increasing production of certain chemicals, notably aspirin and saccharin that had traditionally been imported from Germany. The company also manufactured products and equipment for men at the front, including vermin powder, anti-fly cream and water sterilisation tablets. Boots's laboratories and manufacturing facilities were expanded and almost a thousand women employed exclusively to make over 5 million box respirators (an early type of gas mask) that were desperately needed in the field.

Jesse Boot became Lord Trent in 1929, having handed over the business to his son, John Campbell Boot – a man two years older than Jack – in 1926. When Jesse died in 1931, his son became the second Lord Trent. Renowned for his love of the high life, he ran Boots as his personal empire, building a highly compartmentalised structure in which managers were forbidden to pry into the affairs of other departments.[2] With the onset of the Second World War, the company again fulfilled a vital role. Alongside their regular work, Boots employees took up civic roles as air raid wardens and first-aiders, with John Boot himself serving as the Regional Commissioner for Civil Defence for the North Midlands, even as he continued to run the company. With rationing imposed, the firm manufactured saccharin equivalent to some 700,000 tons of sugar, which was by then in short supply. It distributed educational leaflets about planting and producing food in support of the 'Dig for Victory' campaign, even sowing some 40 acres of land around its factories with vegetables to supply its staff canteens. As in the First World War, Boots was there once more to supply water sterilisation tablets and, crucially, penicillin – the new wonder drug to combat infections. Overall, it added into its roster some 30 drugs that had previously been made only in Germany. Moreover, the company built warehouses to protect supplies from bombing and refrigeration facilities to store insulin for diabetics. All of this serves as but a snapshot of what Boots contributed to the war effort, during the course of which it lost 381 members of staff and 33 shops.

For all its good work, the company took a financial pummelling. Heavily overdrawn, it ultimately required two share issues in the early 1950s to return to an even keel. While John

Boot was borderline despotic in his management style, he did retain one confidant who commanded his total faith: Roundell Cecil Palmer, 3rd Earl of Selborne. Born into the aristocracy in 1887, Selborne was always destined for a life on the political front line and became Assistant Director of the War Trade Department during the First World War. Come the Second World War he served as Minister of Economic Warfare from 1942 to 1945, in which role he oversaw attempts to disrupt Germany's economy, its food supplies and production chains. Selborne would eventually become vice-chairman of Boots in 1951, but he was a key figure in setting the company's post-war path long before then.

When he and Boot were looking for individuals to carry the faltering business forward, Jack was an obvious target: a first-rate research scientist with impeccable connections and an almost unrivalled knowledge of biochemistry and nutritional health. Here was a man with a proven track record of incisively getting to the heart of practical problems, possessing an eye for granular detail with a grasp of the big picture. Such was his reputation that his mere presence brought prestige to any project with which he was associated, not to mention attracting funding. In a fast-changing world, he might also be the bridge to connect the academic and commercial worlds like no one else.

There was another reason why Jack seemed an ideal fit. John Campbell Boot wanted to get a foothold in an increasingly important market – one with which Jack had compelling crossover. Underpinning Jack's career had been a profound understanding of the importance of food to public health. From his fundamental research into the chemistry of vitamins to his hands-on role in the development of the National Loaf and food drying technology, and on to his efforts to prevent famine in war-torn Europe, it was the thread that carried through all his labours. The two World Wars threw up ample proof of the importance of secure food lines both for health and national security. At opposite ends of the scale, the U-boat threat in the First World War had highlighted the dangers of over-dependence on imports, while the Dig for Victory campaign had hammered home the advantages of strong domestic production.

Jack was thoroughly engaged with new biochemical methods of enhancing food production but he was also well versed in the dangers threatened by weaponised biochemicals. He had written his study on the contamination of food by chemical weapons in 1937, which almost certainly drew on his experience investigating 'a biochemical problem of a somewhat unorthodox type' 23 years earlier. Then, when he set about revising that study in 1940 at the behest of the Ministry of Food, he paid visits to Porton Down – the Ministry of Defence's secretive scientific research centre in Wiltshire – where he conducted experiments and collected data on decontamination and the effects on food exposed to gas contamination.

Who better, then, to be involved in Boot's quest to establish his company as a purveyor of herbicides, pesticides and fertilisers. Boot's interest in a field he believed had massive potential for growth was longstanding, as evidenced by the firm patenting a copper-based fungicide back in 1931 to control mildew and blight in an array of crops. This was based on the 'Bordeaux mixture' of copper sulphate and slaked lime. So successful was it that the product remains on the market today. Boot then developed an experimental garden at his home in Nottingham's Lenton neighbourhood, which was operating as early as 1935. By 1945 he hoped pesticides and herbicides would be the answer to his company's economic travails. The pressure was on from the government to maximise yields from homegrown crops, and to develop the new chemicals that would dominate the marketplace. It was a priority that became even more pressing after Britain's farmers were forced to make do without rotenone, a plant-based insecticide from Malaysia, when its importation ceased after Japan's invasion of its near neighbour. Meanwhile, a study of new weedkillers and pesticides in 1943 had returned promising results, with fivefold increases in oat and wheat yields – proof for the powers-that-be that their thinking was on the right lines.

As the government concentrated on increasing the amount of land available for growing crops and increasing the yield that each acre could produce, the landscape of Britain underwent a post-war transformation. Trees were felled, hedgerows pulled up and wildflower meadows destroyed. In their place came vast fields of wheat and crops for animal fodder. Altogether, somewhere in the region of an extra 10,000 square miles of UK countryside was turned over to farming. The age of intensive agriculture had arrived; land lying fallow was regarded as land squandered and wasted. Where intensive new methods quickly compromised soil fertility, crop rotation was recommended. But the main thrust of official advice was to trust in the extensive use of pesticides, herbicides and artificial fertilisers. Farmers were compelled to change age-old mindsets or risk being left behind. Officials were increasingly heavy-handed in enforcing the use of agrochemicals, with failure to comply invoking serious punishments including confiscation of land. Chemical utopia reigned. For the companies delivering the chemicals, competition was cutthroat and relentless but the potential rewards were correspondingly huge. Corporate giants like ICI, Hoechst, Bayer, Merck, DuPont, Monsanto, the Rockefeller Company and Standard Oil slugged it out.

Jack had not, of course, found his way to Nottingham by replying to an advertisement in the newspaper or by putting himself through a robust selection process. Negotiations instead took place through back-channels. As a chemist of international repute, decorated across the continents and with pre-existing knowledge in the agrochemicals arena, Boots was determined not to miss out on him. They deployed all their natural advantages in what turned out to be a classic example of the old boy network in action. Jack was not merely a man whose name they had heard on the breeze of London – and in Selborne's case, Westminster and Whitehall – chatter. They were all personally known to one another, members of both the Savile Club and the Savage Club. It is not hard to imagine Jack, Selborne and Boot sat together in some sumptuous wood-panelled room, sipping brandy as the latter pair launched their charm offensive to persuade Jack that his future lay a little over a hundred miles north of London.

Whatever was said, it did the trick. In return, Jack was given whatever he needed. Boots developed new laboratory facilities at Lenton and at Thurgarton, just a few miles away. By 1952, the company controlled about 4,500 acres of English and Scottish farmland – a significant investment for its pesticide research programme. Yet it made virtually no effort to advertise its work in the field. On the contrary, the company seemed intent on drawing as little attention as possible to itself. Perhaps it was feared that too much talk of industrial agrochemicals would unsettle Boots's regular customers who looked to the company for the medicines that kept them and their families safe from coughs and sniffles. A scour of the corporate history and the key biographies of the Boot family reveals virtually no mention of the firm's agrochemical activities.

Nonetheless, if you dig deep enough, the telltale clues are there. Take, for instance, a brochure for an 'Industrial Fair' held at London's Olympia exhibition centre in 1947. Boots occupied stand no. A.1193, the company write-up listing its many product ranges. Tucked away in between 'Pharmaceuticals, Fine Chemicals and Veterinary Products' and 'Toiletries, Cosmetics, Industrial Chemicals, Galenicals, Potassium Permanganate and Saccharin' were 'Horticultural Products'. It is known, too, that Dr Lloyd Stocken, who conducted biochemical research out of the University of Oxford during the war and was particularly renowned for his work on the effects of chemical weapons, had gained significant experience of sulphur compounds in a previous role with Boots. In other words, agrochemicals were indubitably an important strand of the company's work.

In 1953, Boots filed three patents related to pesticides; it filed another three in 1954, and five in 1956.[3] Each of these was the result of years of research and refinement – projects that began under Jack's supervision, even if they were completed under his successor. Among Boots's biggest successes in Jack's time was the selective weedkiller MCPA (as found in the product branded Cornox), which became a major seller for the company and was highlighted in its annual report of 1950, with Jack singled out for praise.

Yet just as Boots were reluctant to promote their work in this sector to the world at large, so Jack's part in it was downplayed to the point of silence after his death. His Royal Society obituary, for one, is hazy on his role at the firm, emphasising only – briefly – his contribution to Boots's veterinary science division. A far more family-friendly division, one might think. Meanwhile, Jack's successor as scientific director at Boots, Gordon Hobday, seemed almost at pains to belittle his predecessor's efforts. He dismissively suggested Jack had been chiefly responsible for 'tropical disease research which lacked commercial potential'.[4] A future company chairman, Hobday quickly moved Boots away from such altruistic but commercially unappealing pursuits, instead focusing on medications to address the more profitable 'lifestyle' illnesses of the West like heart disease and diabetes. Eventually, he would lead the team that developed Ibuprofen.

The reasons why Boots might have wanted to be discrete about its development of agrochemicals are not difficult to fathom. The time, effort and resources required to develop a viable product were immense, commensurate with the profits to be earned from a success. Given what was at stake, secrecy was a necessary strategy to ensure competitors could not steal a march. But agrochemicals was also a shady business, where the potential medical and environmental impacts of synthesised chemicals in the food chain were only in the early stages of being understood.

There was something else too – it did not take much to turn the chemicals that could maximise crop yield and support life into weapons that spread death.

LIFE AND DEATH   16

The fear of chemical and biological weapons was a relatively new phenomenon but one that bore down heavily on Jack's world, the culmination of decades of bitter experience.

A little after eight in the evening of 30 October 1938, the American CBS radio network's programme of live music was interrupted by a breaking news bulletin. It reported evidence of unusual explosions on the planet Mars, the first of several bulletins that evening. The next relayed news of an unidentified object falling on to a farm in New Jersey. As the bulletins racked up, it became evident that some sort of alien invasion was taking place. Panic quickly gripped towns and cities across the United States, terrified mobs were said to be taking to the streets and the CBS switchboard was lighting up. Just over half an hour after the first report, a new bulletin claimed an alien gas attack on New York was under way.

These broadcasts would go down in history. There was, of course, no alien attack. Instead, this was a radio drama based on H. G. Wells's *The War of the Worlds*. The production was the brainchild of Orson Welles, who years later would attempt to document on film the real-life horrors of La Grand Terre. The bulletins that night in 1938 were a sophisticated put-up job but they played into genuine fears and vulnerabilities. The drama was fake, the terror genuine.

A year later, the British people and their government were in an elevated state of fear that chemical weapons might soon be used against them in the event of war with Germany.

This was not the result of some unfounded collective paranoia. The public was terrified because they had seen at first hand the results of poison gas within the last quarter-century. They remembered the thousands dead and the hundreds of thousands more who bore the scars – physical and mental – of being gassed. There were plenty still alive who could give their own accounts of being in Belgium at the Second Battle of Ypres in April 1915. Jean Giono, the writer who followed the Drummond case so closely, was among the First World War's gas casualties, losing his eyelids and eyebrows in an attack in 1918. In October of the same year, there was a notable Allied mustard gas attack in the Ypres Salient that resulted in multiple casualties, including a rather obnoxious corporal who was temporarily blinded as he retreated from his dugout. His name was Adolf Hitler. It does not do to impose too much amateur psychological analysis upon one of history's most wretched mass murderers, but there is a case to be made that this experience played some part in his seeming reluctance to deploy chemical weapons during the Second World War. As we shall see, Germany had potent new weapons in its chemical arsenal going into that war, and the history of the Holocaust provides devastating evidence that Hitler had no ethical objection to using gas against his fellow man. The fear that doing so might provoke his enemies to do likewise, with terrible consequences for his own side – of a type he himself had endured – appears a plausible explanation for his reticence.

The international response to the use of gas in the First World War was self-contradictory, albeit understandable. On the one hand, there was a 'Never Again' movement. Article 171 of the 1919 Treaty of Versailles took a punitive position with regard to Germany, prohibiting 'the use of asphyxiating, poisonous or other gases and all analogous liquids, materials or devices ... their manufacture and importation'. Six years later, the League of Nations organised a conference in Geneva which agreed a 'Protocol for the Prohibition of the Use of Asphyxiating, Poisonous or Other Gases, and of Bacteriological Methods of Warfare'.[1] In effect, the use of chemical and biological weapons by any country was now banned.

But there is always a gap between intention and application. With mistrust on all sides after the atrocities of 1914–18, no one wanted to be caught napping. Even as the world's nation states agreed not to utilise such weapons, they were manufactured and stockpiled at an alarming rate – the US and Germany being in the vanguard. In post-First World War Britain, Winston Churchill served variously as Minister of Munitions and Secretary of State for War. He was among those reticent about ruling out the use of such weapons altogether. In a May 1919 memorandum, he wrote:

I do not understand this squeamishness about the use of gas ... It is sheer affectation to lacerate a man with the poisonous fragment of a bursting shell and to boggle at making his eyes water by means of lachrymatory gas ... The moral effect should be so good that the loss of life should be reduced to a minimum. It is not necessary to use only the most deadly gases: gases can be used which cause great inconvenience and would spread a lively terror and yet would leave no serious permanent effects on most of those affected.

Over in Germany, Haber continued at the cutting edge of development, with his institute developing a cyanide-based insecticide, Zyklon. Come the Second World War, one particular formation, Zyklon-B, would become the notorious chemical of choice for the extermination of innocents in the Nazi death camps. By then, however, Haber was dead. He had suffered heart failure at a hotel in Basel, Switzerland, back in January 1934 as he travelled to take up a new position at a research institute in Palestine. With his Jewish heritage counting against him in Hitler's Germany, he had been forced from his beloved fatherland. As Albert Einstein would later reflect: 'Haber's life was the tragedy of the German Jew – the tragedy of unrequited love.' For several months in the early stages of his exile, he was invited to the UK to work in Cambridge by, among others, Frederick G. Donnan. A prominent physical chemist, Donnan spent most of his career at UCL, where he would have been well known to Jack Drummond. But not everyone was able to overlook Haber's dark contributions to humanity; Ernest Rutherford, the father of nuclear physics, refused to acknowledge him or shake his hand.

For all the international pledges to abstain from the use of chemical weapons, realpolitik dictated that they remained a very real threat. Little wonder that the British government approached the coming Second World War so warily, contemplating the employment of chemical weapons not just against combatants but potentially against the civilian population as well. Without a crystal ball to enable them to see that the war would pass without such deployment – a minor miracle, one might think – they were responsibly planning for the worse. As the story of Zyklon attests, the histories of agrochemicals and chemical weapons are tightly bound together. The progression from, say, a herbicide or a pesticide to a chemical weapon can be chillingly short. A herbicide kills weeds and other plants deemed a nuisance by the user; a pesticide kills insects and other organisms deemed a nuisance by the user; chemical weapons kill human beings deemed a nuisance by the user. It is simply a matter of the degree of toxicity and small changes to the chemical structure.

In broad terms, the knowledge garnered from the chemical weapons used in the First World War significantly drove the development of herbicides and pesticides in the inter-war period, which in turn informed the development of new, even more appalling chemical weapons. Two businesses feeding into and off one another – one to support human life, the other to destroy it.

In Germany in the 1930s, a young scientist called Dr Gerhard Schrader was working for IG Farben, then the world's biggest chemical company. In 1934, Schrader, still only 31 years old, was put in charge of a unit tasked with developing a pesticide to kill weevils in grain silos. He scoured the scientific literature and discovered the work of Will Langer, published in 1932 by the University of Berlin.[2] Langer had shown that a compound consisting of an organic ring of carbon with phosphorus attached had just the insect-killing properties Schrader was after. This group of chemicals were called organophosphates. Organophosphates are the most common insecticides in use today, under names including Malathion and Parathion. They are, for example, a significant element of the sheep dip that farmers use to rid their animals of irritating infestations, working by effectively uncoupling the nerve from the muscle in targeted organisms. In fact, such compounds are commonly doused by parents over the heads of their beloved children in the ongoing battle with head lice.

Around 1937, Schrader got to work on adapting and improving the structure of known organophosphates to make them even stronger. His resulting compound of cyanide and phosphorous was so potent that he almost killed himself and his team, and was disappointed when he realised that it was far too toxic to be used as an insecticide. However, some-one in IG Farben brought it to the attention of the German government, which was by then on a war footing. Mussolini had already used chemical weapons in the Italian conquest of Abyssinia (Ethiopia) back in 1935, in flagrant disregard of the Geneva Protocol. The League of Nations stood by powerless. Nobody really thought the next war would be a clean one.

Schrader continued to tinker with his compound, which was named tabun after the German for 'taboo', and evolved an even deadlier version that became known as sarin. In short order, sarin went into field trials, was fast-tracked into pro-duction and was soon being stockpiled ready for use as a weapon. But now the high command faced a dilemma. Sarin was a direct product of Schrader's survey of publicly available academic literature. If he could find it, the thinking went, then so could the Allies. And if the Germans launched an attack, they could expect the same in return. This threat proved deterrent enough to ensure that the German sarin stockpiles were left undisturbed. That was fortuitous, because in fact the Allies not only had no comparable stockpiles but had no knowledge of the weaponised compounds. They only learned of tabun and sarin during the clean-up of Europe after the war. The German soldiers driving the trucks carrying the deadly load made sure to tell the Allies to be careful, then got as far away as possible. Britain's chemical weapons planning involved only the use of old-fashioned phosgene on the nation's beaches in the event of Nazi invasion. If Hitler had so desired, he could have killed millions with the sarin he possessed, perhaps with impunity. The world had had a very close shave.

What might Jack's role have been at this intersection of agrochemicals and chemical weapons? He was in a unique position. Not only was there his research work over several decades into the impact of herbicides, pesticides and chemical weapons on crops, he was also part of the Ministry of Food team that was pushing for increased yields and therefore more and better pesticides. His biochemical knowledge would have left him in no doubt as to the uncomfortable military potential of the chemicals under development.

The centre of Britain's chemical weapons research was Porton Down, which Jack is known to have visited. One of its most positive contributions to the war effort was the development of British anti-Lewisite, or BAL, which was originally an antidote to the dreaded chemical weapon Lewisite, but later discovered to also be an effective medication to treat metal poisoning. Both Boots Fine Chemicals and ICI produced BAL in bulk in the war, although it was thankfully not needed to treat Lewisite poisoning. ICI also undertook much innovative work in organochlorines, including the development of benzene hexachloride (BHC; also called hexachlorocylohexane or HCH) used to protect grain and troops from infestation. Jack acted as a consultant for ICI throughout this period, and while there is no definitive evidence that he worked on the compound, nor is there proof that he didn't. It would certainly have been within his wheelhouse.

During his time at Boots, the company focused on developing herbicides and pesticides based on chlorine. Among its greatest successes was Cornox, in which the active ingredient was MCPA, a herbicide recently brought to market by ICI designed to kill weeds while leaving cereal crops unaffected. Jack was a man who had always advocated expansive testing to ensure the safety of such products but the race to introduce new money-spinners was such that Cornox was not subject to the sort of strength-testing that might have been expected. It was eventually taken off the market when other related herbicides were shown to contain dioxin and were linked to cancers and foetal abnormalities. The infamous Agent Orange, used with such cruelly destructive impact in the Vietnam War, is a chemical offspring of the Cornox group of herbicides.

Developing agrochemicals is not the same as developing chemical weapons, of course. But the overlap is striking. To ignore the link is to stick one's head in the sand. On 6 August 1952, when the Drummond murders were still headline news, the *Birmingham Gazette* ran a story on the case. It explained how Jack had joined Boots in 1946 and was elevated to its board of directors two years later. A spokesman for Boots confirmed that his death marked 'a very great loss to the firm and to the country'. Then the report makes a bold assertion. 'His work,' it claims, 'was "top secret" and the firm refused to comment on it.' This paints a very different picture to that subsequently presented by Boots of a man who had thrown himself into altruistic but unprofitable work in the fields of veterinary and tropical medicine. If he was involved in 'top secret' work related to the search for new chemical compounds that might directly impact on issues of national security, it would explain Boots's rather hush-hush attitude to Jack after his death.

There were curious goings-on behind the scenes, too. As soon as they got word of the killings, the management at Boots jumped into action. They immediately contacted the British Consul General in Marseilles regarding documents in the Drummonds' Hillman that they urgently wanted to retrieve. Within the week, the Consulate sent a note back to one E. L. Archer at Boots inquiring: 'I take it you were able to collect all the documents and papers you were after.' A little later, a new request from Nottingham: 'We should like to have an inventory of the car's contents so that we may know if there are any further business papers of importance to us.'

The exchange raises many questions. What was the documentation that the firm so desperately wanted back? Why was it in Jack's car anyway when he was meant to be on a family holiday? What was so important that Boots saw fit to seize what was, after all, evidence at the scene of a crime? And why were the British authorities so eager to assist a private company? About a month later, a further fascinating letter was sent to the Consul General, pressuring the staff there to hurry up and send a death certificate so that 'we are able to claim on a very substantial insurance policy which was taken out by this company on behalf of Sir Jack'. Why had the firm insured him so heavily? Was Jack involved in especially risky work? Was there an expectation, even, that something bad might very well happen to him?

THE GENTLEMAN SPY?   17

Suggestions that Jack had been some sort of spy, already doing the rounds by the time Gaston Dominici faced trial, were given little credit by most sober-minded observers. In the decades since, journalists and writers have generally assumed a default position that such stories are the preserve of cranks. Conspiratorial ramblings from those forever paranoiacally seeking some hidden agenda where the truth is too mundane for their tastes.

Conspiracy theorists have a habit of being their own worst enemies, clinging to the feeblest of evidence, manipulating fact and delivering their cases with an unsettling mix of aggression and unflinching faith. Common sense is routinely cast aside in favour of a litany of assumed facts and alleged deceptions that hold up to little scrutiny. The Bartkowski allegations are a case in point. In the end, the sensible majority reach their own conclusions, and the conspiracy theorists with their peevish insistence are left to lick their wounds. In the case of the Drummonds, the idea that their tragedy was somehow part of a wider picture of espionage and official secrecy seemed not only unbelievable but faintly obscene: as if the family's suffering weren't enough of a story in itself, it was necessary to overlay a plot more suited to a Saturday matinee or an airport crime thriller. There is much to be said for such scepticism. However, is it also possible that the desire to avoid joining the ranks of the self-deluding conspiracy theorists has blinded subsequent generations to a series of uncomfortable details about the case that warrant much closer inspection?

We might start with Roundell Palmer, the Earl of Selborne, the wartime government minister who was a key figure in Jack's appointment to Boots. As has already been noted, prominent among the conspiracy theories was that Jack was undertaking a secret mission for the SOE, perhaps involving gold or maybe delicate personal correspondence belonging to the prime minister. They are allegations so 'out there' that they are easy to dismiss. Where is the evidence trail? Of course, there is not one, so the assumption becomes that all suggestions that Jack was involved with secretive government work of any kind should be treated as risible. But then we must address the more inconvenient aspects of the presence of the Earl in the Drummonds' story, because in his role as Minister of Economic Warfare, responsibility fell to him for the running of the SOE. It was his job to be on top of what was going on in occupied Europe and to direct the organisation's covert operations. As such, he wielded significant influence on the UK's wider military strategy and had an almost unrivalled insight into the military capabilities of Europe's various combatant nations.

It is possible, with a little reframing, to now see Jack's post-war move to Boots in a different light. At first sight, it was an appointment that made good economic sense to Jack himself, even if it left many former colleagues perplexed.

They wondered how a man whose career had been built around doing important work for the public good, both in academic and governmental capacities, could content himself with surrendering his skills to the private sector on research that seemingly could never rival the impact of his earlier work. Veterinary medicines, pesticides, even searching for treatments for tropical diseases – none of it would have the immediacy of saving your country (and perhaps even an entire continent) from starvation, or the importance of conducting Nobel-level research into vitamins.

But given that Jack's appointment was facilitated by Selborne, could it not have always been intended that Jack would straddle the gap between state and commercial interests? Selborne knew him to be a safe pair of hands who understood the needs of government. An ideal fit to slot into Boots, where his scientific background would make him a gift to the agrochemicals programme, which neatly dovetailed with enriching the nation's bank of knowledge around chemical weapons. Espionage was never much about James Bond-type figures low-flying single-seater aeroplanes through perilous mountain ranges or miraculously fighting off terrifying assailants. In reality, the intelligence services would have considered a sharp-witted man with his ear to the ground, a position in the upper echelons of high commerce and a foothold in delicate international markets as being worth his weight in gold. The business world has long been an excellent natural habitat for the intelligence-gatherer. One might be forgiven for thinking that Jack's own decision to join Boots would have been quite simple if he knew it would involve ongoing service to the nation too. Lord Selborne was a man who could provide just that guarantee. Jack's association with Selborne does not of itself prove he was a government operative, but the fact that one of the nation's foremost espionage ringleaders was not only in his social circle but an important figure in his professional life is at the very least noteworthy.

The movements of Jack and his family in the days leading up to their deaths also raise a number of questions not adequately answered by an insistence that they were mere holidaymakers. Take, for instance, the choice of location outside La Grand Terre where the Drummonds chose to camp that night, halfway between the villages of Peyruis and La Brillanne on the busy N96 road that cut through the river basin from Aix-en-Provence to Grenoble. Their Hillman was parallel parked very close to the edge of the road, next to a prominent milepost, in full view of the highway where headlights would shine into the car each time a vehicle passed. A most curious setting when a space under a shady mulberry tree was available just a matter of metres away, out of sight of the road. Indeed, it is highly doubtful whether the family even planned to camp out for the night, since they had left their tent back in Villefranche.

There is something distinctly fishy about this entire leg of the trip, which began with the Drummonds retracing their steps all the way back to Digne on 4 August, having only arrived in Villefranche three days before. Having taken seven days to get to their destination from Nottingham, one might have expected them to enjoy it a little longer before embarking on another long road trip. The Hillman might have been a desirable vehicle in its day, but it was hardly the most comfortable for hour after hour, trundling along at 40 miles per hour on France's still-war-damaged roads. And for what? Ostensibly to satisfy Elizabeth's demand to watch a bullfight in Digne, one hundred miles away through the mountains.

Such events were relatively common in the region. The proximity to Spain and the long tradition of parading Camargue bulls and horses meant that there were events in virtually every village during the summer months. Even today, the long-horned black bulls, elegant white horses and Camargue cowboys (*les gardians*) can be seen careering around villages, pursued by the local youth determined to grab on to the bulls' horns as spectators gaze on, sipping local rosé or pastis. There was no need for the Drummonds to go so far out of their way, several hours' drive back to Digne. Moreover, no lesser figure than Jean Giono once described Digne's bullfight as 'extremely ugly and unattractive'. It certainly seems an odd choice of attraction for a ten-year-old girl known for her sensitivity, especially when there were more family-friendly bull-running events much closer by.

There are other curious aspects to their journey. The drive to Digne can be done in around two to three hours today, but in the Hillman in 1952, a target of four to five hours would have been more realistic. The bullfight started at 4 p.m., so a departure time of, say, 10 a.m. would have been more than adequate. In fact, the Drummonds left Villefranche at around 6 a.m. It was going to be a long day, with plenty of time to kill. Yet, the Drummonds apparently decided to drive the most direct route on this part of the journey, up the Route Napoleon. However, on the way back, they apparently took the more roundabout route via the N96 as Anne was said to dislike the more mountainous roads. That may have been the case, but it seems counterintuitive to choose a much longer journey home, late at night after what must have already been an exhausting day. Guy Marrian, the patriarch of the family the Drummonds met in Villefranche, told police that his friends enjoyed sleeping in the open air, hence they left

their tent behind on the Riviera. But then why bother clog-
ging up the Hillman's limited boot space with a tent all the
way from England in the first place if you don't intend to
make use of it?

It was widely assumed that the Drummonds were unfamiliar with the area around Lurs, first-time visitors who stumbled
upon their curious camping site. However, witnesses emerged
with testimony that hinted that their presence may have been
less a matter of chance than it appeared. A local postman,
Francis Perrin, told investigators that on the morning of
4 August, when the family were meant to be driving their
direct route to Digne, he had seen a car like their Hillman
and with British plates. It was, he said, driving carefully down
the steep road that leads from the Ganagobie plateau and the
village of Lurs to the main road by the river. Moreover, it contained three passengers – two adults and a child in the back.
The road Perrin described is indeed steep, the views from the
top panoramic. There is the old monastery up there on the
plateau and it's a great place for a picnic. It is impossible to
know for sure that the postman had spotted the Drummonds,
but there cannot have been many such vehicles in the vicinity,
and fewer still containing that composition of people. If it
wasn't the Drummonds, then it was a mighty coincidence that
such a similar group should have passed what would become,
only hours later, the murder site. And if it was Jack, Anne and
Elizabeth, then they bookended that curious day with time
in the area. For two days, Perrin sat outside the courtroom
where Gaston Dominici was tried, but he was never called to
the stand and the court never heard his evidence.

A journalist from *Paris Match* later found three other
witnesses who each claimed to have seen a family matching the description of the Drummonds and driving a car like

their Hillman. According to these witnesses, the group was camping near Lurs on the evening of 31 July or 1 August, at least three days earlier than the bullfight and when the Drummonds were meant to have been forging their way down to Villefranche from Nottingham. They slept in a tent described as being 'bell shaped' and with a central pole, while the woman of the group was said to have been wearing a black dress.[1] However, the lead was never significantly followed up after Guy Marrian convinced the British Consul General in Marseilles, E. C. Bateman, that the Drummonds' tent did not meet the description (an assertion he backed up in writing to Scotland Yard and *Paris Match*). An inventory of effects found in the Hillman after the murders also showed no black dress. There was, however, a dark skirt and blouse among the family's effects, which could certainly have been mistaken for a dress at distance. Nonetheless, the evidence was deemed too tenuous to be treated seriously.

None of these sightings can be taken as definitive proof that the Drummonds were present in the area prior to the evening of the 4th. But there is suddenly a real possibility that they had been there that morning, and perhaps three days previously too. The various witnesses were not constructing webs of obvious deceit. There is no clear reason why they should lie on these matters, and their accounts would be humdrum were it not for the fact that they may have been describing people who went on to be murder victims shortly afterwards. What if the sightings were genuine? What if Marrian had made a mistake about the tent? He had, after all, never seen it erected. It was Marrian's account that served to undermine the testimony of these several witnesses with no obvious motive to mislead. Essentially, the official thinking went that they must all have been mistaken because Marrian had the family elsewhere at the crucial times. But if they weren't mistaken after all, a picture builds of the Drummonds making a specific beeline for the area around Lurs. Did they have some pre-arranged appointment there? Or else were they scoping it out for reasons unknown?

Guy Marrian was repeatedly a source of crucial information for the original investigating team:[2] the only man who, it was thought, could reliably fill in the gaps as to the Drummonds' movements in the days before the killings and regarding what their plans had been. For Marrian, the story was very straightforward. His old friend Jack and his family had come to France to enjoy a break away, making the best of what France had to offer the discerning tourist. He was the one who confirmed that the Drummonds arrived in Villefranche on 1 August, when others claimed to have seen a family fitting their description in Lurs. It was he who told the police that Elizabeth had been eager to return to Digne for the bullfight, and he who explained they had taken a direct route to the venue and a circuitous one on the way back. He too who expounded on their love of camping beneath the stars, and who confirmed that the *Paris Match* witnesses must have been mistaken. And it was Marrian who told the police erroneously that Jack did not speak French.

Marrian was also the source of a claim that the Drummonds had opted to camp on the night they died because Elizabeth had wanted to do so. He later expanded on this, claiming that the young girl was eager to go for a midnight swim in a river. This helped explain their choice of venue so near to the Durance but there is something vaguely unsettling about the assertion. Elizabeth was a ten-year-old described by those who knew her back in the UK as of a nervous disposition. Would Jack and Anne really have agreed to take her to a setting where she could swim in a fast-flowing and treacherous river in the pitch dark, even if she had truly wanted to do so? The answer is surely not. Yet Marrian's testimony was consistently accepted at face value and helped define the Drummonds as tragic tourists, in the wrong place at the wrong time. However, as we shall soon see, Marrian made one critical claim – that Jack was unfamiliar with Lurs – that must be considered very doubtful. It might have been a genuine mistake, but if he was wrong about this, what else that he said needs closer scrutiny?

Guy Marrian, born in 1904, was thirteen years Jack's junior. When Guy was studying chemistry at UCL between 1923 and 1930 (working towards his doctorate for the latter five years), Jack became a mentor to him. The older man's infectious enthusiasm was crucial to persuading Marrian that he wanted to specialise in biochemistry and he would describe Jack's lectures as 'thrilling'. Academically strong, notably sporty and a good all-rounder, Marrian possessed qualities that appealed to Jack, who no doubt saw echoes of himself in the younger man. Marrian was eventually offered £50 per year to teach part-time at the college, and Jack sent him to Paris to undertake research into the question of whether vitamin D deficiency affected appetite and therefore exacerbated the effects of starvation. The French posting was necessary because British regulations around ethics at the time prevented several of the experiments that Marrian's team was able to undertake abroad. Meanwhile, Jack gave Marrian's wife Phyllis a job in his laboratory at UCL.

Marrian went on to become an expert in lipids and the adrenal cortex, especially oestrogen. Through Jack, he found an appointment in Toronto, Canada, but returned to the UK in 1938 – just a few days before the Munich Crisis – to take up the biochemistry chair in Edinburgh. In September 1939, he was drafted along with several other colleagues to undertake research work on a chemical weapon, a poison gas called arsine, which at the time was considered the most likely to be used by the Nazis. While he was involved in this perilous enterprise, he sent Phyllis and their two children back to Canada for safety, joining them in 1941 to work at the Suffield Chemical Warfare Station in Alberta. It was only in 1943 that Guy returned to Britain, his family following him to Edinburgh in 1944 when the risk of invasion had reduced.

Clearly, Jack and Marrian were close colleagues with overlapping interests. They discussed their respective work lives with each other, and it is evident that they would have had much to talk about in respect of Jack's work in agrochemicals and Marrian's background in chemical weaponry. But when, in the aftermath of the murders, journalists started speculating that Jack had worked for the British intelligence services, Marrian dismissed the claims out of hand. Furthermore, he insisted that the trip to the South of France was all pleasure and no work. Just two old chums bringing their families together. However, in the 2000s, author James Fergusson wrote a book about the killings called *The Vitamin Murders* and managed to track down one of Marrian's daughters. She had been in her twenties at the time of the killings and although she was reluctant to speak to Fergusson, she denied having ever met the Drummonds before that holiday, insisting the families were not close. Was this a case, then, of the two men meeting to talk shop under the pretext of a cosy family holiday?

Marrian became a key defender of Jack's reputation, deflecting suggestions that the Drummonds were anything other than innocent tourists. His evidence went untested, his assumed infallibility used to undercut the evidence of others, even though much of what he claimed could not be corroborated. Even when he changed his story to the police – as he did on several points, including over whether or not Jack had stated his intention to camp on the night of the killing, and whether or not the family had got lost for several hours on one of their drives – he was never questioned about it in court. Yet if one chooses to doubt him, then the whole edifice starts to crumble. For example, if his hearsay evidence about the Drummonds' movements is disregarded, we might decide that the weight of other evidence backs Jack's reported presence in and around Lurs over several days at the start of August 1952. If we then consider that Jack took some oddly circuitous routes between his various destinations in France, selected the most unlikely of camping spots, and made time for a powwow with an old pal from the chemical weapons business, the assumption that he was just an innocent holidaymaker starts to look rather less stable.

Among the many strange vignettes during Gaston Dominici's trial was one involving Phyllis Marrian. She accused Gaston of touting for a tip when he showed her and Guy around the murder site. The spectators in court were outraged, as was a much wider audience internationally when it was reported in the press. It was a turning point. Public opinion towards Gaston collapsed from its already precarious position. Gaston was forced to listen to many unpleasant things being said about him during the trial and for the vast majority of the time, he took it with extraordinary passivity. But Phyliss's words cut him, prompting a rare outburst. He rose to his feet and shouted that she was a liar. 'I am a good Frenchman,' he insisted in his Provençal dialect. Amid a trial replete with lies and inconsistencies, Dominici clearly felt this was a misrepresentation too far. For most of the rest of the world, though, what the Marrians said was taken as gospel. Because what on earth might they have to gain, or hide, by telling an untruth that painted the blackest picture possible of the defendant?

The evidence suggesting that Jack was in France in August 1952 not for a holiday but for some other highly secretive reason has, until now, been circumstantial. A theory etched as much in the gaps in the story as in its substance, but with some solid groundings. We can track Jack's career and say with assurance that it included stints as early as the First World War undertaking confidential work for the government. There is the public record of his research into the impact of chemical weapons on food and crops before the war, which we may safely assume continued to overlap with the research projects he oversaw at Boots – a company that subsequently conspired with the British authorities to extract papers from the murder scene as a top priority. Then there is the holiday itself, with its various puzzling aspects. That the answer to the riddle of the Drummond murders lies with the palpably unsafe conviction of an old peasant farmer who suddenly mined unheralded depths of depravity seems unsatisfactory to say the least.

When the rumours of Jack's involvement in espionage were whirling ahead of Gaston Dominici's trial, the Drummond family's solicitor – a Maître Delorme, who had been appointed by the French authorities – feared that they might spike the entire prosecution. As a safeguard, he requested from the British government an official letter to use at the trial if challenged, stating that Jack was not involved with the British intelligence services.[3] Delorme's intervention spurred a flurry of secret communications between the British government, the embassy in Paris and E. C. Bateman, the British Consul General in Marseilles. Today, in the National Archives at Kew there is a copy of the requested letter, which states: 'We have confirmed that Sir J. Drummond was never employed as an intelligence agent, and you would be quite safe in emphatically denying any story connecting him with any such activities.'

This, though, was the final version of a letter that had clearly been through several drafts.[4] An attached handwritten note in the Foreign Office file, credited to one C. G. Kemball, reveals as much. It states that 'we would rather that Meade [a government official] put nothing in writing at all but if Maître Delorme satisfies Meade that a letter on the above lines would be desirable, we do not demur'. It then suggests a rewording of the first draft of the letter, omitting the crucial words 'Il n'a jamais fait parti de l'intelligence service' ('He never worked for the intelligence service'). It is a subtle but potent adjustment, allowing for the possibility that Jack undertook work for the intelligence services without ever being formally employed to do so. However, there was an extraordinary addendum to the final draft: 'It does not appear to me conceivable that any member of the Foreign Office could put their name to such a letter.'[5]

Instead, it was suggested approaching the Ministry of Food for a 'purely formal certificate confirming Sir J. Drummond's employment with them during the war years', which is not the same thing at all. If the letter's content was truthful and not designed to mislead or misrepresent, why should there be reluctance to attach an individual official's name? On the other hand, if the letter gave an incomplete picture, disassociating it from any individual would have provided far greater scope for plausible deniability later on. As denials go, it was altogether rather mealy-mouthed and evasive. In fact, it is the kind of partial denial that only reinforces the suspicion that Jack was involved in some sort of clandestine intelligence work after all.

There is, in addition, a very brief entry in the *London Gazette*, that official outlet for all government and military announcements, dated 26 April 1949.[6] Under staff movements at the Admiralty, it notes that as of 1 March, J. C. Drummond was removed from the list as Honorary Commander of the Royal Naval Reserve. Unmentioned in any biographical profile, it turns out that Jack held a senior commissioned officer rank within the RNR. It was a position with some heritage too. One rank below Commander is Lieutenant Commander, the most famous holder of the office being a fictional character: the secret agent James Bond. The title was bestowed upon him by his creator, Ian Fleming, who himself held the same rank when he worked in Admiralty intelligence from 1939. Why might Jack have been granted a rank superior to even Fleming? If it was a purely honorary title, why was he given it, why was more not made of the honour, and why was it withdrawn? Moreover, why the RNR, when Jack's military associations were with the army? He certainly didn't receive any training to prepare him for life on a ship, in port or with the Coastguard, as other members of the RNR customarily did. But he would undoubtedly have been a useful asset alongside Fleming *et al.* in naval intelligence. The lack of transparency and public acknowledgement around the posting leads one to suspect that this is the most likely explanation for his appointment. Moreover, it turned out that he already had a close contact within the organisation, as we will soon see. Such a posting would, one might think, have made it viable for Jack to undertake foreign intelligence operations for, say MI6, while never being specifically within the employ of that organisation. In other words, as could be inferred from the Foreign Office's weasel-worded note, it was possible that Jack was used as a secret agent without being employed as one, just as it is possible to give someone a lift in your car without being employed as their chauffeur.

This official unwillingness to talk about Jack in the round is evident even in his obituaries. The official journal of his first scientific family, the Biochemical Society, declined to publish one at all, despite Jack's enormous contribution to its history as a multi-term president and secretary.[7] What, the question lingers, was the cause of their reluctance to celebrate him? Was it because of what could not be said about him? Of what they wished to remain hidden?

The most significant obituary, as we have seen, was thus written by F. G. Young on behalf of the Royal Society, a club of which Jack had been a largely unenthusiastic member. Although extensive and well-crafted, the obituary nonetheless contained a number of errors. This perhaps reflected Young's reliance on information from Jack's old scientific colleagues, some of whom had been professional rivals. But Young also found his path blocked repeatedly when he turned to the authorities for greater background detail. In one missive, he wrote:

> I know from my personal contacts with him during the war that he made very many visits abroad on most confidential matters, but although they were undoubtedly highly confidential at the time, it would be very valuable to give some general outline of his activities in this connection since it was in part his great ability to get on with all types of people that made him such a valuable international catalyst at this time.[8]

Young repeatedly pressed for information but he did not get an answer, at least not one that he felt able to put into print. There was a flurry of official correspondence preceding publication in November 1954,[9] with strong indications that Young had knowledge of Jack that he was being pressured not to publish. As he noted in one letter: 'I do not think that any of the information given could now be held to transgress the Official Secrets Act.'

Jack's legacy was at this point in the hands of an officialdom that was evidently determined to keep significant elements of his life away from public view.

THE TRANSATLANTIC CONNECTION

18

Jack, as we know, was a cultured man. Food and drink, theatre and travel – these were a few of the things that gave his life structure away from the research lab and the lecture theatre. But travel was part of his day job too, seeing him venture to the continent and beyond, far and frequently. He was notably skilled as a linguist, speaking French and Spanish, along with some Russian and German. Ahead of a trip to the Soviet Union in 1936, his preparation not only included language lessons but extended to eating in Russian restaurants and immersing himself in Russian music, ballet and literature. He undertook a similar cultural deep-dive ahead of a trip to Spain just prior to that country's brutal civil war.

While a professor at UCL in the 1930s, he and Mabel enjoyed a high standard of living as stalwarts of the London arts and social scene – a position no doubt easier to uphold in the absence of children. Nonetheless, it must have been a challenge to maintain their high-rolling on only Jack's salary of approximately £1,000 per year (equivalent to about £42,000 today). As far as records show, Mabel did not have an income of her own, coming from that generation where wives routinely didn't work unless family finances absolutely decreed it – a shame as she was obviously a talented chemist in her own right. Yet we know that Jack travelled to the USA by cruise liner at least nine times between 1924 and 1935, spending up to two months away each time. Surviving records reveal he made a trip each year in that period except for 1926 and 1932, with Mabel accompanying him on most of them. Either UCL had an unfeasibly generous attitude to supporting faculty and their spouses on foreign trips, or the Drummonds had alternative means of finance.

Nor did Jack ever settle for cattle class. The records show that he always either travelled first class or cabin class.[1] Mostly he went with the Cunard Line and on later trips indulged in the unfettered opulence of first-class travel on board the *Queen Elizabeth* and *Queen Mary*. Although several of his earlier trips were taken during the summer months, when his university responsibilities were at their lightest, in 1928, 1933 and 1934 he went in the springtime, when presumably his students were embarking on their most intensely busy stretches of the academic year. Exactly how much each trip cost is difficult to assess, but an adult one-way fare would have been around the 40-guinea mark (a guinea having been worth a pound and a shilling, and a measure of currency typically used for pricing up luxury items). Today, that 40 guineas equates to around £3,000. In other words, a return trip for a couple (and Elizabeth also travelled with the Drummonds in later years) would have cost the equivalent of £12,000. Factor in additional travel expenses for a six- to sixteen-week stay and the bill would have eaten up most of Jack's annual UCL income if he had to stump up for it himself.

New York was his most frequent destination, a city beset by economic depression in the 1930s (and one where Jack could not even hope to get a decent glass of something stiff before the end of Prohibition in 1933). Ethel Merman, America's powerhouse singing sensation, boasted she could hold a note longer than the Chase Manhattan Bank – a fact she attempted to prove by maintaining a high C across sixteen bars of the Gershwin classic 'I got Rhythm'. New York was still the Big Apple, wonderful and exciting and vibrant, but these were bleak times. Yet something kept drawing Jack back. Nor did the rate of his visits subside with the onset of war. As Lord Woolton recalled in his memoirs,[2] and as was reiterated in the Royal Society's obituary, Jack made 'many transatlantic visits' to organise the flow of food supplies resulting from the Lend-Lease Act and to vet claims of food innovations, as well as being present at Hot Springs in 1943 for the conference that laid the foundations for the UN and the Food and Agriculture Organisation. There were a further three documented post-war trips as well, in 1945, 1949 and 1951. The middle one of these saw Elizabeth join her parents on a luxurious voyage that must have made her feel like a princess. The 1951 trip lasted fully four months. Every time, Jack's itinerary involved a stint in New York.

We know that in 1942, Jack took flights to New York that were paid for by the Rockefeller Foundation. Once there, he met with Wilbur A. Sawyer, one of the Foundation's officials. A note survives in the Foundation's files in which Jack thanks the 'RF' for its hospitality and the kindness shown to him.[3] In return, he offers to 'look after' two scientists employed by the Foundation who were due to come to the UK: Virgil P. Sydenstricker and Arnold Peter Meiklejohn. Sydenstricker, born in 1889, was charged with developing nutritionally sound war rations for American troops, while Meiklejohn, a Briton twenty years Sydenstricker's junior, would go on to become a nutritional adviser to the United Nations Relief and Rehabilitation Administration. Both subsequently worked alongside Jack Drummond in trying to save the lives of the starving survivors of the Belsen concentration camp.

This 1942 trip was by no means Jack's first interaction with the Rockefeller Foundation, which had been founded in the city in 1913. It was the creation of the Standard Oil magnate John D. Rockefeller – along with his son John Jr and their business colleague Frederick Taylor Gates. Rockefeller Sr's father had been a travelling snake-oil salesman who was variously accused of rape, burglary, arson, counterfeiting and, over a period of 34 years, bigamy. His mother, though, taught him the values of hard work, saving and giving. John certainly threw himself into his labours, although he also displayed streaks of his father's callousness. Having originally made money selling whisky at inflated prices to Federal soldiers, he invested heavily in the then-emerging oil industry. By 1880, within a decade of its foundation, his Standard Oil Company had a virtual monopoly on refining in the US and controlled 60 per cent of the world's oil supply. In 1911, the authorities demanded the break-up of the company into many smaller ones in a bid to curb its anti-competitive antics, but the dissolution only swelled Rockefeller's personal wealth. The first dollar billionaire, he accumulated a fortune frequently reckoned to be the largest of any individual in modern history. The Foundation was his grand philanthropic gesture, of the type popular in the American Gilded Age.

Rockefeller had already founded an eponymous Institute for Medical Research in New York in 1901, and an associated hospital opened in 1910. It is possible these projects were driven by personal tragedy, his grandson having died in 1901 from scarlet fever. The institute's Biomedical Research

Centre concentrated on studying those infectious diseases then considered the greatest threats to human health, and there were early and dramatic successes in combating meningitis, syphilis, sleeping sickness, hookworm and yellow fever. Causal links between particular cancers and viruses were also made, and Oswald Avery, who joined the institute in 1913, led efforts to develop the first pneumonia vaccine. In 1944, Avery would enjoy his greatest success as part of the team that identified for the first time the substance that transmits hereditary information in living organisms: DNA.

But that was all some way ahead. Back in 1910, Rockefeller Sr was said to have been deeply affected after reading a report on the quality of teaching for American and Canadian doctors. Its author was Abraham Flexner, brother of the first director of the Rockefeller Institute, Simon Flexner. Its conclusions about the appalling state of medical education in America was one of the stimuli which led Rockefeller to set up the Foundation three years later. He wanted to fundamentally reform the bank of medical knowledge at home and abroad, so medical research and public health became key pillars of the new Foundation's remit. Its first grant of $100,000 was given to the American Red Cross before 1913 was out. More money flowed to found the Johns Hopkins School of Public Health, Harvard's School of Public Health and Toronto University's School of Hygiene, and there was financial support for many other institutions and public health programmes. Staff at the Foundation routinely crossed over with the Rockefeller Institute for Medical Research, and the organisation's international reach was extended across continents through an International Health Division, which provided help, for instance, to build new medical centres in Peking and Brussels. It was not long before Rockefeller's eyes fell upon London.

London represented an obvious home for his investment, since it lay at the heart of what was then still a vast empire. The London School of Hygiene and Tropical Medicine, a world leader in tropical disease research as it trained doctors to treat administrators and military personnel in tropical outposts of the British Empire, was the first UK recipient of a grant in 1914. It allowed the school to move to new central London premises by 1920. But it was the next recipient that was of rather more relevance to Jack.

In 1919, Jack faced a career crossroads that saw him opt to take a position at UCL, where he quickly rose through the ranks to become a professor in August 1922. His salary in this latter post was a generous £500 per year to begin with, which doubled within two years so that he was getting more than many older colleagues. In terms of the population at large, the average salary for a man at this time was £200 per year, and slightly less than half that for a woman (numbers that rose only by a small proportion in the following two decades). Jack was thus relatively well enumerated but, nevertheless, had some foreboding about the college's economic circumstances. 'I am greatly looking forward to working with Starling and Bayliss [Ernest Starling and William Bayliss, renowned physiologists],' he wrote, 'and I have great hopes of getting a school of Biochemistry going there. There is also the attraction of academic circles. My only pessimistic moments are when I think of the penniless condition of the College to which I am going.'

It is likely Jack was being a little disingenuous, since he almost certainly knew that UCL was already in discussions with the Rockefeller Foundation. They were negotiating a deal to fund a state-of-the-art laboratory for the department of biochemistry within physiology, and for the Foundation to put up the money for a new professorial chair and to pay the associated staff. Vast sums of money were in play. The Rockefeller 1920 annual report discusses 'the drawing up of agreements looking toward Foundation co-operation ... making a total from the Foundation of approximately $4,000,000 toward the entire plan of development'. That $4 million is worth over $50 million today. The Rockefeller annual report of 1923 was able to celebrate the fruits of this investment, with photos of King George V and Queen Mary opening the new buildings on 31 May 1923.[4] In the same year, the physiology department at Oxford University was also provided with funding, allowing it to move from three small rooms to a new building fitted out with the latest scientific mod cons. At the time, the department was led by Rudolph Peters – later Sir Rudolph – a chemical weapons expert whose achievements included the development of British anti-Lewisite.

UCL's records from this time are scant, mostly destroyed by fire in 1941 after its archives took a direct hit during the Blitz. But among those documents that were salvaged are the personal record cards for Jack covering the years 1919 to 1924. In each case, the accounting column is overwritten in red ink with payments received from the Rockefeller Foundation to cover part of Jack's salary.[5] Because of the fire damage, it's impossible to say how long this arrangement continued, although a document in the Rockefeller Institute's own files shows a payment was made to Jack during his employment at Boots, suggesting some level of sponsorship throughout his career. Once he was installed at UCL in the 1920s, he set about building his department with the help of the Rockefeller coffers. His first appointment was Charles Harington, who came with a degree from Cambridge University and a PhD from Edinburgh. Jack promptly sent him to the Rockefeller

Institute in New York to study with D. D. Van Slyke (chief chemist at the Rockefeller Hospital), before he returned to UCL and became a professor on his way to serving as director of the National Institute for Medical Research in the 1940s. Today, Harington is best known for synthesising thyroxine, the thyroid hormone.

Another interesting appointment of Jack's was Bernard Katz in 1935. Katz, who would eventually be knighted, was a young physiologist who left Germany after Hitler came to power, on account of his family's Russian-Jewish heritage. He specialised in the biochemistry of nerves and once noted: 'It is my belief that in the near future this research on chemical transmission will lead to a better understanding of the intimate nature of mental disease and psychical disturbances.' His studies of organophosphate compounds and their effect on the nerves informed the development of various nerve gases and emerging pesticide compounds. His appointment at UCL was strongly supported by the head of its physiology department, the Nobel laureate Professor A. V. Hill, who went on to serve as a wartime cabinet scientific adviser under Winston Churchill. Intriguingly, though, there exists a memo from the Rockefeller Foundation to Jack, thanking him for making the appointment and suggesting that it made the process easier for the Foundation to approve a grant that Jack had applied for.[6] They had clearly wanted to get their man into the post.

A year after he employed Katz, Jack undertook a tour of Europe, ostensibly learning about the nutritional scene across the continent through visits to laboratories and other institutions in Holland, Germany, Czechoslovakia, Austria, Hungary, Yugoslavia, Switzerland, Poland, Russia and Finland. It was a mammoth undertaking, lasting from January to May, at a moment when Europe was already lapsing into disarray. Fascism was installed in Germany and Italy, Spain was on the brink of civil war, Russia was about to embark on its Great Terror, all played out against the backdrop of the Great Depression. Despite these inhospitable conditions, Jack ventured on – and the entire enterprise was funded by the Rockefeller Foundation.

The first documentation relating to the tour is correspondence dating to late 1934, when the head of the Foundation's European office, Daniel P. O'Brian, wrote to Alan Gregg, who was then the director of its Medical Sciences Division and would later become the Foundation's vice-president.[7] O'Brian suggested a 'critical survey' of the field of nutrition in Europe that would 'afford interesting possibilities', and Gregg urged him to sound Jack out about the project. He was, they concurred, the perfect man for the job. Another memo between these two powerhouses of the Rockefeller Foundation reveals that their principal research interest lay in the interaction between nutrition, the nervous system and mental disease. It was therefore decided that the money to fund the study should come from the budget of its psychiatry programme, rather than that of the medical sciences (which didn't work in the field of nutrition). Jack was duly wined and dined and promised ongoing financial support as he agreed to the grand tour, for which the Foundation awarded him a special short fellowship. According to the Foundation's own paperwork:

> The Fellowship Programme was to allow D to make personal contact with scientists in the field of nutrition in Continental Europe in order to have an opportunity to form an opinion of the direction and potentialities in the different centres. Fifteen countries including the USSR will be visited.

He will prepare an account of his impressions and findings which should prove valuable to RF officers in their consideration of projects in the field of nutrition ... This will get League sponsorship for the nutritional survey, including its economical, sociological and political aspects. It was judged that there was no conflict between this special study and the general plan.

It is to be assumed that the 'League' referred to is the League of Nations, the forerunner of the UN, established in 1920 in a bid to hold peace together after the First World War. Although the US was never itself a member, the Rockefeller Foundation afforded the League major financial support from the outset and maintained a long-term commitment, as evidenced by the Rockefellers' role in later deciding where the headquarters of the successor UN would be. Amid fierce competition between nations and individual cities to host it, New York won after John D. Rockefeller Jr bought and donated an eighteen-acre site on the East River at a cost of some $8.5 million. Ahead of Jack's 1936 trip, it is not clear what conflict there might have been between the so-called 'general plan' and a simple nutritional survey. Regardless, and despite the political turmoil consuming the continent, Jack set out and engaged with scientists across a great sweep of Europe, giving him unique insights that the Foundation was able to mine.

So what if Jack was closely aligned with the Rockefeller Foundation? Its impressive philanthropic contributions were hard to argue with. Yet the story is not quite so simple as that. While there can be no doubting the much good that the Foundation was responsible for, it was not an unequivocally benevolent picture. In particular, delving into its activities in the fields of psychology and psychiatry (particularly relevant given the funding source for Jack's 1936 trip) unearths certain grounds for disquiet.

In 1930, David Edsall, the dean of Harvard's Medical School, reported to the Rockefeller Foundation trustees: 'Psychiatry now is dominated by elusive and inexact methods of study and by speculative thought ...' This was bad news for the Foundation, which sought to restore the discipline to respectability, convinced that it held the key to social progress on many levels. As was noted in its annual report of 1932:

> Special attention has been given to the field of psychiatry ... How badly needed is knowledge in this field may be inferred from the economic, moral, social and spiritual losses occasioned by the criminally insane, the delinquents, the feeble minded, the emotionally unstable, and the psychopathic, and the widespread but preventable anxieties, tantrums, phobias, complexes and unbalanced behaviour of otherwise normal human beings. Stress is therefore needed on studies throwing more light on the function of the nervous system, the role of internal secretions, the factors of heredity, the diseases affecting the mental and physical phenomena, and in general the whole field of psychobiology.

Back in 1904, Ida Tarbell had published *The History of the Standard Oil Company*,[8] laying bare shocking discoveries about Standard Oil and casting Rockefeller Sr as a ruthless tyrant. Rehabilitating the family name became a priority and it was a process that had to be embarked on again when, in 1914, John D. Rockefeller Jr was castigated for his role in what became known as the Ludlow Massacre. Twenty-one men, women and children were killed in Colorado after the National Guard opened fire with machine guns on unarmed striking miners and their families at one of the Rockefellers' mines. Aside from any philanthropic considerations, the dynasty had a profound interest in understanding the psychology of the public and how its mood and thoughts might be influenced and manipulated.[9,10] A skill notably useful to those with political aspirations.

In its bid to better understand the human mind, the Foundation spared little effort and expense. In the 1920s, it created the Medical Sciences Division, first under the leadership of Richard Pearce until 1930, and then Alan Gregg. It was effectively a psychiatry division, channelling the Foundation's funding and research in this area. Analysis of its annual reports from as early as 1920 until the 1940s shows that the Foundation donated to virtually every major institute and research centre involved in psychiatry around the world. By 1946, in Britain alone it had funded psychiatry-related research at UCL, the Maudsley, the Tavistock Clinic and the Universities of Bristol, Cambridge and Edinburgh, as well as giving funding to the Medical Research Council.

Most disquieting of all was the Foundation's support for studies into the now discredited field of eugenics, which seeks to select desirable heritable characteristics to 'improve' future generations, particularly with regard to humans. Its godfather was the English polymath Francis Galton,[11] who in 1904 established a laboratory at UCL, making it the first British university to officially study eugenics. In due course, his work was recognised and supported by the Rockefeller Foundation, which rated highly his statistical analysis of experimentation on everything from human twins to sweet peas, concluding that the evidence supported the greater influence of nature over nurture.

This played into the hands of politically motivated figures on both the left and the right who manipulated the idea that there existed social hierarchies in which particular groups had inherent characteristics. In Britain, for example, the Mental Deficiency Act of 1913 identified people who were 'mentally or morally defective' and legally prevented them from having children. Galton's ideas gained enormous traction, including in the United States, where they were used to support policies of racial segregation and enforced sterilisation. According to John Foster Dulles, a trustee of the Rockefeller Foundation and Secretary of State under President Eisenhower from 1953 to 1959, eugenics was the means by which it would become possible to 'eliminate the weakest members of the population'. Over in Nazi Germany, Galton's work was ultimately hijacked to provide a justification for the Holocaust. The sad truth was that corporate philanthropists like Rockefeller were supporting scientists and officials who perverted the results of their studies to justify political actions.

In the financial year 1928–9, for instance, the Foundation released a grant of $317,000 to build and support the Kaiser Wilhelm Institute for Eugenics Anthropology and Human Heredity in Berlin. This was a laboratory that employed the notorious Dr Josef Mengele before his wartime transfer to Auschwitz, and where there was a particular focus on experimentation on twins, as well as on schizophrenics. From the mid-1920s to the mid-1930s, the Foundation spent millions funding German scientists and continued to do so even as the evidence built that Hitler was using their work to justify his mistreatment of the Jews and other social groups deemed 'defective'. Even after the Second World War, when the atrocities of the Holocaust and the horror of the so-called eugenics research conducted by Mengele at Auschwitz came to light, the Foundation continued its support in the discipline, granting over $20,000 to the Galton Laboratory at UCL in 1946.

There was never a suggestion that Jack's research strayed over into eugenics, but it is notable that he was being funded from a pot of money that did also go in that direction. Moreover, in broader terms, he was attached to an organisation that enjoyed significant sway domestically and internationally, while itself having relatively little accountability. Its reach was extraordinary and its influence inevitably extended beyond public health and into the spheres of politics and public affairs. Aside from its hefty influence on the creation and direction of both the League of Nations and the United Nations, it wielded softer influence too. In the 1930s and 40s, the Foundation was an important funder of research into propaganda and psychological warfare (Orson Welles' *War of the Worlds* providing researchers with a brilliant case study in mass persuasion and panic). In 1954, with the Cold War in full swing, John D. Rockefeller Jr's son Nelson was appointed by Dwight Eisenhower as Special Assistant to the President for Foreign Affairs. His job was to advise on how different government departments could counter threats posed by the Soviet Union, and he quickly earned the nickname Special Assistant to the President for Psychological Warfare. In due course, Nelson Rockefeller would serve as both the Republican Governor of New York and as Vice President to Gerald Ford in the 1970s.

On the one hand, it is possible to marvel at the way the organisation helped mould the global landscape in the twentieth century. On the other, one can ponder whether it had too much influence for a non-democratically elected organisation. Regardless, it is clear that Jack not only had a long-lived association with the Rockefeller Foundation, he relied to some extent on its generosity to bankroll his life's work. Jack remained in receipt of the Foundation's money even after he resigned from UCL in 1945. Furthermore, it gave him access to America's corridors of power. If his regular visits to the US over a period of decades are anything to go by, these were corridors down which he frequently trod. There is nothing to suggest that Jack had any involvement in the shadier work of the Rockefeller Foundation – no link to eugenics, nor to its programmes of psychological and psychiatric research, even if data from his 1936 European trip might have been made use of in this direction. But merely by being in its pay, Jack was in a vulnerable position.

His association with the Rockefellers was always downplayed, warranting barely more than a passing mention in his obituaries and hardly referred to elsewhere in the public record. That is strange considering it made him a 'player' on both sides of the Atlantic, a man with an unrivalled network of contacts to go with his unique stock of knowledge. Factors that made him perhaps as valuable an asset in New York and Washington as he was in Nottingham and London. But just how valuable?

THANK YOU FROM WASHINGTON

19

On 15 January 1948, Jack arrived at the American ambassador's residence in London, wearing his smartest suit and tie. A short while later, Colonel Ernest Bomar, the military attaché, presented him with the US Medal of Freedom (with silver palm). This was a major accolade, to stand alongside his knighthood, his share of the Lasker Prize and the many other international honours that had come his way in the years prior. The Medal of Freedom had been inaugurated by President Truman in July 1945 as a means of honouring civilians who had performed 'an especially meritorious contribution to the security or national interests of the United States' during the Second World War.[1] It could be awarded by any of the Secretary of State, the Secretary of Defence (previously War), or one of the Secretaries of the Army, Navy or Air Force, although eventually John F. Kennedy would reconfigure it as a presidential award and the highest civilian honour the nation could give.

Squirrelled away in the archives of University College London is a shabby box containing eleven of Jack's awards and decorations. Several of them are in their own red or black leather cases, and a few are wrapped only in the delicate brown paper that dates to 1952 when they were originally put into storage. Sitting proudly among them is the Medal of Freedom with its silver palm (it could also be bestowed with bronze or gold palm, or none at all). According to the Orders and Medal Society of America,[2] the type of palm associated with the honour directly correlated to the number of Americans or Allies rescued thanks to the actions of the recipient. If the recipient's actions involved the rescue of up to 15 Allies, there was no palm; between 16 and 35 warranted bronze; 36–75 silver; and more than 75, gold. Overall, from some 5,300 medals bestowed, only about 350 came with a silver palm and just 79 with gold. In the period 1945–50, very few medals were given, no more than five each year, a fact that emphasised their prestige, but even when they were awarded more regularly in the late 1950s, they retained great kudos. There is, however, no citation attached to Jack's medal in the UCL archives to provide background on why his was awarded.

Tracking down the reasons proved a feat of detective work. A thorough search of the OMSA archive returned no reference to Jack, although the organisation asserts that the medal was issued primarily to those who assisted Allied soldiers in escaping or avoiding capture by the enemy, and for 'underground operations in the interest of security of the United States'. The publicly held Harry S. Truman Papers provide information on early recipients,[3] listing all the awardees from 1945, 1946, 1947 and 1949 (with between two and five recipients in each of these years) but unhelpfully it has no information for 1948, nor any explanation as to why this is the case. The page for that year is simply blank. For 1949, the information returns, with details of four awards, of which three went to women active in the French Resistance and responsible for saving hundreds of lives. An indication, at least, of the calibre of recipients.

Perhaps a scour of the National Archives would prove more fruitful. Surely the *London Gazette* would record the accolade among its lists of awards, honours and military medals granted to UK citizens. After many hours scrolling through fragile and imperfect microfiche films, a picture eventually emerged of the British recipients. Most striking was their seemingly small number. The *Gazette* contains only thirteen verifiable reports of Britons receiving the silver-palmed version of the medal between 1946 and 1952, and only one recipient getting the golden palm.[4] Of the legible records, all citations involved 'underground' or 'intelligence' activities. Jack Drummond is again not mentioned.

The first non-American recipient was a British citizen, Sir William Samuel Stephenson, who received his medal with gold palm in 1946. A colourful character with the wartime intelligence, codename 'Intrepid', the Canadian-born Stephenson was perhaps the most senior and influential British intelligence agent in the Second World War. After a distinguished career in the First World War, he enjoyed a stellar business career between the wars and became a close confidant of Churchill. In 1940, as newly appointed Prime Minister, Churchill posted him to the US under the guise of a British passport control officer. His real task was to covertly set up the British Security Coordination (BSC) service, an organisation that represented MI5, the SIS (now MI6), the SOE and the Political Warfare Executive, and which was active in North America, South America and the Caribbean. His base of operations was a room in the Rockefeller Centre, from where he soon rose to become the most important British intelligence figure in the western hemisphere. His contributions included establishing, on Canadian soil, Camp X, a base for training some 2,000 covert agents who went on to serve in all the major theatres of the war. Additionally, he was instrumental in the creation of the Office of Strategic Services (OSS; the body that would become the Central Intelligence Agency, or CIA), and persuaded President Roosevelt to install his old friend William J. 'Wild Bill' Donovan at its head. The OSS forged a close alliance with its British and Canadian counterparts during the war. Stephenson is also credited with playing a major role in propagandising the conflict, shifting American public opinion from a neutral position in 1940 to a pro-war one by the end of 1941. As Ian Fleming commented in 1962: 'James Bond is a highly romanticised version of a true spy. The real thing is ... William Stephenson.' The Bond novel *Goldfinger* is said to be based on a real (although never put into practice) Stephenson scheme to steal nearly $3 billion in Vichy gold reserves.

One year after Stephenson received his Medal of Freedom and before Jack got his, Francis Cammaerts was awarded the same honour, with silver palm. The only British recipient that year, he is a figure with whom we are already familiar as the SOE leader of the French Resistance network that crisscrossed the left bank of the Rhône and took in the territory where the Drummonds met their end. It is further evidence of the prestige of the award, and that Jack was in the company of some of the most courageous and daring men on the planet, often involved in work of the most secretive type. It is curious, then, that there is so little in the official record to explain Jack's award. But hidden away in a report issued by Boots in 1948, an answer presents itself. Introducing Jack as a new director, the piece – less than a page long – notes his recent award, and quotes the official citation (which remains elusive) in stating that the award was made for 'exceptionally meritorious achievement which aided the US in the prosecution of the war against the enemy in Europe'. While serving as scientific adviser to the Ministry of Food:

> He rendered outstanding service by his unusual professional knowledge and ability, his excellent scientific training, keen understanding, and respect for the important problems existing with regard to the nutritional status of the civilian population of North-West Europe.
>
> He further contributed to the general plans of operation by his splendid co-operation, interest, and assistance, which cemented the relationships of British, French, and American public health officials, and made possible the achievement of the well co-ordinated programme of mutual understanding and accomplishment, thereby meriting the praise and recognition of the United States.[5]

The mystery is solved. Or is it? Although the magnitude of Jack's contribution to the war effort from the viewpoint of nutrition cannot be overstated, the citation fails to satisfy in certain respects. Assuming the report accurately quotes the official citation (despite the difficulties in corroborating this), the stated reasons seem off-kilter with those of, for example, Stephenson and Cammaerts. Jack's work around nutrition was already well celebrated, not least by the Americans, who had acknowledged it through the award of the Lasker Prize. But accepting that the US government was intent on recognising him separately, if it was for his contribution to keeping millions well fed and nourished, surely the medal should have come with a gold palm in accordance with the 'lives saved' protocol described by OMSA. This raises the possibility that his expertise around the 'nutritional status of the civilian population of North-West Europe' was merely a convenient cover story to attach to the award. The question arises: if this was a medal customarily bestowed to acknowledge significant 'underground operations in the interest of security of the United States', might Jack's have been given for reasons other than those stated in the Boots report?

Such a suggestion might seem preposterous were it not for the wealth of circumstantial evidence that exists to indicate Jack's involvement in covert activities. As already explored, there is copious evidence pointing to him discreetly providing the government with intelligence on chemical weaponry. We know too of his close ties to the US via the Rockefeller Foundation, which in turn had the ear of Washington. If he were undertaking clandestine activities for the British authorities, it does not take much of a stretch to contemplate that he extended his services to the mother country's greatest ally too. It would place Jack's award into a neat chain of association. Stephenson, the previous year's British recipient, famously based himself in a Rockefeller property. The following year's recipient, Cammaerts, made his name directing operations in the very territories where Jack would soon be killed. But if Jack was working for the Americans as well as the British, what might he have been doing?

The most obvious answer is that – just as he did with the British – he shared his knowledge, expertise and insights into the development of chemical weapons. Given his governmental and commercial associations, his freedom to travel widely across the continents and his extensive network of contacts (built with British and US assistance), he was perhaps unrivalled in his ability to deliver valuable intelligence in this area. But there is another intriguing possibility that could have similarly made use of these attributes.

Towards the end of the war, when the Allies had gained the upper hand in Europe and Hitler's demise was all but assured, the Americans and the British set their minds to a knotty problem: what to do about the army of skilled scientists who had given their efforts to the Nazi cause? Among them were some of the elite minds on the planet, the sort of intellectual heavyweights who could mastermind weapons like the V2 rocket – a totem of both terror and engineering brilliance. The Allies feared such assets slipping out of Allied-occupied zones before they could be rounded up, free instead to offer their services to the highest bidder. In particular, there was concern that German scientists would shift allegiance to the Japanese, so prolonging the war in the Pacific. But Washington and London (not to mention Moscow and Paris) also realised there was much to be gained if all that cerebral talent could be harnessed to the Allies' cause.

From February 1945, the Supreme Headquarters Allied Expeditionary Force (SHAEF) established a section devoted to analysing thousands of scientists who were working or had worked for the Axis powers, pinpointing those who posed most danger – and equally, most potential benefit. There was an emphasis on those working in the aeronautic and nuclear fields, but the list of targets extended to chemical and biological weapons, ballistics, electronics, photo optics, medicine and many other scientific branches besides.

In July that year, the Americans put Operation Overcast into action, extracting target scientists and their families. They were initially housed at a camp in Bavaria, before being transported out of Europe and over to the United States. When the operation codename leaked to the public in the coming months, it was redesignated as Operation Paperclip – a wry nod to the clips attached to the files of particular individuals identified for extraction. The programme received official White House approval from President Truman in September 1946 and over the course of the 1940s and 1950s, somewhere between 1,500 and 2,000 scientists, engineers and technicians made the journey from occupied Europe to America.

While the initial motives had been to shorten the war in the Pacific and to benefit America's post-war research programmes, the speedy onset of the Cold War added a new dimension. The US, UK and USSR had rubbed along well enough when faced with a common enemy, but now the divisions between East and West were coming to the fore. Paperclip evolved into a race to deprive Moscow of the scientific talent the Americans feared might ultimately swing the direction of the Cold War. The competition was intense. On the Soviet side, over 2,000 German scientists were forcibly recruited in a single night in 1946. But although the Kremlin picked up many highly rated brains, the Americans arguably emerged with the crème de la crème. Perhaps none came to be more famous than the German aerospace scientist Wernher von Braun, one of the creators of the V2, who was among the first to reach the US as part of Paperclip and subsequently helped NASA win the race to land a man on the Moon. In 1969, the year that Neil Armstrong took a giant leap for mankind, von Braun was one of four former Nazis brought to America by Paperclip to receive NASA's Distinguished Service Medal, its highest award.

Britain's version of Paperclip was called Operation Matchbox and helped the UK acquire over 500 scientists, while Canada and Australia also received personnel via the UK. Secrecy was a vital component of these operations. The governments in each of the participating countries knew that the general public would struggle to stomach employing those who had been active in the German war machine, including some involved in war crimes such as the use of slave labour and the practice of abusive experimentation on concentration camp prisoners. Then there were the crimes that might have been. In 1943 the Allies captured a chemist in Tunisia who had previously been employed at a nerve agent laboratory at Spandau in Berlin. He gave his captors a comprehensive overview of the Axis powers' chemical and biological weapons programmes that was so nightmarish that the overseeing British intelligence officer decided his evidence should be categorised as science fiction. Only after the war did the Allies discover the proof that Germany had developed two new deadly substances, tabun and sarin (as described in an earlier chapter), mass-producing them in a factory near Dyhernfurth (now Brzeg Dolny) in Poland, and loading them into bombs and shells. The masterminds behind such innovations were the sort of brilliant but unthinkably dangerous brains that the Allies were trying to yoke to their own ambitions. In December 1946, Albert Einstein (a refugee from the Nazi regime and by this stage a beloved US citizen) put his name to a letter sent to President Truman. It read: 'We hold these individuals to be potentially dangerous carriers of racial and religious hatred. Their former eminence as Nazi Party members and supporters raises the issue of their fitness to become American citizens or hold key positions in American industrial, scientific, and educational institutions.' But it was to no avail. Choices were made at the highest levels to overlook war crimes in favour of seeking the scientific upper hand in the new Cold War reality.

There is no paper trail that neatly links Jack to either Matchbox or Paperclip. Such documentary evidence is necessarily rare in the world of international subterfuge. Yet it was long whispered that he might have been involved in smuggling Axis scientists across borders to build new lives in the victorious nations. Indeed, William Reymond wrote an entire book making the case that Jack was killed by Soviet assassins sent by a Kremlin disgruntled at losing out on key targets. That particular theory was subsequently widely debunked, not least because released KGB files suggest that the organisation never had Jack in their sights, or even on their radar. But is it so outlandish to suggest that Jack might nonetheless have played a role in the extractions?

Circumstantially, Jack would have been an ideal candidate for the job: scientifically literate, politically astute, discreet, well-connected across the continent and with extraordinary freedom to travel. Although Paperclip and Matchbox were both running down by 1952, similar programmes continued throughout the decade, overseen by national intelligence agencies established for the purpose. We know too that the British were keeping a keen eye on scientists from the chemical and biological warfare spheres, among them Dr Gerhard Schrader, the creator of tabun and sarin, although ultimately he opted to remain in Germany. Who better than Jack, one might think, to vet such characters, especially given his close association with Lord Selborne, who in turn could call upon his web of highly trained agents to assist in extractions and transportations.

With that in mind, it is worth returning to that collection of medals in the UCL archive. Among them, without any identifying documentation, is one that appears to have three Cs interlinked. On closer inspection, it is possible to make out that the letters in fact read 'CCG'. This award derives from the Control Commission Germany, the caretaker mechanism looking after local government in Allied-occupied post-war Germany between 1945 and 1949. Jack worked for the commission from 1945 until he started at Boots in 1946, and remained associated with it when he undertook a nutrition survey in Germany on behalf of the Foreign Office in 1948–9.[6] It was the Control Commission that oversaw the execution of Operation Matchbox in this period, so Jack, with his remit to roam, was ideally placed to lend a hand. Incidentally, it is also worth noting that back in the 1930s, the Rockefeller Foundation had provided funding for the relocation to the US of scholars under threat from the Nazis. It contributed to two main schemes (the Refugee Scholar Program and the Emergency Committee in Aid of Displaced Foreign Scholars), which together helped over 300 scholars move out of Europe, including eminent figures like Leo Szilard, who played such a vital role in the subsequent development of the atomic bomb. This was all around the time when the Foundation was paying for Jack to travel far and wide across the continent.

Then we come to the day of Jack's murder, and the reported sightings that morning of a group in a car fitting the description of the Drummonds. They were, according to the reports, descending from the plateau above the Lurs river basin where the Ganagobie Abbey was situated. The isolated abbey – home to a single priest, Father Lorenzi – had been a bastion of wartime French resistance, a Maquis stronghold well known to both the SOE and to the Jedburgh teams involved in the Allied landings. Lorenzi had been the Resistance's faithful and doughty protector, giving away nothing. If you were looking for a safe house to quietly hold and then move on foreign scientists, you could do much worse. Moreover, Lorenzi would not have been the only Catholic priest to lend a hand in Paperclip and Matchbox, providing assistance to navigate secret escape routes – or 'ratlines', as they were called. In the view of the Vatican, the communist Soviet Union posed a far greater existential threat than a few academics from the losing side in the war. After the Drummond murders, Lorenzi maintained his characteristic low profile, providing very little information to help the police and keeping his distance from the journalists who overran the place. Gaston Dominici had worked the land up at the abbey when he was a young man, long before he could afford to buy La Grand Terre. He and the priest had remained friends ever since, as evidenced by a series of letters later published by Gaston's grandson Alain. If Lorenzi was aiding the Matchbox or Paperclip operations, Gaston would have been one of the select few who might have had any inkling.

A picture builds in which it is conceivable that Jack had important business in the area that day. Or perhaps it was just an innocent jaunt after all. In the end, it all depends on whether you buy that Jack was just any old tourist, eager to see the sights in a corner of France he was not particularly familiar with.

INNOCENT TOURISTS?   20

Guy Marrian always gave short shrift to rumours of Jack's involvement in classified operations. The idea that he was a secret agent, he suggested, was preposterous, and he eagerly discredited all evidence that pointed towards Jack's trip being anything other than touristic. The apparent multiple sightings of a family like the Drummonds in a British-plated Hillman in the days leading up to the murders? The witnesses, he argued repeatedly, must have been mistaken. To the best of his knowledge, Marrian insisted, Jack had never been to Lurs or the surrounding area before.

This makes the discovery of an old diary on a municipal rubbish tip on the outskirts of Nottingham all the more problematic and intriguing. Within a week or two of the murders, a thirteen-year-old boy called Marshall Hughes was rummaging through the tip in Long Eaton, a town about equidistant between Nottingham and Derby, with two friends, Barry and Frank. They were poking through the detritus with sticks when Hughes turned up a small, black pocket diary from 1947, in good condition save for burn marks in one corner. On the front page were Jack's name, address and phone number, along with his identity card details. There was no doubting to whom it belonged. The teen, who quickly made the link with the French murders recently featured in the newspapers, took his plunder home and showed it to his mother. She at first considered it of no practical use to investigators since it was some five years old. However, after a chance encounter, she shared it with a local councillor, who in turn passed it to Wilfred Thompson, managing director of the local newspaper, the *Long Eaton Advertiser*. He alerted the Long Eaton police to the discovery and after eight days of investigation, they established that a dustman called Fred Broughton had collected the diary in the rubbish bin of Jack Drummond's house in Nuthall. The diary now made its way to Scotland Yard, but there it fell into a black hole. Seemingly, it was in the Yard's possession for at least two years, during which time it did little other than gather dust. Then it simply disappeared without trace, missing from Scotland Yard's files. A press attaché from the Yard told the weekly *France Dimanche* that they had 'no item in our possession concerning the Drummond Affair' and that 'if this diary exists it must be the French Police who have it'. Alas, they did not.

What we know of the diary's contents today is what can be gleaned from press reports. *France Dimanche* undertook an investigation and published an article on 22 August 1954 that included an interview with Michael O'Hara, editor of the British weekly *Sunday Empire News*. According to this piece, the diary confirmed Jack's 'exceedingly frequent' travel to Europe in 1947. His favourite destinations were Holland, Belgium, Switzerland and France, and he made several visits to Basel, Eindhoven and Utrecht – all towns noted by *France Dimanche* as 'known for their counter espionage activities'. Critically, it was also revealed that Jack had been to Lurs that

August, where he had had a six o'clock meeting one evening with an unnamed contact. Throughout the diary, none of the names of people he met with on his trips was listed, although names of work colleagues and daily contacts were mentioned. Unfortunately, none of those whose hands the diary passed through made their own independent notes as to his various assignations.

The article then claimed that Wilfred Thompson had met with an unnamed chemist who was a former colleague of Jack's. According to *France Dimanche*, this source had claimed to Thompson that 'JD had been in permanent contact with the officers of MI5 (the British Counter Espionage Agency) and had made throughout the war numerous visits to France and Belgium on their behalf. These were always treated as clandestine visits.' But over in France, Sébeille was unmoved by the potential breakthrough, telling a *Dimanche* journalist that 'the case is closed, Gaston has confessed. All the rest is literature ...'

According to Thompson, the authenticity of the diary was 'indisputable'. There is no obvious reason to doubt his account of its contents. A local journalist, he made no wild claim that it held the key to identifying the Drummonds' killer. He did not write books off its back, or make a movie. Simply, he reported how it illustrated Jack's prodigious travel (of which we know much already) and, vitally, showed that he was not a stranger to Lurs – a detail that potentially changes our entire understanding of the crime. In its light, the Drummonds' presence on the road outside La Grand Terre, by a milepost perfect for a rendezvous, seems much less likely to have been a chance occurrence while on holiday. Given its unsuitability as the camping site it had been presumed to be, that Jack intended to be there for some other reason becomes the logical assumption. There were, meanwhile, persistent (although unverified and widely doubted) rumours that he had been parachuted into the area back in 1943 or 1944, as well as visiting in 1947.

The diary's singed corner suggested that an attempt had been made to burn it but had failed, as if it had been at the edges of a bonfire before being scooped up and disposed of in the dustbin. Certainly, someone was intent on getting rid of it in short order after the discovery of the murders. By pure chance, this particular document was saved and discovered but it begs the question, what else was burned? And who was so keen to cover Jack's tracks? Boots, of course, had already made their presentations to the British authorities in France to clear the Drummonds' car of papers that it seemingly considered sensitive. Might a company representative have similarly been granted access to the family home to lift any-thing else that could cause embarrassment? Or should eyes instead be turned towards the intelligence services? There is no doubt that someone was on a mission to tidy.

In the months after the deaths, the nutritional scientist and government scientific advisor Dorothy F. Hollingsworth – a colleague of Jack's – entered into various correspondences in search of Jack's papers related to his government work. She was also engaged in helping to write Jack's obituary for the Royal Society. She learned from one Miss Margaret Grey, Jack's former secretary at the Ministry of Food, that there existed a 'diary he kept of visits to the Netherlands, Germany (including Belsen) and other European countries', although Miss Grey (by then living in Canada) did not know where it was. This revelation prompted Hollingsworth to investigate, but without success. A short while later, she reported to another correspondent that 'the diary he [Jack] kept of these visits abroad was, I understand, destroyed by his mother-in-law after his death'.[1] Why this desire to do away with potentially valuable documentary evidence of his work? Did Mrs Wilbraham simply want to free herself of reminders of the past, or did she know (or perhaps someone else told her) that Jack's diaries contained secrets best left untold?

———

While the road by La Grand Terre would have made a great location for a meet-up or drop-off related to Operation Paperclip and/or Matchbox, there was another obvious local draw for Jack. There is a large chemical factory just seven or so miles up the road, on the Drummonds' assumed route, at a place called Château Arnoux. Opened in 1916, the factory specialised in producing chlorine and helped meet the First World War demand for chemical weapons including chlorine gas, phosgene (carbamyl chloride) and mustard gas (dichlorodiethyl sulphide). The factory had been owned by Péchiney since 1950 and had recently been visited by President de Gaulle, consolidating its reputation as an asset of national importance. It was also a major employer in the region, not least providing work for a large number of Communist-supporting former members of the Maquis. A number of relatives of the Dominicis were among the staff too. James Fergusson, author of The Vitamin Murders, discovered that agrochemicals had been produced at the site since 1927, and as of 1952 it was producing the organochlorine pesticides HCH and lindane. In addition, it manufactured chlorinated solvents, including PVC, that were close cousins of MCPA, the herbicide developed by Boots.

There can be no doubt that the factory would have held more than a passing interest for Jack. By chance, there was a public footpath that cut directly across the site, so it was easy to stroll through and perhaps even discreetly take a few pictures if the mood took him. But there must also be the possibility that he had cultivated a relationship with a contact or contacts within the establishment on previous trips to the area. A source, say, who could provide him with more in-depth insights into just what was going on within the factory walls. It was the sort of unglamorous intelligence work that James Bond might have rolled his eyes at, but just the sort of information that both Boots and the British government would be delighted to have in their back pocket. Boots were, after all, utterly convinced that the Drummond car contained papers of interest to the company, and rallied the British authorities to help retrieve them. Moreover, a high-end camera is one of the few items known for definite to have been stolen from the crime scene.

Tellingly, there is a strong body of evidence to indicate that the Drummonds had interacted with other people in the days before the killings. There were multiple sightings of a 'second Hillman', in particular the evidence of the young gendarme in Digne, although its existence and the identity of its purported passengers have never been confirmed. There was also a report of a Triumph sports car with British plates near to the scene of the killings. After a dedicated search, a vehicle matching the description (including a partial number plate match) was found stored in a garage in Lyon. Its owner, a Canadian man, was questioned but his alibi was deemed rock solid.[2] His name was Peter Gerard Martin and he was 20 years old. He had come from Canada the previous year and lived in London. He had bought the car in a garage in New

Cross, London, a few weeks before crossing into France with a companion and driving to Cannes. He was due to return to London and then travel back to Canada on 9 August, but instead, for reasons still not clear, he tucked the car away in the garage in Lyon (150 miles north of the murder site), went hitchhiking in Switzerland, returned for the car on 26 August when the furore around the Drummonds was dying down, and returned to London. His itinerary allowed for a rendez-vous on 4 August, but with his alibi accepted (with little in the way of questioning), he was not deemed worthy of further investigation.

Perhaps most significantly, a local traffic policeman reported seeing a young man and woman, dressed in black, leaving Digne in a Hillman (and in an obvious hurry) a few minutes after the Drummonds on 4 August. This unidentified pairing stopped to ask the officer directions to Château Arnoux, home of the chemical factory. Despite a massive search and public appeal, neither the couple nor their car was ever traced, nor was the officer's evidence heard in court. Guy Marrian, predictably, poured cold water on the reports. Remarkably, however, some Belgian tourists developed their holiday snaps when they returned home from their summer holidays in France and discovered they had captured images of the Drummonds relaxing and interacting with a young couple. The Belgians had followed the story on the news and immediately recognised Jack, Anne and Elizabeth. They sent the pictures to the French police but the photos subsequently disappeared before they could be introduced at trial. Were these Jack's accomplices in whatever illicit (or, at least, under-cover) operation he was executing in the Durance Valley in 1952? If they had been mere fellow travellers casually encountered, it is surprising that they subsequently disappeared from view quite so comprehensively given the levels of interest around the case just then.

———

With some justification, the assumption has been that if the Drummonds were outside La Grand Terre on the night of 4/5 August 1952 for reasons other than camping, the real motive for their presence likely rests with Jack. For all the reasons outlined in this book, he is the family member most likely to have led them there. But it is long overdue that we take a closer look at Anne Wilbraham. Was she merely bending to Jack's will when she set about catching a few hours' sleep under the Provençal skies that night? Or should we credit her with greater agency?

The story of the Drummond affair is full of strong women compelled by social expectation to play supporting roles behind their men. From Gaston's put-upon wife, his daughters and his sons' spouses to Anne's mother back in England, there is a cast of women who exude strength and spirit but whose voices are heard much more quietly than those of the men whose actions, foibles and flaws dominate the piece. In accounts of the murders over the years, Anne has rarely been allowed to play anything other than the tragic victim, the loving mother and the second wife, and, just occasionally, Jack's secretary too.

Her role as his co-author on *The Englishman's Food* perhaps serves as a suitable metaphor. By the time of its publication, she had already been acknowledged for her role in handling data for G. E. Friend's academic book *The Schoolboy: His Nutrition and Development* and was credited as co-author with Jack on a paper published in the *Lancet* about the tragic nutritional experimenter William Stark. It was a paper very different from any other that Jack published at the time, leading to the suspicion that Anne may in fact have been the driving force behind its scholarship, while Jack's name and reputation paved the pathway to its publication. Regardless, *The Englishman's Food* easily superseded it to become the pinnacle of both Anne's and Jack's literary achievement – an act of astounding scholarship involving the analysis of books and manuscripts going right back to Tudor times, originating in multiple countries and written in an array of languages. It is difficult to imagine that Jack had much time to undertake the necessary and copious research considering his many other professional distractions during the period of the book's composition in the late 1930s.

Easier, instead, to imagine Anne as the prime mover, building on the work of that *Lancet* paper, deep-diving into the historical literature and plundering museum archives for inspiration. She was independent, earned her own money (which must have been significant), cared little for societal norms and clearly had the intellectual ability to write the book, not to mention the strong language skills required to wade through tomes in Old French. If it was indeed her passion project, Jack's academic status would have again been the key to its publication. Given that he was about to leave Mabel to take Anne as his new wife, he would not have lacked the motivation to help where he could. This interpretation can never be proven but is credible.

Yet how quickly Anne's contribution was downplayed. When the second edition arrived, post-murders, she was all but written out of its creation in the preface by Norman Wright, Jack's successor as Scientific Advisor to the Ministry of Food. Worse was to come in 1991 when a reprint of this

edition by Pimlico arrived with a new introduction by the
food writer Tom Jaine. In the marketing blurbs, this edition
was referred to as 'Jack Drummond and Tom Jaine's book'. A
case study in how women are erased from history.

The early twentieth century saw significant strides in
terms of female enfranchisement but the world Anne inhabited in the 1930s, 40s and 50s remained resolutely a man's
one. There were greater opportunities for women to work,
especially during the war, but ideally only until they settled
into domestic bliss as a wife. The year 1946 saw publication
of a government-sponsored book entitled *Charter for Health*.[3]
It provides a summary of recommendations from a committee
set up by the British Medical Association under the chairman-
ship of Jack's old partner-in-crime, John Boyd Orr. All bar one
of the committee's 22 members were male, a fact reflected in
the book's contents. Page 43, for instance, notes: 'The kitchen
is the housewife's workplace. The mother's occupation is to
be prime minister of the home, to feed, clothe, and minister
to the needs of the family and above all, to bring children into
the world.' Four pages later, on 'the training of girls':

> The education of girls should be designed to teach them the
> art of home-making. At present eight out of ten girls leave
> school at the age of fourteen. In the secondary, schoolboys
> and girls often receive the same education, which is unre-
> lated to the future life of many of the girls. The struggle for
> equality with boys has confused identity and equality. With
> the introduction of the New Education Act, the curriculum
> for girls should be revised and related more nearly to the
> home. Girls should be instructed in the buying and prepa-
> ration of food, in practical housekeeping, in the decoration
> of the home, in the care of infants and in home nursing.

A little later, a final insult: 'Girls may also be helped to acquire good taste in appearance, clothes, furniture, manners and morals, which will be of more value to them in homemaking than academic knowledge.' But Anne kicked back against the prevailing orthodoxy. She worked before and after marrying Jack. A look into her background reveals a character who continually defied expectations.

Anne Wilbraham was born on 9 December 1907. As of 1911, she lived at Belmont in Surrey with her 36-year-old mother, Constance Georgina, her 39-year-old father, Roger Eustace Wilbraham, and Edith Dorothy Caroline, her older sister by fourteen months. Roger was a lawyer based at 1 Hare Court, Temple in London (presumably a barrister, although he was known to introduce himself as a solicitor). The household employed two servants and Anne enjoyed a well-heeled upbringing.

Her sister married Gerald Vere Borlase Burgoyne in 1929, when Edith was 23 and he was 30. Gerald's father had died when the boy was young and he had been sent to live with his grandparents and six servants. His grandfather was Peter Bond Burgoyne, a wine merchant considered the father of the Australian wine industry in Great Britain. With Jack's love of wine and close friendship with André Simon, it is likely that the pair met at some point.

Edith and Gerald's marriage did not last the distance, and he remarried in 1941, just a year before his death at the tragically early age of 42. He left an estate valued at £41,647, equivalent to £2–3 million today. One of those who inherited was the Hon. Lancelot William Joynson Hicks, an MP and solicitor who later served in Churchill's government as Parliamentary Secretary to the Ministry of Fuel and Power. Edith was remarried in 1942, at the age of 35, to Major Donald

C. Cameron of the Royal Canadian Army, thereafter moving to Canada where she had two children. Cameron, at the time a brigadier, was mentioned in relation to chemical weapons in a book published in 2014 entitled *In Peace Prepared: Innovation and Adaptation in Canada's Cold War Army*. Yet another link into the world of chemical warfare for the Drummonds – a frequent trope in their story.

Anne was in her twenties for most of the 1930s, when her occupation was recorded as a secretary. She made several visits to Marseilles over that decade, always in the company of her father (who would die in 1951, thus mercifully being saved the pain of his daughter's murder). They always sailed first class, with each trip lasting about a month. On one voyage, British Fascist leader Oswald Mosley was among their fellow passengers, although it is not known if they had any contact. The trips certainly helped develop Anne's Francophone skills, though – abilities that would come in handy when working on *The Englishman's Food*.

By 1939, Anne, now 32 years old, lived in an apartment of her own in Rossmore Court, St Marylebone in London – a highly desirable location adjacent to Regent's Park, and difficult to afford on an average secretary's wage. While here, she volunteered as a part-time air raid warden. Intriguingly, her name appeared in the ARP (Air Raid Precautions) register of addresses as 'Wilbraham' but it was crossed out and changed to 'Drummond', despite her being designated a spinster. It would be another year before she married Jack, who lived at this time in a flat a conveniently short walk away, across Regent's Park in Hallam Street. Anne later joined him there.

So, where was Anne getting the money to supplement her pay packet so that she could afford her expensive accommodation and London's exorbitant living expenses? She had no inheritance that we know of. Her mother seemingly left the family home at some stage in the 1930s, taking a flat for herself in Sloane Square instead, so the Wilbrahams' finances were under some strain. Jack was certainly in no position to bankroll her. After their deaths in 1952, probate records confirm that Anne was independently wealthy: she left an estate of over £17,000 (equivalent today to nearly a million pounds sterling) whereas Jack left less than half that amount, just £6,680.

A clue to her independent wealth may be hidden in an announcement in June 1940 in the *Chelsea News*, which detailed Anne's marriage to Jack on the 15th of the month in Marylebone. Alongside a description of her blue two-piece with matching hat and veil (complemented by a spray of orchids), there was a mention of her work: 'Miss Wilbraham is engaged in the Admiralty Intelligence Department.' This was information presumably provided by her proud parents. A later newspaper article, from around the time of the murders, stated that Anne was 'was engaged in government research work'.

Anne was described in Jack's obituaries variously as his student or his secretary, but she never worked at UCL or for the Ministry of Food. Logic therefore suggests that their association must have begun at the Admiralty. Was Anne his secretary within the intelligence department? It would certainly have been a job well within her capabilities. Perhaps she was even the senior party? Her lifestyle suggests she was better remunerated than most secretaries of the day. What we know for sure is that she did not give up the job even after her nuptials at Marylebone just a month after Churchill had taken over at No. 10 and days after the miracle of the Dunkirk evacuation. It is also notable that after the Drummonds moved to

Nottingham, Elizabeth attended a boarding school close to home. Was it convenient for her to board so that Anne might carry on her duties for the Admiralty?

Naval intelligence was a small, intimate gang housed in Room 39 at the Admiralty, where everyone knew everybody else. As well as working together on academic treatises, we must consider the prospect that Mr and Mrs Drummond were also colleagues in intelligence work. Anne's presence in the intelligence department consolidates suspicions that Jack's RNR ranking was granted to support his position there too. The 1952 trip to France perhaps ought to be seen as a mixture of business and pleasure not just for Jack, but for them both. There was reportedly uncharacteristic friction between the pair the night before they left England. Jack was, unusually for him, the worse for wear through drink and rowed with Anne. Was there some aspect of the trip that was anxiety-inducing to one of them? Were they squabbling about the upcoming rendezvous amid the sightseeing? Was one of them – were both of them – now doubting the good sense of bringing Elizabeth along on a trip that incorporated some aspect of their professional work? Was it perhaps even the case that it was Anne, and not Jack, who was the driving force in bringing the family to the bend on the road near Lurs where they were destined to be struck down?

The odds are against ever conclusively establishing why the Drummonds were there that night. But that they were there for a reason other than tourism is, at the very least, a distinct possibility and, given the weight of evidence, a likelihood. It seems safe to say that the Drummonds' days as innocents abroad ended long before that summer of 1952.

CHERCHEZ L'HOMME 21

All the indicators are that the Drummonds parked up by mile-post 32, just along from La Grand Terre, for a reason other than its suitability for camping. Jack, Anne, or possibly both of them had alighted on the spot as ideal for a secretive ren-dezvous with a person or persons unknown. Perhaps they intended to meet with someone who could pass on sensi-tive information about the goings-on at the chlorine factory. Alternatively, they may have been laying the groundwork for the extraction of another scientist from the continent for redeployment in the UK or North America. They might even conceivably have been there to oversee the physical handover of an individual – perhaps in cahoots with the mysterious cou-ple in whose presence they had been seen earlier in the day.

Accepting that there was a clandestine reason for them being there that night, it is natural to then assume that the Drummonds' deaths were pre-planned, or at least that their assailants had the expectation of a confrontation. Elizabeth (and perhaps Anne too) may have been considered by the attacker(s) as unavoidable collateral damage in a mission to disrupt Jack's and/or Anne's activities. The list of potential assassins is considerable. They could have originated from a party aggrieved that Jack was engaged in an act of commercial, and potentially military, espionage. On the other hand, for all of his absence from the KGB's files, any involvement in removing valuable ex-Nazi scientific assets from Europe had the potential to invoke the ire of the Soviet Union. Or perhaps this was a case of more local resentment from those who had suffered terribly at the hands of the Germans only very recently. In this heartland of French communism and wartime resistance, the mere presence of an interfering non-Frenchman may have been enough to open old wounds. Vengeance was a common currency here, so did someone local hold a grudge against Jack for his actions in the war?

There is a problem with this thesis, though. The murders were carried out with none of the gruesome finesse of planned executions. The murder weapon was both unsubtle and unsuitable. Why choose an ageing rifle, unwieldy and oversized, to carry out a get-in-get-out assassination? Why not, say, a much smaller, more accurate weapon with a silencer? Nor is it feasible to think that professionals would have had to resort to the horrendous beating that Elizabeth suffered, and then left the crime scene quite so chaotic and with the murder weapon so easy to find. Moreover, there was never any real doubt that the gun originated locally. Even acknowledging that the Drummonds were at the location by design, the murders were undoubtedly an act of impetuous and disorganised violence. Incompetent and inept.

So, we find ourselves back at Gaston Dominici. The old peasant farmer who waited for his autumn years to show himself as a mass murderer. Patriarch of a moderately dysfunctional family, whose collective fear of authority cast them into a pit of self-incrimination. A man who, in his mid-seventies, blamed the slaughter (when not denying all knowledge of it) on his untameable sexual urges. According to the famous 'Ockham's razor' theory of the fourteenth-century philosopher William of Ockham, when weighing up competing theories, it is always wisest to follow the simplest one that poses fewest impediments. Dominici has, for decades, seemed to represent this path of least resistance – partly as a result of his portrayal by the French police and judicial system, and partly because of his own personal foibles and those of members of his family.

But impediments spring up at almost every turn. The absence of compelling forensic evidence. The murder weapon never proved beyond doubt to have been his, nor shown to have been fired by him that night. No remotely credible motive, nor any patterns of behaviour established to suggest a penchant for such extreme violence. There is in the end only his confession – offered and retracted time and again, full of inconsistencies and unlikelihoods – and the accusations of his sons, mired in doubt and acrimony. Changeable words uttered in moments of utmost stress by a family in meltdown. Who can really credit the claims of lust (turned to bloodlust) from an elderly man who needed a walking stick to get about, nor the even more fanciful idea that the much younger Anne succumbed to his passions with her husband and child in close proximity? If we pose the question 'Did Gaston Dominici murder the Drummonds?' the jury remains out but our conclusion must surely be that he likely did not.

Who else then? The million-dollar question. One to which we may never have the answer for sure, given the mismanagement of the investigation and the passage of time. Yet still there is room for informed speculation. There is a figure who played a crucial role in bringing down Gaston Dominici, a man the old farmer and his son came to revile and who himself was once the prime suspect in the case. By carefully supplying the police with evidence that firmly put the focus on Dominici, he was able to shrug off official suspicions and retreat quietly into the background. His name has largely remained hidden in the shadows over the decades since but the time seems ripe for a re-evaluation. This one-time prime suspect's name is Paul Maillet.

—

The Dominicis and the Maillets knew each other of old. Paul's father Auguste and Gaston were contemporaries. Both had laboured hard over the years to make something of themselves, but by the time of the murders it was Gaston who had the most to show for his work. Auguste Maillet had once been a prosperous café owner but these days scratched a living from the land. Paul considered that Gaston rather enjoyed lording it over his father, which did not sit well with him.

As children, Paul had been at school with Clovis and Gustave, and was particularly friendly with the former. He had even played the role of peacemaker several years earlier when Clovis sought to reconcile with his family after choosing a career on the railways over the one planned for him on the family farm. The pair now worked together for SNCF, the state rail operator, where Paul was a plate-layer. He lived about a mile away from La Grand Terre with his wife and four children. During the war, he had been a leading figure in the local Maquis but now, aged 37, he was better known as the small, wiry, blustering leader of the local Communist Party cell in Lurs. Like the Dominicis, the Maillets were a large family and Paul sat at its centre. Little went on that he didn't get to hear about. While he could be affable, he also had a reputation as the sort of man you didn't want to make an enemy of.

In early police interviews, he claimed not to have been near La Grand Terre on the night of the murders. He was at home with his family, he insisted. It was never the most fireproof of alibis and, since he was known as a regular visitor to the Dominicis, there has long been speculation that – despite his denials – he and his brother were present for the celebrations that Gaston hosted to celebrate the *arossage* (the watering of his fields). He was certainly there at lunch the next day, when the extended Dominici clan gathered to establish a strategy in response to the tragedy on their doorstep. It was widely reported that the farmhouse also entertained a wider collection of local Communist Party officials who contributed their own thoughts and opinions. With family members in shock and clearly contemplating the involvement of one another in the killings, a policy of non-cooperation with the police (initially polite but less so over time) was implemented. In the early days of the investigation, it seemed as if Gaston and his sons could rely on a 'red wall' of Communist Party protection around them. Commissioner Sébeille came up against a barricade of silence that the Party worked hard to maintain. Maillet himself was suspected of being responsible for inserting disparaging articles about the investigation into the local communist press.

He seems to have done his level best to look after the Dominicis in those early days – the least he could do if he were indeed the killer. But there was a fly in the ointment. Maillet himself came under increasing suspicion. The police heard whispers in the local community that they should take a closer look at him. They were sent anonymous letters pointing the finger at Maillet and even accusing him of involvement with a previous murder. It was suggested that just as he put up a wall of protection around the Dominicis, he had one around himself too because he was privy to the secrets of the Maquis. Not long into the investigation, a local woman claimed that she had seen the murder weapon, or a rifle very similar to it, hanging in the Maillets' kitchen, and Sébeille received an anonymous letter alleging similar – an accusation denied, as might be expected, by Maillet and his family. But when Clovis had his extreme reaction upon first being shown the weapon, isn't it just as likely that he fell to his knees in dismay not because he recognised it as being from the family home but because he knew it to be that of his old friend? He would have known that to implicate the influential Maillet had the potential to cause as many problems for himself as accusing his own family. Sébeille certainly came to think Maillet might have been his man at this stage of the investigation, as did Sébeille's celebrated detective father.

A little over three weeks into the investigation, Sébeille paid a visit to the Maillet household. Paul was out at the time. The officer took the carbine with him and showed it to Paul's wife, Ginette, and their four children, none of whom admitted to recognising it. Officers then undertook a search of the property and turned up two Sten guns concealed in an oven. These were, Ginette explained, war souvenirs. Unfortunately for Paul Maillet, they were also illegal to possess. Additionally, they were proof of his love of powerful, war-vintage assault weapons. On top of that, it seemed that he had been stealing electricity from the grid – further ammunition that the police could use to make his life uncomfortable.

Suddenly finding himself a man under scrutiny, Maillet's benevolence towards the Dominicis ran dry. Within weeks, he would tell Sébeille that Gustave Dominici had discovered Elizabeth still alive but had left her to die. Then, a little later, another shocking revelation, that Gustave had confessed to witnessing the murders from an alfalfa field at La Grand Terre. The implication was clear – Gustave was covering for someone in his family whom he knew to be the killer. These were game-changing moments in the investigation. Popular support seeped from the Dominicis and all other lines of investigation were now secondary to the pursuit of Gaston. Under such intense pressure, and abandoned by someone who until then had seemed so vital to their protection, the family turned in on itself. Their trust in an old friend – one they may have had good reason to suspect was the Drummonds' killer – had been inverted against them. By then, they had also committed themselves to upholding Maillet's original statement that he had not been at La Grand Terre on the night of the murders.

If Maillet was guilty of the triple murder, he had hit upon the perfect way to divert suspicion and inject poison into the Dominicis. With his own life at stake, the price of betraying an old man he didn't much care for was one that likely seemed not too high. There was, nonetheless, a premium to pay. He was stripped of his local office within the Communist Party, which was uncomfortable with his behaviour on several counts. The discovery of the Sten guns did not play well for the Party when sections of the press implied that Maillet had been stockpiling weapons with insurrection in mind. But it was the sudden turnaround with regard to the Dominicis that really raised hackles. With Maillet initially at the forefront of the cheerleading, the Communists had put their weight behind proclaiming the family's innocence. Now all of that work was being undermined, with a faithful Party man poised to take the fall on the word of a supposed comrade. The

Dominicis ran a vitriolic campaign to discredit Maillet, who was shunned by many of his neighbours. On one occasion, a length of wire was stretched across a path to knock him from his motorcycle. But the police now treated him as an asset and not a suspect.

Maillet's behaviour was notably odd at the re-enactment of the crime prior to Gaston being charged. He was seen to prowl around the site, chain-smoking, a broad smile on his face, and interacting with Sébeille in a chummy way. It was a curious event, punctuated by Gaston's apparent suicide bid when he attempted to throw himself from a railway bridge, but Gaston was generally calm in his relations with everyone on the day save for Maillet. The old man lost his cool with him, calling him a 'punk' and an 'assassin' and suggesting that he was the real owner of the murder weapon. To add to the strangeness of it all, Sébeille was heard to congratulate Maillet on 'witnessing his victory' – an utterance that seemed to confirm an unhealthy relationship between investigator and former suspect.

The murmurs around Maillet's potential guilt contin-ued through to the trial. Eye-witnesses had reported seeing two men by the murder site around 1 a.m. on the night of the killings, providing descriptions that did not obviously fit any of the Dominicis. In the witness box, Gustave inti-mated that Clovis had on several occasions cast suspicion on Maillet in the immediate aftermath of the crimes. Similarly, Gaston's son-in-law, Clément Caillet, testified that Clovis had suggested to him that the Rock Ola M1 belonged to Maillet – striking testimony about a witness now adamant that his own father was the murderer. Then there was Caillet's wife and Gaston's daughter, Augusta, who claimed that the confession Clovis supposedly heard their father utter over the family dinner table had been misheard. Gaston did not say 'I killed', she claimed, but 'He killed', which she further suggested was in reference to Maillet. Yet none of this mattered in the end. As soon as the jury convicted Gaston, Maillet was in the clear. But if Maillet was in fact the killer, how might the murders have played out?

———

It is coming up to one o'clock on the night of 4/5 August. The Drummonds are parked close by the old farm, easy to spot for those that need to find them but without drawing undue attention. Jack has prepared well for his meeting. He has scouted out the location in the days prior, reacquainting himself with an area he already knows and meeting contacts (including the couple driving the other Hillman). Now he is anxious to get the night's work over with so that the family can return to enjoying their holiday. He is not fearful, though. He expects a routine operation and carries no weapon. Besides, he would not dream of bringing Anne, let alone Elizabeth, to a rendezvous that he thinks has even the slightest chance of turning nasty.

His hope had been that the business could be concluded early enough that they could start making their way back to Villefranche. He had not come with the intention of camping, and had therefore left the family's tent back at their accommodation on the Riviera. But things have not gone entirely to plan. There has been a delay and it is now far too late to embark on the long journey home. The family prepares for an uncomfortable night's sleep. Anne has not even brought night clothes so must sleep fully dressed. Elizabeth gets the best of it, being granted the back seat of the car for her bed.

Jack and Anne will sleep under the stars, on camp beds that happen to still be in the boot.

Meanwhile, up at the farm, festivities are in full swing. Among the guests is Gaston's grandson, Zézé. Later, he will deny being present but his protestations are fragile, not least when he claims to have been miles away early the next morning buying milk from a man who has in fact been dead for two years. (Zézé will offer a masterclass in how to be an unreliable and unbelievable witness.) Paul Maillet is at La Grande Terre too, as is his brother Pierre. It's a good-natured evening and the wine is flowing. Everyone is relaxed – so relaxed that they have been distracted from the job in hand, overwatering the land until it threatens to slip on to the railway line. Gustave goes out to inspect, but Paul carries on drinking.

As he gets into his stride, Paul suggests a few of the guests might like to join him for a bit of late-night poaching – a favourite pastime of his. It is, of course, illegal but everyone turns a blind eye round here. Perhaps he has even brought one of his own rifles with just such a plan in mind; either that or he suggests borrowing one from the Dominicis. Zézé is up for the trip, and Gustave says he'll join when he has finished checking on the landslide. Paul heads out with Pierre as Zézé scurries off to get himself ready.

When Paul steps out on to the road, he notices the Hillman, the one with the British number plates, parked a little way away. He'd spotted it earlier. It irks him that he does not know what its business is. As a man of influence in the area, he doesn't like to be out of the loop. And he has been hearing whispers. Some of his communist contacts at the factory have mentioned that a car like this had been doing the rounds, its driver even taking photos of the site. Alternatively,

Paul has heard – either directly or via Gaston – something mentioned by Father Lorenzi, about visitors up at the abbey.

Alcohol coursing through him, Paul determines to confront the inhabitants of the car. With a rifle cocked under his arm, he will let them know who is in charge around here. But matters soon escalate. Jack sees them approaching. He may even spy them as he is answering a call of nature. When you're on an undercover mission and you see armed men, it is natural to switch into defensive mode. With the safety of Anne and Elizabeth at the forefront of his mind, he decides he must be proactive rather than allow events to overtake him. He raises himself up as large as he can and grabs the first thing that comes to hand as a makeshift weapon.

This is not how Paul has expected the scene to play out at all. He wants to impose his authority but he has not come looking for trouble. Now a red mist descends around him. Adrenalin pumps, and his body urges fight not flight. He quickens his pace towards the stranger, who in turn advances towards him. The foreigner shouts something at him in French but the language barrier is too high, the local dialect too challenging. There is pointing and finger-wagging, someone lays a hand on someone else. Then a scuffle. Paul cannot recall exactly what happens but he strikes out with the gun. The stranger is stunned, reels back. Then Paul is firing. Again and again. A woman screams. He shoots her too. Now from nowhere a child appears. The distraught girl takes in the scene for a fleeting moment, her face crumpling. She fixes eyes with Paul. And then she is running. He chases after her but she is quick. It takes him a while to catch up. He wants to calm her, to explain that he had meant no ill. But she is screaming. 'Ssshhh,' he begs her, but she carries on, trying to wriggle free from his grip. He has no choice, he thinks, raising the butt of his gun and smashing it into her head. He carries on hitting her until she collapses on the ground, barely moving.

Now the panic kicks in. He looks at the weapon in his hands, the blood splattered across his face and clothes. He races down to the water, dowses himself and flings the weapon as far as he can. He just wants rid of it. Then he scrabbles back up the bank. Pierre is there, shock etched across his face. Paul grabs his shoulders, tells him they must leave now. Like that, they disappear into the night. Back at the farm, it has been impossible to ignore the disturbing symphony of gunshots and screaming. A terrifying soundtrack at the end of what had been a good night.

Gaston tells the women to stay where they are as he nervously goes out to check what's going on. When he arrives on the scene, Gustave is already there and Zézé too. In the dark of the night, they pick out the trail of carnage, dread rising in each of them. They call for Paul and Pierre, but nothing. Are the brothers really responsible for this horror, they wonder. And what about each other? In the confusion of these moments, no one can account for where the others were. Paranoia overtakes them. Might one of them have had a hand in this?

They regroup at the house. They agree there is nothing constructive they can do tonight. It is only a matter of time before the police come knocking but they decide to wait till daylight to report the deaths. Then they will adopt a unified 'saw-nothing, heard-nothing' approach to questioning. To speak of what they know, they reason, threatens only to bring more trouble down upon them. Don't go looking for trouble, for fear that it will come looking for you. And so the Dominicis' nightmare begins.

—

Many years after Gaston's death in a hospice in 1965, Paul Maillet continued to proclaim, 'Le vieil homme a tué les Anglais, je n'en doute pas' ('The old man killed the English people, I have no doubt'). Given that he had long ago won that battle in the courtroom, there were those who wondered if the gentleman did protest too much.

Can we say categorically that it was Maillet, not Gaston Dominici or some other person, who shot dead the Drummond parents and battered their young daughter? By no means. Just as with Gaston, there is no damning forensic trail. No certainty that the murder weapon was his. No definitive proof he was at the scene. But there is legitimate suspicion. There is good reason to think he may have been at La Grand Terre that night, providing him with opportunity. We know with certainty that he enjoyed using guns, had an arsenal of his own and that acquaintances harboured suspicions the murder weapon was his. Moreover, his motive is much clearer than Gaston's. Paul Maillet was a local mover and shaker who liked to be on top of local affairs and had a reputation for throwing his weight around. He was much more likely to seek out confrontation with foreign interlopers than Gaston, admittedly a firebrand in his youth but a man who had long ago adopted a slower pace of life. At least several members of the local community always considered him the much likelier culprit. In his favour, he possessed a mental fortitude to assert his innocence and stick to that line unfalteringly. Most importantly of all, he was able to drip-feed the police with information that promised them an easier route to prosecution and took the heat off himself. At first a prime suspect, once he had cast the finger of suspicion in the direction of the Dominicis, there was an almost unseemly rush to remove him from the spotlight.

Paul Maillet might or might not be the man responsible for slaughtering the Drummonds. But he is a viable alternative suspect, and a man who ought to have been subjected to far more vigorous investigation given the shaky basis of the confessions and denunciations that condemned Gaston Dominici. Neither his assertion that he had 'no doubt' of Gaston's guilt, nor his willingness to swear innocence on the life of his children, should preclude us from questioning whether a gross miscarriage of justice occurred – one that denied justice not only to Dominici but to the murder victims whose names were so quickly disassociated from the affair.

AFTERWORD   22

Jack Drummond and Gaston Dominici arrived in the world
some fourteen years and 600 miles apart in the latter stages
of the nineteenth century. Both were born to unmarried
mothers and were orphaned at a young age. Jack became
a brilliant scholar and celebrated public servant; Gaston, a
man who never made it rich, but nevertheless established
himself as a mainstay of his local community, surviving on
work ethic and wits. Theirs were lives on different trajecto-
ries until they catastrophically collided in Provence on that
balmy night in 1952.

The impact of the events at La Grand Terre have reverber-
ated down the years. It has been a story kept alive, at least
in France, by a plethora of books, films and TV programmes.
The merits of the police investigation and the trial continue
to be debated, amid wider questions of how it all reflected
on France. Gaston narrowly escaped with his life but lived
out his remaining years a remote and reviled figure. Nor was
the impact of his conviction confined to him. The Dominici
family irredeemably lost the status built up over many years
among their peers, and the personal toll mounted. A close, if

mildly dysfunctional family had been ripped apart. Gustave's marriage to Yvette broke up and he fell into alcoholism, while Clovis was dead from cancer of the liver before his father won release from prison. The damage was generational. Even Alain, Gustave's son and a baby at the time of the murders, suffered for many years because of the revulsion his family name inspired. He still remembers being forbidden to take a girlfriend out because of her father's disapproval, and how a local school refused to take him as a pupil. Not merely a case of the sins of the father, but of the grandfather. Alain, however, has never been convinced of those sins and has spent his adult life seeking redress, a battle that has exacted its own price on him.

We can look more widely for the aftershocks, too. Not least to poor Constance Wilbraham, her beautiful family ripped from her. It is agonising to think of her – in her eighties, white-haired and neatly turned out – trying to come to terms with the slaughter of her loved ones. What feelings must have pulled at her heart as she curated the few postcards sent by Anne and Elizabeth in the days before their deaths, as she contemplated what to do with Jack's old diaries, or when she stared at the television in the corner of her living room, a gift from Boots. Meanwhile, back in France, Commissioner Sébeille, the man charged with chasing down the architect of all this grief, saw his career go into decline. He was relegated to duties at a local station before eventually retiring in 1962.

Nor should we forget the innocents who lived in the Durance Valley, their towns and villages forever linked with such a notorious crime. Orson Welles saw to it that the people of Lurs in particular would never truly escape its shadow. But of course, our compassion should be preserved most for the Drummonds themselves. Lives of achievement and potential not only cut short but redefined by the natures of their death. Justice demanded – and still demands – that every effort be made to establish the truth of their murders and identify the perpetrator(s). But the final injustice is that the story of their lives has all too often been superseded by their victimhood.

Elizabeth is preserved as the eternal child, the little girl who might have gone on to achieve anything but who remains a symbol of innocence and potential diabolically snuffed out. Anne, meanwhile, has suffered the ignominy of being diminished by history – a woman whose many attainments have not only faded from the memory but have been actively overwritten. A symbol of a damaging, pervasive and longstanding social failure. Then there is Jack, a man who might well have been more widely remembered for his vast contribution not only to British life but to the wider world had he not been condemned to the status of victim. It seems perverse that his homeland so easily allowed him to disappear from its collective memory, even as the crime that claimed him inhabits the French consciousness. Not only was he responsible for saving countless lives threatened by hunger (in Britain, the Netherlands, Germany and Malta), his genius impacted many more. Thanks to the system of rationing to which he was integral, millions had the opportunity to grow and thrive, shielded from the horrific consequences of malnutrition – especially babies, children and nursing mothers.

Yet there is a paradox. The murders deprived us of who-knows-what further accomplishments Jack, Anne and, indeed, Elizabeth might have realised. But with the passage of time, a re-examination of their deaths brings their lives back to the fore. We can see in a new light the extraordinary contributions to public and intellectual life that the family made and which have lain largely ignored since in the public record. It is remarkable to consider, in particular, how Jack's work continues to resonate with the concerns of the modern world. Had he been alive today, it is safe to say he would have been just as engaged in questions of nutrition, public health and best agricultural practice. Indeed, he would probably have been rather depressed at some of the backwards steps we have taken since he figured out how to ensure the well-being of the nation in a moment of extraordinary crisis.

But we can go further. By looking once more at the murders, we are compelled to explore those corners of Jack's and Anne's lives that have been hidden from sight. A complex web of clues points to an existence beyond the one in the public record. One, we can discern, that stretched from Europe to America, working in the realms of state secrecy and at significant personal risk. The great irony is that while this work placed the Drummonds in the path of danger, their murderer likely had no true understanding of why they were on the road outside La Grand Terre that night. Murder mysteries implore us to solve them but the Drummond affair demands more: it calls us to remember how even in tragic stories, good people are capable of extraordinary things. The Drummonds died in the most terrible of circumstances. But they lived life richly and fully and to the benefit of millions who never knew them. Lives well lived, indeed.

The passing of time only confirms that Sir Jack Drummond was a British hero of the first order. A hero long overdue his recognition.

NOTES

1 Recovering the Drummonds

1. See Recommended Reading.
2. A major film, *L'affaire Dominici* was released in 1973 starring Jean Gabin and Gérard Depardieu. It has been rated by Cinema Français as one of the best French films ever.
3. *L'affaire Dominici*, a two-part TV documentary drama produced by TF1 and shown on French TV in 2003.
4. J. C. Drummond and Anne Wilbraham (1939) *The Englishman's Food: A History of Five Centuries of English Diet*, Jonathan Cape; (1957) revised and with a new chapter by Dorothy Hollingsworth and preface by Norman Wright; (1991) reissued by Pimlico with an introduction by Tom Jaine.
5. The first report of the murders was in the late-night final edition of the *Manchester Evening News*, front page, on the evening of 5 August: 'Famous British Scientist and Family Murdered'.

2 Who was Jack Drummond?

1. H. D. Brandon *et al.* (1952) 'Sir Jack Drummond FRS', *Nature* 170, 1131, 27 December.
2. Casimir Funk (1884–1967) wrote a book, *The Vitamines*,

published 1922 by Baltimore Co. A summary of his work is in Anna Piro *et al.* (2010) 'Casimir Funk: His Discovery of the Vitamins and Their Deficiency Disorders', *Ann Nutr Metab* 57, 85–88.

3. J. C. Drummond (1918) 'Some aspects of infant feeding', *Lancet* 2, 482–4.

4. Drummond and colleagues isolated almost pure vitamin A and vitamin E but were unable to prove it. I. M. Heilbron, R. N. Heslop, R. A. Morton, E. T. Webster and J. C. Drummond (1932) 'Characteristics of highly active vitamin A preparations', *Biochemical Journal* 26, 1178–93; J. C. Drummond, E. Singer and J. MacWalter (1935) 'A study of the unsaponifiable fraction of wheat germ oil with special reference to vitamin E', *Biochemical Journal* 29, 456–71; J. C. Drummond, E. Singer, R. J. Macwalter (1935) 'Further observations on the constituents of the unsaponifiable fraction of wheat germ oil with particular reference to vitamin E', *Biochemical Journal* 29(11), 2510–21.

   Pure crystalline vitamin A was made in 1937 by Holmes and Corbet, (Science 1937 85,2195,103) and vitamin E by Herbert Evans *et al.* (*J Biol Chem* 1936, 113, 319); however, the important discovery of the vital accessory food factor was made by Gowland Hopkins in 1912 and Elmer McCollum in 1913.

5. See p. 255, n. 4.

6. 'Food and its Protection Against Poison Gas: The Conservation of Food is Second Only to the Preservation of Life' (1941), HMSO. An extended version of a report Jack had written in 1937.

7. 'On certain aspects of the food position'. National Archives, MAF256/5, 72B. This memorandum was based in science but was understandable and hard-hitting. It pointed out that the machinery for dealing with new inventions and processes for use in wartime was inadequate.

5 Secrets and Spies

1. 'The Tragedy of Lurs' was the name given to the story of the murders by Orson Welles in his 1955 documentary film for his television series *Around the World*. The film was not officially seen by the public for over forty years, one (unsubstantiated) reason being that the French government blocked it. The unfinished film was discovered and finished by the French director Christophe Cognet.
2. *Europa Touring Atlas 1952*. This is likely to have been the road atlas used by the Drummonds to plan their journeys.

6 A Scientific Mind

1. Frank George Young (1954) 'Jack Cecil Drummond 1891–1952', *Biographical Memoirs of Fellows of the Royal Society*, vol. 9, issue 1.
2. The eulogy by F. G. Young is the most quoted obituary, but there were many more. Some are listed here.
   D. F. Hollingsworth and N. C. Wright (1954) 'Drummond, Jack Cecil (1891–1952) – obituary', *British Journal of Nutrition* 8, 319–324; C. L. Evans (1952) 'Sir Jack Drummond, F.R.S.', *Nature* 170, 401–2; H. J. Channon (1952) 'Drummond, Jack – obituary', *Chemistry & Industry*, 905–906; G. F. Marrian (1953) 'Drummond, Cecil Jack 1891–1952 – obituary', *Journal of the Chemical Society*, 357–360; A. M. Copping (1964) 'Sir Jack Cecil Drummond FRS – biographical sketch', *Journal of Nutrition* 82, 3–9.
3. William Dobinson Halliburton (1891) *A Textbook of Chemical Physiology and Pathology*, Longmans Green and Co. Reprinted 2018 by Forgotten Books.
4. Dr W. Bain (1914) *Quart J Exp Physiol* 8, 229.
5. O. Rosenheim, J.C. Drummond (1914) 'A volumetric method for the estimation of ethereal and inorganic sulphates in urine', *Biochemical Journal* 8, 143–51.

6. J. C. Drummond, C. Funk (1914) 'The Chemical Investigation of the Phosphotungstate Precipitate from Rice-Polishings', *Biochemical Journal* 8(6), 598–615.
7. W. D. Halliburton, J. C. Drummond (1917) 'The nutritive value of margarines and butter substitutes with reference to their content of the fat-soluble accessory growth substance', *Journal of Physiology* 51(4/5), 235–51.
8. Charles Booth wrote *Life and Labour of the People*, vols I (1889) and II (1891); Benjamin Seebohm Rowntree wrote *Poverty: A Study of Town Life* (1901). These are two seminal, influential and shocking documents.
9. F. G. Hopkins (1912) 'Feeding experiments illustrating the importance of accessory factors in normal dietaries', *Journal of Physiology* 44(5–6), 425–460.
10. Casimir Funk (1912) 'The etiology of the deficiency diseases. Beri-beri, polyneuritis in birds, epidemic dropsy, scurvy, experimental scurvy in animals, infantile scurvy, ship beri-beri, pellagra', *Journal of State Medicine* 20, 341–68.
11. J. C. Drummond (1918) 'Some aspects of infant feeding', *Lancet* 2, 482–4.
12. J. C. Drummond (1920) 'The nomenclature of the so-called accessory food factors (vitamins)', *Biochemical Journal* 14(5), 660.
13. Britain's first biochemistry chair had been at Liverpool, when Benjamin Moore (founder of the *Biochemical Journal*) had been appointed in 1902. The second was at Cambridge, where Frederick Gowland Hopkins took up the reins in 1914. In 1920, meanwhile, Moore moved from Liverpool to Oxford to establish the third biochemistry chair. Then came Jack at UCL. Not bad for a 31-year-old with no old school connections.
14. André L. Simon (editor) (1952) 'In Memoriam: Sir Jack Drummond', *Wine and Food, A Gastronomical Quarterly*, no. 75: Autumn, 127.

15. J. C. Drummond, A. Z. Baker, M. D. Wright, P. M. Marrian, E. M. Singer (1938) 'The effects of life long subsistence on diets providing suboptimal amounts of the "vitamin B complex"', *Journal of Hygiene* 38(3), 356–73; J. C. Drummond and W. R. Lewis (1938) 'The examination of some tinned foods of historic interest. 1. Historical introduction', *Chem and Indust* 57, 808–14; J. C. Drummond (1939) 'Sources of vitamins A and D', *British Medical Journal* 2, 1112–3; J. C. Drummond, C. H. Gray and N. E. G. Richardson (1939) 'The antirachitic value of human milk', *British Medical Journal* 2, 757–60; J. C. Drummond (1940) 'Sources of vitamins A and D', *British Medical Journal* 1, 36–7; J. C. Drummond (1940) 'Food in relation to health in Great Britain – The historical background', *British Medical Journal* 1, 941–3; H. V. Taylor, J. C. Drummond and M. Pyke (1941) 'Food from the garden', *Nature* 148, 712–4; J. C. Drummond and T. Moran (1944) 'Unconsidered trifles in our diet – Vitamin content of beverages', *Nature* 153, 99–100.
16. J. C. Drummond (1940), 'Margarine', *Nature* 145, 53–5.
17. G. E. Friend, with foreword by J. C. Drummond (1935) *The Schoolboy – His Nutrition and Development*, Heffer.

7 The Englishman's Food

1. See p. 255, n. 4.
2. See p. 255, n. 4.
3. J. C. Drummond, A. Wilbraham (1935) 'William Stark, M. D. An eighteenth century experiment in nutrition', *Lancet* 226, issue 5843, 459–463.
4. See p. 259, n. 17.
5. John Boyd Orr (1880–1971), an academic giant in the world of nutrition and contemporary of Jack Drummond who was awarded the Nobel Peace Prize in 1949 for his research and his work as the first director-general of the United Nations Food and Agriculture Organisation (FAO).

6. John Boyd Orr (1936) *Food, Health and Income: A Report on a Survey of Adequacy Diet in Relation to Income*, Macmillan and Co. Boys from public school (who by no means had a perfect diet) were shown to be on average five inches taller than their contemporaries at charity schools. Meanwhile, vitamin D deficiency had caused the majority of children in Durham and London to show early signs of rickets. It was a close-run thing whether the book would get published at all, but in the end Macmillan – publishers of Rowntree's seminal book decades earlier – stepped in at the behest of one of its partners, future prime minister Harold Macmillan. However, Kingsley Wood's threats ensured that Boyd Orr's colleagues initially felt unable to put their names to the book, so it was published under his name alone. Thanks to his standing up to the bullies, it soon went through three editions (by the second edition, he was able to acknowledge those other contributors) and became required reading on social studies courses in several American universities.
7. Malcolm Muggeridge (1989) *The Thirties: 1930–1940 in Great Britain*, Weidenfeld & Nicolson.
8. Jean Anthelme Brillat-Savarin (1755–1826), *Physiologie du Goût*, 1825.

8 Man of the Moment

1. Earl of Woolton (1959) *The Memoirs of the Rt. Hon. The Earl of Woolton*, Cassel, p. 237. In these memoirs, the author downplays the work of his scientific advisor to his own self-aggrandisement.
2. See p. 256, n. 6.
3. See p. 256, n. 7.
4. Earl of Woolton (1959), *The Memoirs of the Rt. Hon. The Earl of Woolton*, Cassel, p. 1.
5. In 1939, two eminent nutritionists, Elsie Widdowson (1906–2000) and Robert McCance (1898–1993),

experimented on themselves and friends to investigate if
a diet restricted in eggs, fish and meat but with unlimited
calcium-fortified bread, vegetables and potatoes would be
sufficient to maintain health in active people if the rationing
became severe. They took a rigorous cycling and climbing
course to replicate the high activity levels of troops and farm
workers and presented their findings to the government in
March 1940, which gave peace of mind when developing
the rationing policy. The results were kept secret as the gut
side effects were significant. This is reported in Margaret
Ashwell (editor) (1993) *McCance & Widdowson: A Scientific
Partnership of 60 Years, 1933–1993*, British Nutrition
Foundation.

An image of the intrepid guinea pigs can be seen at
https://www.bbc.co.uk/news/uk-england-cambridgeshire-
57594654
6. *Nutrition and Relief Work: A Handbook for the Guidance of Relief
Workers*, written by Jack Drummond and colleagues on behalf
of The Councils of British Societies for Relief Abroad.
7. National Archives, FO 916/847, WO 219/3944, WO 222/208
8. National Archives, FO 916/847, WO 219/3944

10 The Dominicis
1. Jean Laborde (1974) then translated by Milton Waldman,
*The Dominici Affair: French Justice on Trial for the Murder of the
Drummond Family*, William Collins Sons & Co., pp. 39–40.

12 Doubts
1. Jean Giono (1955) *Notes sur l'affaire Dominici suives d'un
essai sur le caractère des personnages*, Gallimard. Subsequently
published in English as *The Dominici Affair*, translated by
Peter de Mendelssohn, London Museum Press.
2. Alain Dominici (1998) *Gaston Dominici: Une vie … chronique
d'un paysan bas-alpin*, Ligne Sud.

3. Martin Kitchen (2017) *The Dominici Affair*, Potomac Books, p. 219.
4. See p. 257, n. 1.

13 A Web of Intrigues

1. Cited in James Fergusson (2007), *The Vitamin Murders: Who Killed Healthy Eating in Britain?*, Portobello, p. 148.
2. *Mussolini: The Final Truth* (RAI, 2004). This documentary proposes there was secret correspondence between Mussolini and Churchill, but doesn't reference Drummond specifically.
3. A speech Churchill gave on 17 February 1933 to the Anti-Socialist and Anti-Communist Union in London. An excellent analysis of this is given at https://richardlangworth.com/mussolini-law-giver
4. William Reymond and Alain Dominici (1997) *Dominici non coupable: Les assassins retrouvés*, France Loisirs/Flammarion.
5. William Reymond and Alain Dominici, 'Lettre ouverte pour la révision', Flammarion, 2003.
6. *L'affaire Dominici*, a two-part TV series in 2003 for the French channel TF1, written by Pierre Boutron, supporting the thesis that the secret service was implicated in the murder.
7. Many letters survived and are at the National Archives at Kew. National Archives, MEPO 2/9393

15 Big Boots to Fill

1. Stanley Chapman (1974) *Jesse Boot of Boots the Chemists*, Hodder and Stoughton, pp. 31–56.
2. Ibid, p. 192.
3. Examples of the patents can be found: https://patents.google.com/?q=(insecticide)&assignee=boots&before=priority:19531231&after=priority:19530101&oq=insecticide+1953+boots

4. James Fergusson (2007), *The Vitamin Murders: Who Killed Healthy Eating in Britain?*, Portobello Books, pp. 172–173. Fergusson researched his book when some of the players were still alive. Gordon Hobday was one, also one of the Marrian daughters and, amazingly, Francis Cammaerts.

16 Life and Death
1. The 1925 Geneva Protocol prohibits the use of chemical and biological weapons in war. The Protocol was drawn up and signed at a conference which was held in Geneva under the auspices of the League of Nations from 4 May to 17 June 1925, and it entered into force on 8 February 1928.
2. Lange was working at the University in Berlin when he synthesised the organophosphate and realised their toxic effects on man. He left Germany to work in the United States and did not continue this line of research.

17 The Gentleman Spy?
1. National Archives, FO 698/47
2. National Archives, FO 698/47
3. National Archives, FO 369/5032, FO 369/4920
4. National Archives, FO 369/5032, KG 11712/72, MEPO/2 9393
5. National Archives, FO 369/5032
6. *London Gazette*, 26 April 1949, issue 38595, page 2053.
7. National Archives, FO MAF 256/5, 48W, 15
8. National Archives, MAF 256/4, 25
9. National Archives, MAF 256/4 SA40, MAF 256/5 SA40A

18 The Transatlantic Connection
1. Ancestry.com
2. Woolton, The Earl of (1959) *The Memoirs of the Rt. Hon. The Earl of Woolton*, Cassel p. 217.

3. A note survives in the Foundation's files in which Jack thanks the 'RF for its hospitality', www.rockarch.org

4. Archives of University College London.

5. Ibid.

6. www.rockarch.org

7. www.rockarch.org

8. Ida Tarbell (1904) *The History of the Standard Oil Company*. This book has come to be known as a masterpiece of investigative journalism with the Ludlow Massacre representing the culminating act of perhaps the most violent struggle between corporate power and labouring men in American history.

9. https://resource.rockarch.org/story/war-of-the-worlds-rockefeller-philanthropies-disinformation-and-media-literacy-in-the-1930s/

10. https://www.cia.gov/readingroom/docs/CIA-RDP86B00269R000900020001-9.pdf

11. Francis Galton (1822–1911) was a polymath and distant cousin of Charles Darwin. His achievements include producing the first weather map and advancing the use of fingerprints in criminal detection. But the question that truly engrossed him was whether human abilities and characteristics are inherited or acquired. Galton himself proposed adoption studies as a research method, including trans-racial adoptions in order to separate the effects of heredity and environment. Whatever his intentions, such studies became co-opted by those intent on using eugenics to justify theories of class and race superiority.

19 Thank You from Washington

1. https://www.trumanlibrary.gov/library/executive-orders/10336/executive-order-10336

(a) The Medal of Freedom may be awarded to any person not hereinafter specifically excluded who, on or after December 7, 1941, has performed a meritorious act or service which (1) has aided the United States in the prosecution of a war against an enemy or enemies, (2) has aided any nation engaged with the United States in the prosecution of a war against a common enemy or enemies, or (3), during any period of national emergency declared by the President or the Congress to exist, has furthered the interests of the security of the United States or of any nation allied or associated with the United States during such period, and for which act or service the award of any other United States medal or decoration is considered inappropriate.

(b) Under special circumstances, and without regard to the existence of a state of war or national emergency, the Medal of Freedom may also be awarded by, or at the direction of, the President to any person, not hereinafter specifically excluded, for performance of a meritorious act or service in the interests of the security of the United States.

2. www.omsa.org
3. The publicly-held Harry S. Truman Papers http://web. archive.org/web/20071013231536/http://medaloffreedom. com/HarryTrumanMedals.htm
4. The recipients of the US Medal of Freedom with silver palms can be found on the *London Gazette* website, but the citations can be seen on microfiche at the National Archives at Kew.
5. http://archives.walgreensbootsalliance.com/ Record.aspx?src=CalmView.Catalog&id=WBA/ BT/28/41/6/10/164&pos=37
6. Bi-zonal Nutrition Survey 1948–9 FO 943/442

20 Innocent Tourists?

1. National Archives, Kew, FO 146/4611, 42. Letter from Dorothy Hollingsworth to Peter Meiklejohn re: Information for the Royal Society obituary June 1953.
2. National Archives, MEPO 2 9393 pts 1/2, 14, 19B, 26, 27, 41B, 62A
3. *Charter for Health* (1946), George Allen and Unwin.

RECOMMENDED READING

About the murders

Arrigoni, Jaques (2008), *Affaire Dominici: Enquête Sur L'histoire*, Éditions Toustemslibre.

Bresson, Pascal, and Follet René (2010), *L'affaire Dominici*, Glénat.

Carrias, Pierre, et al. (1997), *Dominici, De l'accident aux Agents Secrets*, Éditons de Provence.

Dominici, Alain (1998), *Gaston Dominici: Une Vie … Chronique d'un Paysan Bas-alpin*, Ligne Sud.

Fergusson, James (2007), *The Vitamin Murders: Who Killed Healthy Eating in Britain?*, Portobello Books.

Giono, Jean (1955), *Notes sur L'affaire Dominici Suivies d'un Essai sur le Caractère des Personnages*, Gallimard.

Giono, Jean (1956), translated by Peter de Mendelssohn, *The Dominici Affair*, London Museum Press.

Kitchen, Martin (2017), *The Dominici Affair*, Potomac Books.

Laborde, Jean (1972), *L'affaire Dominici, Un Matin d'été a Lurs*, Robert Laffont.

Laborde, Jean (1974), translated by Milton Waldman, *The Dominici Affair: French Justice on Trial for the Murder of the Drummond Family*, William Collins, Sons & Co.

Reymond, William, and Dominici, Alain (1997), *Dominici Non Coupable: Les Assassins Retrouvés*, France Loisirs/Flammarion.

Sebeille, Edmond (1970), *L'affaire Dominici, Toute la Vérité sur le crime de Lurs*, Plon.

Young, Gordon (1955), *Valley of Silence*, Robert Hale Ltd (NB: Young was a journalist from the *Daily Mail* who covered the trial in detail).

(2003) *'Lettre Ouverte Pour la Révision'*, Flammarion. The open letter to the French government was to persuade them to posthumously pardon Gaston Dominici, using the evidence presented in the 1997 book by William Reymond and Alain Dominici. It failed.

Memoirs of Jack Drummond's friends, colleagues and contemporaries

Boyd Orr, Lord John (1967), *As I Recall*, Doubleday and Company.

Bradshaw, Percy V. (1958), *Brother Savages and Guests: A History of the Savage Club 1857–1957*, W. H. Allen.

Bright Astley, Joan (2007), *The Inner Circle: A View of War at the Top*, The Memoir Club.

Cabell, Craig (2008), *Ian Fleming's Secret War*, Pen and Sword.

Jean, Fernand (1987), *J'y étais: Récits Inédits sur la Résistance au Pays d'Apt*, Association des Médailles de la Resistance de Vaucluse.

Jenkins, Ray (2009), *A Pacifist at War: The Life of Francis Cammaerts*, Hutchinson.

Pyke, Magnus (1978), *There & Back*, The Leisure Circle.

Russell, E. John (1956), *The Land Called Me: An Autobiography*, George Allen and Unwin.

Simon, André L. (1957), *By Request: An Autobiography*, The Wine and Food Society.

Woolton, The Earl of (1959), *The Memoirs of the Rt. Hon. The Earl of Woolton*, Cassel.

(1949) *Food*, Burke Publishing Co.

French occupation and culture

Edward, H. R. (1985), *Occupied France, Collaboration and Resistance 1940–1944*, Basil Blackwell.

Grady, Stephen (2013), *Gardens of Stone: My Boyhood in the French Resistance*, Hodder and Stoughton.

Massie, Allan (1989), *A Question of Loyalties*, Canongate.

Maurois, André, translated by Henry Bins (1949), *A History of France*, Jonathan Cape.

Modiano, Patrick (1968), translated by Frank Wynn (2015), *The Occupation Trilogy*, Éditions Gallimard (French) and Bloomsbury (English).

Young, Gordon (1957), *The Cat with Two Faces*, Coward-McCann.

Second World War

Bailey, Roderick (2009), *Forgotten Voices of the Secret War: An Inside History of Special Operations During the Second World War*, Ebury Press.

Binney, Marcus (2005), *Secret War Heroes: Men of the Special Operations Executive*, Hodder.

Committee of the British Medical Association (1946), *Charter for Health*, George Allen and Unwin.

Council of British Societies for relief work (1945), *Nutrition and Relief Work: A Handbook for the Guidance of Relief Workers*, Oxford University Press.

Crowdy, Terry (2016), *SOE: Churchill's Secret Agents*, Shire Publications.

Dulles, Allen (1966), *The Secret Surrender*, Harper & Row.

Escott, Beryl E. (2010), *The Heroines of SOE: Britain's Secret Women in France*, The History Press.

Foot, M. R. D. (2004), *SOE in France: An Account of the Work of the British Special Operations Executive in France 1940–1944*, Frank Cass Publishers.

Fry, Helen (2019), *The Walls Have Ears: The Greatest Intelligence Operation of World War 2*, Yale University Press.

Goodman, Susan (2005), *Children of War: The Second World War Through the Eyes of a Generation*, John Murray.

Hitchcock, William I. (2008), *Liberation: The Bitter Road to Freedom, Europe 1944–1945*, Faber and Faber.

Irwin, Will (2005), *The Jedburghs: The Secret History of the Allied Special Forces, France 1944*, Public Affairs New York.

Macintyre, Ben (2020), *Agent Sonya :The True Story of WW2's Most Extraordinary Spy*, Penguin.

Macintyre, Ben (2007), *Agent Zigzag: The True Wartime Story of Eddie Chapman, the Most Notorious Double Agent of World War 2*, Bloomsbury.

Saika, Robin (editor) (2010), *The Red Book: The Membership List of the Right Club 1939*, Foxley Books.

Shephard, Ben (2006), *After Daybreak: The Liberation of Belsen, 1945*, Pimlico.

West, Nigel, and Roberts, Madoc (2011), *Snow: The Double Life of a World War 2 Spy*, Biteback.

Wilkinson, Peter, and Bright Astley, Joan (1993), *Gubbins & SOE*, Pen and Sword.

Rockefeller and Intelligence

Hughes, Gerald; Jackson, Peter; Scott, Len (editors) (2008), *Exploring Intelligence Archives: Enquiries Into the Secret State*, Routledge.

Hutton, Robert (2018), *Agent Jack: The True Story of MI5's Secret Nazi Hunter*, Weidenfeld & Nicolson.

Jackson, Peter, and Siegel, Jennifer (editors) (2005), Intelligence *and Statecraft*, Praeger.

Jeffery, Keith (2010), *MI6: The History of the Intelligence Service 1909–1949*, Bloomsbury.

Weinberg, Steve (2008), *Taking on the Trust: How Ida Tarbell Brought Down John D. Rockefeller and Standard Oil*, W. W. Norton and Co.

Chemical and biological weapons

Alibek, Ken, and Handelman, Stephen (1999), *Biohazard: The Chilling True Story of the Largest Covert Biological Weapons Programme in the World*, Hutchinson.

Hastings, Max (2015), *The Secret War: Spies, Codes and Guerrillas 1939–1945*, William Collins.

Hunt, Linda (1991), *Secret Agenda: The United States Government, Nazi Scientists, and Project Paperclip, 1945 to 1990*, St Martin's Press.

Mangold, Tom, and Goldberg, Jeff (1999), *Plague Wars: A True Story of Biological Warfare*, Macmillan.

Marrs, Timothy C.; Maynard, Robert L.; Sidell, Frederick R. (1996), *Chemical Warfare Agents: Toxicology and Treatment*, John Wiley & Sons.

Parker, John (1966), *The Killing Factory: The Top Secret World of Germ and Chemical Warfare*, Smith Gryphon.

Schmidt, Ulf (2015), *Secret Science: A Century of Poison Warfare and Human Experiments*, Oxford University Press.

Tucker, Jonathan B. (2006), *War of Nerves: Chemical Warfare from World War 1 to Al-Qaeda*, Anchor Books.

Williams, Peter, and Wallace, David (1990), *Unit 731: The Shattering Exposé of the Japanese Army's Secret of Secrets*, Grafton Books.

Williams, Peter, and Wallace, David (1990), *La guerre bactériologique: Les secrets des expérimentations japonaises*, Albin Michel.

Nutrition, science and food

Bacharach, A. L., and Rendle, T. (1946), *The Nation's Food: A Survey of Scientific Data*, Society of the Chemical Industry.

Ball, Philip (2014), *Serving the Reich: The Struggle for the Soul of Physics Under Hitler*, Vintage.

Boyd Orr, John (1922), *A Short History of British Agriculture*, Oxford University Press.

Boyd Orr, John (1936), *Food, Health and Income: A Report on a Survey of Adequacy of Diet in Relation to Income*, Macmillan and Co.

Boyd Orr, Sir John, and Lubbock, David (1940), *Feeding the People in Wartime*, Macmillan and Co.

Boyd Orr, John (1936), *What Science Stands For*, George Allen and Unwin.

Burnett, John (1966), *Plenty and Want: A Social History of Food in England from 1815 to the Present Day*, Thomas Nelson.

Carson, Rachel (1962), *Silent Spring*, Houghton Mifflin.

Chapman, Stanley (1973), *Jesse Boot of Boots the Chemists: A Study in Business History*, Hodder and Stoughton.

Church, A. H. (1890), *Food: A Brief Account of its Sources, Constituents and Uses*, Chapman and Hall Ltd.

Collingham, Lizzie (2011), *The Taste of War: World War Two and the Battle for Food*, Penguin Books.

Eddy, W. H. (1921), *The Vitamine Manual: A Presentation of Essential Data About the New Food Factors*, Baltimore.

Enock, Arthur Guy (1943), *This Milk Business: A Study from 1895 to 1943*, H. K. Lewis & Co.

Halliburton, William Dobinson (1891), *A Textbook of Chemical Physiology and Pathology*, Longmans Green and Co., reprinted 2018 by Forgotten Books.

Harrow, Benjamin (1910), *Vitamines: Essential Food Factors*, George Routledge & Sons.

Knight, Katherine (2007), *Spuds, Spam and Eating for Victory: Rationing in the Second World War*, The History Press.

Kohler, Robert E. (1982), *From Medical Chemistry to Biochemistry: The Making of a Biomedical Discipline*, Cambridge University Press.

Marrack, J. R. (1942), *Food and Planning*, Victor Gollancz Ltd.

Ministry of Agriculture, fisheries and food (1956), *Domestic Food Consumption and Expenditure: 1954*, HMSO.

Norman, Jill, and National Archives, Kew (2007), *Eating for Victory: Healthy Home Front Cooking on War Rations*, Michael O'Mara Books.

Patten, Marguerite, with the Imperial War Museum (2002), *Victory Cookbook: Nostalgic Food and Facts from 1940–1954*, Chancellor Press.

Pavey, Agnes E. (1948), *Nutrition and Diet Therapy*, Faber and Faber.

Royal Institution (1940), *The Nation's Larder and the Housewife's Part Therein*, G. Bell and Sons Ltd. A series of lectures including one by Prof. J. C. Drummond, 'Food in Relation to Health in Great Britain During the Past Two Hundred Years'.

Shepherd, Sue (2000), *Pickled, Potted and Canned: The Story of Food Preserving*, Headline.

Simon, André L. (1952), *Wine and Food: A Gastronomical Quarterly*, The Wine and Food Society.

Smith, Daniel (2011), *The Spade as Mighty as the Sword: The Story of World War Two's 'Dig for Victory' Campaign*, Aurum Press.

Smyth, James Carmichael MD, FRS (1788), *The Works of the Late William Stark, MD*, printed for J. Johnson, no. 72 St Paul's Churchyard.

The Chemical Council (1953), *Chemistry and Man* (containing a lecture by the late Sir Jack Drummond FRS), E. & F. N. Spon Ltd.

Walker, Susannah (2012), *Home Front Posters of the Second World War*, Shire Publications.

Whitsed, J. de K. (1934), *Diet in the Modern Hospital: A Handbook on Feeding the Sick*, Baillière, Tindall and Cox.

Vernon, James (2007), *Hunger: A Modern History*, The Belknap Press of Harvard University Press.

(1936), *A Catechism Concerning Cheeses*, The Wine and Food Society.

Fiction and non-fiction evoking the atmosphere of the era

Druart, Ruth (2021), *While Paris Slept*, Headline.

Evans, Lissa (2010), *Their Finest Hour and a Half*, Black Swan.

Faulks, Sebastian (2018), *Paris Echo*, Vintage.

Fortescue, Lady Winifred (1937–1948), the *Perfume from Provence* series, Black Swan.

Frank, Otto (editor), translated by Susan Massotty (1997), *Anne Frank: The Diary of a Young Girl*, Puffin Books.

Gardiner, Juliet (2011), *The Thirties: An Intimate History*, Harper Press.

Lloyd, Chris (2022), *Paris Requiem*, Orion.

Lloyd, Chris (2020), *The Unwanted Dead*, Orion.

Némirovsky, Irène, translated by Sandra Smith (2004), *Suite Française*, Chatto and Windus.

Orwell, George (1933), *Down and Out in Paris and London*, Victor Gollancz.

Orwell, George (1937), *The Road to Wigan Pier*, Victor Gollancz.

Pagnol, Marcel (1962), translated by W. E. van Heyningen (1988), *Jean de Florette* and *Manon des Sources*, Éditions Julliard, Prion. A story about local people set between the wars very close to the site of the murder.

Sheers, Owen (2007), *Resistance*, Faber and Faber.

Various (circa 1925), *Fifty Amazing Secret Service Dramas*, Odhams Press.

ACKNOWLEDGEMENTS

Stephanie would like to thank her husband, Prof. Anthony Campbell CBE, for collaborations over many years, his support, archive searching and many adventures chasing L'Affaire in France. Also thanks to Georgie, Emma, Lewis, David and Neil for their encouragement and interest. Thanks to Phil, Laoise, Ann and Sally who read various stages of the manuscript and fell in love with Jack Drummond and to my bookclub friends who helped instill my love of writing. To French friends who ignited the flame of interest, *Merci*.

Dan would like to say thanks as ever to Rosie, Charlotte and Ben for their unstinting support.

We would both like to thank our amazing agent, Andrew Lownie, for believing in the story, his enthusiasm and support. To Ellen, Connor and the team at Icon, a big thank you. Connor's guidance has been excellent and made the process enjoyable.

The research for this book would not have been possible without the professional work done by the archivists at the National Archives at Kew, the Wellcome Trust, the Bodleian Library, the Boots Walgreen Archives and the Museum of English Rural Life. Please carry on your excellent work.

Our thanks to Mark Smith for medal identification and Alain Dominici for discussions and access to his extensive collection of images.

Every effort has been made to contact rights holders. If any have been inadvertently overlooked, the publisher will be pleased to make the necessary arrangements at the first opportunity.

INDEX